THE HIDDEN CURRICULUM

The Hidden Curriculum

FIRST GENERATION STUDENTS
AT LEGACY UNIVERSITIES

RACHEL GABLE

PRINCETON UNIVERSITY PRESS

PRINCETON & OXFORD

Requests for permission to reproduce material from this work should be sent to permissions@press.princeton.edu

Published by Princeton University Press
41 William Street, Princeton, New Jersey 08540
6 Oxford Street, Woodstock, Oxfordshire OX20 1TR

press.princeton.edu

ISBN 978-0-691-19076-1
ISBN (e-book) 978-0-691-20108-5

British Library Cataloging-in-Publication Data is available

Editorial: Peter Dougherty and Alena Chekanov
Production Editorial: Jenny Wolkowicki
Jacket design: Layla Mac Rory
Production: Erin Suydam
Publicity: Alyssa Sanford and Kathryn Stevens
Copyeditor: Kelly Clody

This book has been composed in Arno

Printed on acid-free paper. ∞

Printed in the United States of America

10 9 8 7 6 5 4 3 2 1

CONTENTS

List of Figures and Tables vii

Preface ix

Acknowledgments xvii

1 The Creation of the First Generation Student   1

2 Preparation: A Shifting Self-Assessment   13

3 On Academic Experiences   52

4 Mapping Social Life   95

5 Negotiating Belonging and Critique   127

6 The External Influences on Alma Mater   149

7 Advice to Campus Leaders from First
  Generation Students   176

Appendix 203
Bibliography 221
Index 231

FIGURES AND TABLES

Figures

2.1 Percentage (in category) of senior respondents
"less" prepared, by high school, gender,
underrepresented minority   31

2.2 Percentage (in category) of senior respondents
"less" prepared, by first generation, public high
school, female, Latinx   34

3.1 First and continuing generation academic
satisfaction   60

3.2 Academic majors, first and continuing
generation   64

4.1 First and continuing generation social
satisfaction   96

4.2 Extracurricular involvement, first and continuing
generation   104

5.1 Belonging, first and continuing generation
seniors   142

Tables

2.1 Self-Reported Preparation, First and Continuing
Generation Sophomores and Seniors   29

2.2 Self-Reported Preparation by High School,
Gender, Race/Ethnicity   30

A.1 First and Continuing Generation Student
Invitation and Participation Rates   209

A.2 Repeat Participants, by Cohort (2015, 2016)   210

A.3 First and Continuing Generation Participant
Demographics   211

PREFACE

THE TITLE of this book—*The Hidden Curriculum*—is borrowed from a commonly used phrase among education scholars that describes the tacit rules of educational practice. If you learn those rules well and follow them closely, you will not only succeed in the particular educational context in which you find yourself but you will likely also come to believe in the naturalness, universality, and inevitability of the norms and values these tacit rules uphold.[1] Education scholars often use the phrase "the hidden curriculum" pejoratively to describe a process and set of everyday practices that, while remaining unacknowledged and unexamined, nonetheless serve to maintain the status quo or support a dominant worldview.[2] They hope that the act of identifying, acknowledging, and examining the hidden curriculum will enable those subject to

1. Defined by Philip Jackson in his 1968 *Life in Classrooms*, the hidden curriculum comprises what Michael Apple in his summation of Jackson calls, "the norms and values that are implicitly, but effectively, taught in schools and that are not usually talked about in teachers' statements of end or goals." See Philip Jackson, *Life in Classrooms* (New York: Holt, Rinehart, and Winston, 1968). See Michael Apple, *Ideology and Curriculum*, 3rd ed. (New York: Routledge Falmer, 2004), 78. For additional reading, see Ishmael Baksh, "The Hidden Curriculum," in *Teaching, Schools and Society*, eds. Evelina Orteza y Miranda and Romulo Magsino (New York: Taylor and Francis, 1990), 170–89. For further reference, a comparative table of theories related to the hidden curriculum can be found in Fula Damla Kentli, "Comparison of Hidden Curriculum Theories," *European Journal of Educational Studies* 1, no. 2 (2009): 83–88.

2. For examples of this use of the term, see Khan, *Privilege*, 105; Ballantine, Hammack, and Stuber, *Sociology of Education*, 349–78; Lee, *Class and Campus Life*, 146; and Jack, *Privileged Poor*, 86.

it—students, teachers, staff, and parents—to interrogate the presumed norms and values such a system upholds. As a form of cultural or social critique, to recognize and evaluate the hidden curriculum is therefore to disavow the naturalness, universality, and inevitability of the worldview it supports. Its critique also acknowledges the dimension of social interaction that, while unspoken, nonetheless wields a sizable influence on interpersonal and intercultural relations.

Every educational context has its hidden curriculum, and to identify it one may look to those for whom the educational context in question initially seems unfamiliar, surprising, or strange. At elite, highly selective universities for whom a sizable proportion of their undergraduate classes are graduates of feeder schools and the children of alumni, first generation college students who have little to no prior experience with such forms of education may offer crucial insights into the form and function of the hidden curriculum. Additionally, those who might on the surface appear as natural "insiders" may also critique the unacknowledged values upheld by this system, while newcomers may have an interest in hiding or "passing" in order to achieve personal goals. Rather than representing a single or coherent set of values, the hidden curriculum may actually comprise a congeries of contested aims and attitudes from different parties within and without the educational institution, straining for the right to define and claim the purpose of education.

Nowadays, it seems commonly assumed that first generation students have difficulty adjusting to college because they do not yet have a mental library of cultural knowledge associated with the hidden curriculum at their specific university. Therefore, the goal for concerned university administrators, staff, and faculty is to identify the hidden curriculum on their campus and educate first generation students in its complexity of expectations so that they can maximize the opportunities offered them in college. Embedded in these efforts is the assumption that continuing generation students were taught the tacit norms and rules of the hidden curriculum by their college-educated parents and the social context of their youth.

In this book, readers will discover that indeed students rightly believe there is a hidden curriculum operating in their classrooms, extracurricular organizations, and residence halls. However, it is not the case that one can neatly divide those who are aware of that curriculum from those who are not and correlate that with students who have college-educated parents and those who do not. Nor can we pinpoint a set of uncontested norms and attitudes that define a universal hidden curriculum. Instead, a hidden curriculum is often a site of contestation concerning what the institution represents, whom it serves, and how it defines success. This book shows how students from both first generation and continuing generation backgrounds grapple with the hidden curriculum in convergent and divergent ways as they identify, pursue, and achieve their goals for college and beyond. By listening to them, we can learn how to make colleges better for all students.

This book aims to examine the hidden curriculum at two historically elite universities, Harvard and Georgetown, both of which are steeped in tradition and yet strive for greater inclusivity. Here I follow ninety-one first generation students (i.e., those whose parents did not graduate from a four-year college) and thirty-five continuing generation students (i.e., those with at least one parent with a baccalaureate degree) from their sophomore through senior years in college. As it turned out, the first and continuing generation students in this study critiqued or celebrated their experiences in college at similar rates. However, the lessons that first generation students found initially surprising, but later learned to recognize and to varying degrees adopt or critique, helped illuminate each university's hidden curriculum. The act of making explicit the heretofore tacit expectations for how to behave in college serves practical as well as normative ends. On the one hand, transforming tacit expectations into explicit guidance for future first generation students promises to inform and expand advising and counseling practices, student affairs programming, and faculty guidance on how to best support their students' academic success. On the other hand, unearthing the hidden curriculum grants universities a powerful opportunity for auto-critique in a new era of expanded opportunity: whom does this university serve and what are its obligations to its constituents?

This book toggles between the two aims of practical guidance and normative critique as it traces the contours of Harvard and Georgetown's hidden curricula. The settings here are two universities intimately connected to the nation's highest echelons of power and wealth. The students' experiences are shaped in large part by their primarily residential campuses, sited just minutes from two of our nation's most expensive urban centers—Boston and Washington, DC. The process of unearthing and examining an institution's tacit norms can be applied across many different types of campuses undergoing a growth period in first generation college student attendance. From rural and suburban liberal arts colleges to state flagships, colleges can benefit from the insights of the participants in this study, which can provide opportunities for first generation students, continuing generation students, faculty, and staff. If universities wish to make good on their diversity and inclusion promises, they must first uncover and interrogate the ends their individual hidden curricula serve and who is excluded by the implicit norms that guide behavior in their classrooms and on their quads. Not all of the lessons here will apply to all types of postsecondary institutions; however, the power of their critique, especially as it makes explicit what there is to gain and what can reasonably be altered to foster inclusion and help all students to thrive, can galvanize honest campus discussions across the gamut of universities and colleges.

This book owes a special debt to William Bowen, Martin Kurzweil, and Eugene Tobin's *Equity and Excellence in Higher Education*, which made a strong case for income-sensitive admissions preferences, many of which came to benefit first generation college students at highly selective institutions.[3] From a qualitative perspective, this book seeks to ask questions similar to theirs regarding the academic and social experiences of first generation students attending elite schools. It also seeks to foreground the students themselves and deploys lengthy or intact quotes as often as possible to include as much of the participants' perspectives as possible. In this manner, I borrow techniques established by Richard Light in *Making the Most of College: Students Speak Their Minds* and Ken Bain in *What the Best College Students Do* to allow students themselves to explain why and when they succeed (and by their own definitions), what they believe the university does for them and for their futures, and what advice they can offer campus leaders to maximize college-going opportunities and experiences for future cohorts.[4] While I do not take a disciplinary stance to answer such questions, I do seek to engage with disciplinary scholars in the footnotes. As such, I hope the reader may follow along with the participants' narratives in the body of the text and the scholarly conversation in the notes below.

The book is organized as follows. The first chapter begins with a brief overview of the historical development of the term "first generation," as well as the contexts at Harvard and Georgetown that galvanized administrators' concern for supporting and including the growing number of first generation students on each of their campuses. It briefly outlines the multi-institutional research project, the *First Generation Student Success Project*, that convened administrators and faculty from four universities—Brown, Duke, Georgetown, and Harvard—to study the experiences of first generation students on their campuses, to share insights, and to serve as sounding boards for one another as they evaluated approaches to supporting and including their increasing percentage of first generation students.

3. Bowen, Kurzweil, and Tobin, *Equity and Excellence in American Higher Education*.
4. Light, *Making the Most of College*; and Bain, *What the Best College Students Do*.

The second and third chapters focus on first generation students' shifting self-assessments of their academic preparation, as well as the successes and challenges associated with their academic experiences in college. Rather than attempting to unify the academic narrative among first generation students, I explore the variations and internal complexities in how first generation students and their continuing generation peers describe the academic process. First generation students were more likely to draw on themes of motivation and overcoming hardship, and to narrate academic successes as a series of slow or even false starts, meteoric rises, and, at times, savage disappointments. In contrast, continuing generation students tended to exhibit stable attitudes toward the academic core of their experiences. Some treated faculty members as coaches and coursework as exercises that would allow them to achieve external goals unrelated to any specific academic content. Others viewed the process as one of incremental self-actualization through a balance of mentorship and increasing autonomy. At times, they considered the experience to be a series of somewhat tedious transactions that would ultimately confer the brand name degree that promised to open doors and smooth pathways to future professional success. In each of these cases, it was notable that continuing generation students did not describe an academic roller coaster, whereas first generation students were more likely to do just that, casting it as either exhilarating or terrifying. I explore why the academic narratives among first and continuing generation students diverge and how they might indicate a relationship between familial experience with college and individual expectations of what college can and should do for the person.

While the second and third chapters focus on academics, the fourth and fifth chapters explore first and continuing generation students' social experiences in college. In the fourth chapter, I compare first and continuing generation participants' descriptions of their friend groups and their extracurricular involvement, again with an equal focus on internal variation and overlap as well as understanding the differences among the two groups of students. The fifth chapter traces the varied ways in which first generation students respond to perceived social pressure to adapt to behavioral expectations in academic and social encounters on campus. When or whether they chose to disclose their first generation status, as well as the identities they chose to exhibit in different contexts, underscore a complicated negotiation of status and role within the larger campus community. Significantly, first generation students were no more likely than their continuing generation peers to express a mismatch between their personal identities and their college. Like them they narrated their identities as college students in terms of belonging, recognition, assimilation, and social critique. They did, however, consider their first generation status to be a reason for conflict when it arose. Some first generation students elected to "pass" as continuing generation students. Others expressed pride in their first generation status, and still others criticized the university for their sense of isolation and lack of fit on campus. The complicated negotiations of identity disclosure underscore the liminality of this status, one that is intergenerationally unstable and largely a result of a cultural association in the United States that conflates educational achievement with merit.

The sixth chapter identifies three factors that were outside the university context but that played a role in first generation students' evaluation of their college experiences. These included whether they had prior connections to their college or to a college of a similar type, how they perceived university officials' treatment of their parents, and whether they had specific plans for postgraduation early in their senior year. The final chapter of this book offers policy suggestions gleaned from the prior six chapters. It provides programmatic advice to administrators seeking to align their campus practices with a mission of inclusion. Some of the suggestions are low- or no-cost, while others are cost-intensive.

This concluding chapter is intended to galvanize discussion on campuses, but it can also serve as a useful tool for debate in contexts that may at first seem quite distinct from the two universities described in this book. In all cases, I implore administrators, faculty, staff, and students to scrutinize the hidden curriculum on their own college campuses and to evaluate the suggestions in this book against their particular missions, contexts, and histories.

ACKNOWLEDGMENTS

FIRST AND FOREMOST, I am deeply grateful to the undergraduate participants of the *First Generation Student Success Project*. Your insights and advice are the hand that guided this book. Thank you for sharing your experiences, committing your time, and trusting that your engagement—be it practical instruction, excoriating critique, or unbridled celebration—is a crucial ingredient to sustaining and improving the quality of collegiate experience for future students.

Just as the undergraduate participants in this project fashioned it with their words and insights, so too did the faculty and administrators who listened and responded to its findings. Thank you to the conveners of the *First Generation Student Success Project* for your dedication to improving the college-going experience for not just first generation but all students: Charles Deacon, Christopher England, Melissa "Missy" Foy, Patricia McWade, and Jennifer Nguyen at Georgetown; Anya Bassett, Thomas Dingman, William Fitzsimmons, Richard Light, Jasmine Waddell, and Robin Worth at Harvard; Maitrayee Bhattacharyya and James Miller at Brown; and, for two years of this project, Beth Fox and Christoph Guttentag at Duke University. Thank you to the alumni supporters and anonymous donors who provided funds for gift cards for student participants. To Thomas Healey, thank you for your dedication to this project and for your many crucial insights during its four years. This book owes a special debt to Anya Bassett, Richard Light, Jennifer Nguyen, and Christopher England, all who served as principal investigators and ushered the approvals for research through the university Institutional Review Board (IRB) processes at Harvard and Georgetown. A more extensive description of the project's original aims, participant recruitment, and research methods is located in the *Appendix*.

Thank you to my dissertation committee, Richard Light, Anya Bassett, and Julie Reuben, for your wisdom and guidance as I shaped the evidence from this project into my doctoral thesis. Your thoughtful critiques and unflagging support of me as a neophyte scholar improved my confidence and my analysis of this work more than you can know. For the opportunity to present on this work, I thank the organizers of the University of Richmond Advisor Lunch Series; the Harvard Higher Education Leaders Forum; the Virginia Commonwealth University Equity and Inclusion Leadership Symposium; the Harvard Summit on Excellence in Higher Education; the Georgetown University Teaching, Learning, and Innovation Summer Institute; and the Georgetown University Alumni Admissions Program Chairmen's Conference.

To Peter Dougherty from Princeton University Press, thank you for the pleasure and the opportunity to work with you as I shaped my dissertation research into a book. I would also like to thank the anonymous readers who provided constructive feedback and timely suggestions for improvement on the proposal and draft. Thank you also to Alena Chekanov, Leslie Grundfest, Kelly Clody, and the editorial staff at Princeton University Press, who were exceptionally supportive in bringing this manuscript to its final form.

Finally, thank you to friends and family who believed in this project from the beginning and whose support was invaluable in accomplishing its goals. Amy Cheung and Bruce O'Brien each graciously permitted me to overstay my welcome at their homes as I traveled to Boston and Washington, DC, to complete interviews. Bryan McAllister-Grande and the late Brendan Randall were intellectual companions throughout the doctoral journey. John Rosenberg's enthusiasm for this work was galvanizing at exactly the right time, while Jennifer Grogan's generous feedback on the manuscript helped me bring it to the finish line. My colleagues at Virginia Commonwealth University inspire me daily with their relentless commitment to student success and their optimism that higher education can and should help people from all backgrounds achieve their American Dream. In particular, I'd like to thank Jill Blondin, Christina Marino, Barbara Ingber, my students in VCU Globe, my colleagues in the Global Education Office, and my colleagues in the Office of the Provost. Finally, I thank family and dear friends for supporting and sustaining me throughout this journey: Kathy Taylor and Ed Chase; Frank and Melissa Gelder; LaVerne and the late Ed Gable; Larsen and Grace Gable; the late Miriam and Robert Burgess Sr.; Robert, Vicki, and Gail Burgess; the California Gable clan; and Peter and Margaret Huber. To my husband Eric, thank you for being my dearest companion, my most insightful reader, and my strongest supporter. To Ned and Martin, thank you for the joy of watching you make this world your own.

THE HIDDEN CURRICULUM

1

The Creation of the First Generation Student

COLLEGE HAS ALWAYS been viewed as a vehicle for opportunity and social mobility for talented students, regardless of background. Yet college, especially the most exclusive ones, can also seem to be a bastion of privilege. New evidence suggests that wealthy universities educate wealthy students, with many universities enrolling more students from the top one percent than they do from the bottom sixty percent.[1] What does the college experience look like for those who enter the most storied halls of what we might call "legacy" institutions without the family wealth and prior experience of many of its alumni? What does college do for those who enter its gates presumably carrying less privilege and with more to gain from attending such institutions than the well-off scions of college-educated parents?

---

1. See Chetty et al., "Mobility Report Cards."

On the Creation of the First Generation College Student

The term "first generation college student" appears everywhere nowadays.[2] There are first generation college student centers and programs dedicated to establishing footholds for first generation students on college campuses across the country. First-in-the-family narratives embroider politicians' stump speeches, university leaders' commencement addresses, and memoirs of industry titans and sage professionals of all stripes. The deployment of a "first generation college" narrative harks to an ongoing cultural commitment to educational opportunity and higher education's role in fulfilling the American Dream.[3] As a nation, we are aspirationally committed to incorporating outsiders and newcomers, although we also recognize that we have a history of slamming doors and ousting parvenus. If first generation students have the

---

2. This term has been used with and without a hyphen. I have chosen not to use the hyphen in my own writing about first generation students, but the reader will note that the hyphenated use, "first-generation," will appear in direct quotes from scholars who deploy the hyphen.

3. At the outset of Karabel's *The Chosen: The Hidden History of Admission and Exclusion at Harvard, Yale, and Princeton*, a landmark study of selective admissions at Harvard, Yale, and Princeton, Karabel emphasizes a tension between two divergent ideas on what is fair in educational practice: one seeks "equality of opportunity," or essentially a meritocratic system that awards the best prepared students with the best possible education; and another seeks "equality of conditions," or a system that shares educational goods among students with varying levels of academic mastery and diverse academic interests. Karabel's history of selective admissions tells the story of how "equality of opportunity" became the dominant path chosen by the most prestigious colleges and universities in the twentieth century, and the social ramifications of that path—some positive and others negative—for ethnic minorities, the urban and rural poor, and women. For excellent reviews of the concept of merit in the United States and its relationship to higher education, see Kett, *Merit: The History of a Founding Ideal*; Lemann, *The Big Test: The Secret History of the American Meritocracy*; and Menand, "Why We Have College" and "The Graduates." Finally, for critiques of the concept of meritocracy in elite admissions, see Guinier, *Tyranny of the Meritocracy*; and Warikoo, *Diversity Bargain*.

opportunity to succeed and do so on par with their peers who come from families where college is already a part of life, then their success indicates that higher education is meeting its goal to enable opportunity, however imperfectly. This is perhaps even more potentially salutary on an elite college campus, the presumed proving ground of future professional, academic, and industry leaders, and populated largely by the children of America's economic upper and upper-middle classes. First generation college students who attend our nation's "legacy" institutions are poised to offer crucial insights into the opportunities and challenges of deploying education as a primary path to mobility and social change. But who are the first generation students who attend America's top institutions, and what do they want their campus leaders to know about them and do to help them achieve their educational and personal goals?

The answer to the first question—*who are they?*—can be difficult to parse. First generation college students are commonly defined as the first in their family to attend a four-year college.[4] By entering college, they are engaging in a vocational path that is potentially distinct from that of their parents. As such, they are presumed unable to rely on their parents' experiential knowledge to aid their college-going choices, but beyond this commonality, they comprise a heterogeneous group. In her qualitative study of first generation college students at an elite liberal arts college, sociologist Tina Wildhagen remarks on the rising interest in the category "first generation" beginning in the early 2000s, just as the actual rate of first generation college students reached a nadir.[5] She

4. Most universities and foundations follow Susan Choy's 2001 definition for the National Center for Education Statistics: the student with neither parent having attained a bachelor's degree. See Choy, *Students Whose Parents Did Not Go to College*, 1–34.

5. Wildhagen, "'Not Your Typical Student'." Wildhagen, quoting prior research, contends that at the same time that the interest in first generation college students spiked among administrators, beginning in the early 2000s, the actual numbers of first generation college students plummeted from thirty-nine percent in 1971 to sixteen

points out, as do other scholars,[6] that the categorization of first generation college students, while potentially useful for admissions offices and university leaders, does not always sit well with the students it intends to describe. These students constitute multiple social class, ethnic, and racial categories, are native and nonnative born, and arrive in college with varied high school experiences. They are equally as likely to consider their first generation status as nonessential to who they are and what they intend for their futures as they are to be invested in expressing a first generation identity. Those who self-identify as first generation college students by joining first generation student groups or disclosing this status to their peers do not always represent the heterogeneity and multiple interests of those who fit the status. Moreover, personal identification with the status changes over time and based on context: who is asking and why they are asking it shapes the choice to disclose as much as the individual's personal commitment to the category.

In prior decades, the term "first generation" referred to the pioneering group of students who integrated a school: one would read about "the first generation" of African American or female students to gain access to colleges that previously barred their entry. The fact that a student's parents may not have attended college appeared less salient than other categories. Terms such as "scholarship boy," "low-income student," or "minority student" served to shape research questions about outsider or newcomer status, particularly in exclusive or unequal collegiate settings.[7]

---

percent in 2005. See Victor Saenz, Sylvia Hurtado, Doug Barrera, De'Sha Wolf, and Fanny Yeung, *First in My Family: A Profile of First-Generation College Students at Four-Year Institutions Since 1971* (Los Angeles: Higher Education Research Institute, 2007).

6. See Thai-Huy Nguyen and Bach Mai Dolly Nguyen, "Is the 'First-Generation Student' Term Useful for Understanding Inequality? The Role of Intersectionality in Illuminating the Implications of an Accepted—Yet Unchallenged—Term," *Review of Research in Higher Education* 42 (March 2018): 146–76.

7. For examples, see Richard Hoggart, *The Uses of Literacy* (Washington: Essential Books, 1957) and Rodriguez, *Hunger of Memory*. For in-depth historical accounts of

Memoirs by journalists and academics who dealt with divided loyalties between home and college, or the cleft habitus resulting from social migration—for instance, Alfred Lubrano's sensitive portrait in *Limbo: Blue-Collar Roots, White-Collar Dreams*— offered intimate truths regarding those who were the first in their family to attend college.[8] Current researchers are still very much invested in questions about how race, social class, and gender influence the unequal experiences and outcomes of education for students.[9] They are also concerned with how schools might overcome these inequities. It has only been within the past twenty years that the additional category of first generation college student has become a salient topic of research. However, rather than reflecting an identity feature, this categorization signals a status in flux: once the first generation student graduates from college, the relevance of this status recedes.

The second question—*what do they want their campus leaders to know about them and do to help them achieve their educational and personal goals?*—is the focus of this book. The vast majority of first generation college students in the United States today attend less selective institutions, and their primary goals are to graduate and find meaningful, well-paid work.[10] Administrators at such schools

---

how the language of access and assistance (regarding financial aid and other tools) in elite higher education changed over time, see Cary, "Tradition and Transition"; Karabel, *Chosen*; and Keller and Keller, *Making Harvard Modern*.

8. Lubrano, *Limbo: Blue-Collar Roots, White-Collar Dreams*. *Cleft habitus* is a term deployed by Pierre Bourdieu in his extensive analyses of the personal effects of social mobility, including dis-ease in both old and new contexts. See Bourdieu, *Distinction: A Social Critique of the Judgment of Taste* and *The State Nobility: Elite Schools in the Field of Power*.

9. For just a few excellent recent examples not addressed in other places in this book, see Stuber, "Talk of Class"; Stuber, Klugman, and Daniel, "Gender, Social Class and Exclusion"; Mullen, *Degrees of Inequality*; Harper, "Black Male College Achievers" and "Am I My Brother's Teacher?"

10. Research comparing first and continuing generation student outcomes from a national perspective are important for understanding the baseline differences in these two groups of college-goers. Examples of this quantitative work include Engle

evaluate success or failure of the programs they implement by measuring how well first generation students do in comparison to their continuing generation peers.[11] First generation students who attend elite colleges graduate at very high rates and ultimately find remunerative work at rates equal to their continuing generation peers.[12] So the question is not whether they graduate, but rather, whether they are afforded with the opportunities to thrive and achieve the goals they establish for themselves in college and beyond. Does their attendance at an elite institution provide them with the opportunities and pathways they anticipated when they first elected to attend, or that they established through the course of college? If so, what does that process look like? And what does it mean to the students themselves?

Elite colleges and universities have recently launched initiatives to attenuate or entirely remove barriers to access for low-income

and Tinto, *Moving beyond Access*; Terenzini et al., "First-Generation College Students"; Warburton, Bugarin, and Nuñez, "Bridging the Gap"; Pike and Kuh, "First- and Second-Generation College Students"; and Jenkins, Miyazaki, and Janosik, "Predictors that Distinguish First-Generation College Students from Non-First Generation College Students." See also Bowen, Chingos, and McPherson, *Crossing the Finish Line* for an outstanding and detailed analysis of public university graduation rates based on race, gender, parental education, high school grades, test scores, and the selectivity of the university.

11. One recent national study indicated that the national average graduation rate for first generation college students was around 27.4 percent in the first decade of the twenty-first century, compared to 42.1 percent for students with college-graduate parents. See DeAngelo et al., *Completing College*, 9.

12. Graduation rates among first generation students at Harvard were ninety-six percent and at Georgetown were ninety-four percent during the time of this study, while their overall graduation rates at these institutions were only a fraction higher. Two years after the participants in this study graduated, I was able to verify the employment or graduate attendance of approximately ninety percent of the first and continuing generation participants, with approximately equal employment rates and comparable sectors of employment among both groups. Most recent graduates were launched into careers or graduate preparation in the fields they described as their early career goals during senior interviews, with the modal employer category for both first and continuing generation as the corporate or financial industries.

students, many of whom would be first generation college students. These efforts include eliminating financial obstacles, as well as sending a message to low-income and first generation students that they can achieve success at an elite college and feel like they belong there. Likewise, administrators and dedicated alumni have focused on addressing first generation student transition to college through a variety of outlets. Among these are first generation student programs, funds, and alumni mentorship initiatives as well as retooled academic advising and training for residential and advising staff.

In short, the experiences of first generation students (many, though certainly not all, of whom are also from low-income backgrounds) attending highly selective colleges offer insights into the mechanisms of social mobility through educational attainment. They also provide a test of social reproduction: are certain doors open or closed to first generation students because of their birth origins or parental influence? Studying the social and vocational pathways that students take after they arrive on campus, and the opportunities afforded them while in college and upon graduation, will help scholars to discern whether and under what conditions social reproduction occurs despite institutional efforts to maximize the potential of social mobility for all students.

I explore the questions above through the stories and insights of ninety-one first generation college students and thirty-five of their continuing generation peers attending Harvard and Georgetown University between 2012 and 2016. The participants, who entered college in the fall of 2011 or 2012, comprise a diverse range in terms of gender, race and ethnicity, birthplace origin, cultural/regional upbringing, and high school experiences. These students, 126 in all, spoke of their transition to and progress through college, including their highs and lows, challenges and accomplishments, over the course of four years. Interviewed first as sophomores and again as seniors, they explained how they changed over time and, in many instances, took the opportunity to revise earlier assessments of their college experiences. By asking the same battery of questions to both first generation and continuing generation students, I have been able to draw comparisons and note differences in the reported college-going experiences between the two samples. A demographic breakdown of the first and continuing generation participants can be found in table A.3 in the *Appendix*. The *Appendix* also provides further details concerning the initial goals of the study upon which this book is based, researcher roles and involvement, participant recruitment, data collection, interview analyses, and the iterative process of reporting and reanalysis.

It is often assumed that there is a fundamental difference in college-going between first and continuing generation students. Instead of beginning with this assumption, this book tests that assumption, and where appropriate, clarifies what differences do exist and whether they are differences of degree or kind. Also, first generation student identity and experiences tend to be treated as monolithic by higher education researchers,[13] but I found notable variation in the extent to which first generation students self-identified as such, as well as the degree to which they believed their first generation status impacted their experiences in college. This book traces the variability of the first generation experience in order to identify conditions that foster successful outcomes.

It is not inconsequential that these participants attended an elite university. By undergoing the admissions and enrollment process, they have indicated their ability and willingness to compete at very high levels of academic rigor. Most of the participants in this study were valedictorians, salutatorians, and top extracurricular competitors in their high schools. They have traveled, sometimes

13. Wildhagen advocates against a "monolithic" categorization of first generation students in "'Not Your Typical Student.'" See also Thai-Huy Nguyen and Bach Mai Dolly Nguyen, "Is the 'First-Generation Student' Term Useful for Understanding Inequality? The Role of Intersectionality in Illuminating the Implications of an Accepted—Yet Unchallenged—Term," *Review of Research in Higher Education* 42 (March 2018): 146–76. Recent comparative higher education scholarship critiques the tendency toward monolithic student categories. For excellent examples, see Jack, *Privileged Poor* and Lee, *Class and Campus Life*.

great distances, both physically and psychologically from their homes and communities. And by attending an elite university with a significant endowment, they have been afforded opportunities—internships, laboratory research, study abroad, and fellowships—that they might not otherwise secure or that may not be as readily available at less endowed or less selective colleges.

There are also perceived risks to enrolling in an elite college, especially one that may be characterized as a "legacy" institution due to its history, character, and endowment. Some first generation students, especially those from high schools with fewer advanced course offerings, may arrive feeling less prepared for college than their peers. They may worry about their "fit" with the university, or that they may not "catch up" to their better prepared peers. They may feel conflicted about the friends and family they left at home, or have trouble balancing the expectations from home and school. They might face financial pressures that their continuing generation peers seem not to have, thereby exacerbating the perceived difference between themselves and the "typical" elite college student. This study asks whether and under what conditions these issues are raised by first generation students, and details, given their responses and suggestions, what policies may be implemented to maximize a sense of belonging and fit.

The contemporary social context of the term "first generation" is a factor in this study. The term "first generation" was not widely deployed in higher education research or used as a classification in university recruitment until the early 2000s, a period that coincides with a decline in first-generation college attendance rates from thirty-nine percent at their peak in the early 1970s to under fifteen percent in the early 2000s. The effort to recruit and retain high achieving first generation students at elite universities speaks to their desire to provide opportunities to qualified students regardless of background and their fear that many qualified students are "under-matching" or not attending college at all.[14]

---

14. On the perils of "under-matching," see Bowen, Chingos, and McPherson, *Crossing the Finish Line*.

At Harvard, the active recruitment of first generation students can be traced to former university president Lawrence Summers's launch of the Harvard Financial Aid Initiative (HFAI) in 2004. The financial aid initiative was designed to support students from low- and middle-income families who might not otherwise consider Harvard because they assumed it was financially out of reach. It simplified the financial aid process by eliminating the student loan requirement and the parental contribution expectation for families under a set income threshold. Originally, families with an annual income under $40,000 were expected to pay nothing toward their children's tuition; that threshold has risen over the years to its current $65,000 income threshold. Currently, families that earn between $65,000 and $150,000 are expected to contribute up to ten percent of their household income toward tuition. The intended message from HFAI is simple: "Anyone can afford Harvard."[15]

However, first generation students are not necessarily low-income students, and low-income students are not always the first in their family to graduate from college. At Harvard, the active recruitment and enrollment of low-income students involves current students and alumni telling the stories of their Harvard experience. For some, this included a narrative of being first in the family to attend college. For instance, during the freshman orientation program known as "Opening Days," one reading assignment included an essay by alumnus David Tebaldi titled "Choosing the Color of My Collar," concerning one first generation student's experiences attending Harvard after the implementation of HFAI. However, this author's focus was primarily concerned with social class differences on campus, not the experience of being first generation, per se.

More open discussion about what it means to be a first generation college student, or "first gen," began at Harvard with the cre-

15. Harvard College Griffin Financial Aid Office website, https://college.harvard.edu/financial-aid/how-aid-works/harvard-financial-aid-initiative, accessed June 16, 2019.

ation of a first generation alumni special interest group in 2012 and a first generation student organization in 2013. Since the inauguration of these two organizations by the dedicated students and alumni who launched and expanded them, coupled with the efforts of the university to support and publicly discuss first generation experiences and challenges at Harvard, the term has become more of a fixture in the discussion of diversity and inclusion on campus.

At Georgetown, the development of the first generation category also began in the early 2000s with a fundraising effort to increase financial aid and replace loans with grant packages for high-achieving, low-income recruits. Upon the conclusion of a major capital campaign in 2003, the Georgetown Offices of Undergraduate Admissions and Financial Aid created the 1789 Scholarship and its attendant Georgetown Scholarship Program (GSP). Students who receive the 1789 Scholarship are automatically invited into the GSP, a financial aid and program support office.[16] The GSP specifically targeted first generation college students and has evolved considerably since its inception in 2004. It hosts a variety of programs throughout the year, as well as provides mentorship and leadership opportunities, emergency funds, and other financial resources for its members. The GSP has become an integral part of the larger Georgetown community, standing alongside other well-established programs such as the Community Scholars Program (a.k.a. "Community Scholars"), a rigorous summer transition program originally dedicated to supporting students from the DC public school system, and the Center for Multicultural Equity and Access, which hosts Community Scholars and seeks to increase racial and economic diversity and inclusion on campus.

Harvard and Georgetown are just two among scores of highly selective colleges and universities that have implemented dedicated support systems and programs for first generation students

---

16. The Georgetown Scholarship Program website may be found here: https://gsp.georgetown.edu/

over the past decade.[17] Their activities undoubtedly affect how first generation students experience and evaluate their time in college. This study assumes that the experiences of first generation students attending Harvard and Georgetown were in part due to the evolution of such programs. It also assumes that national trends in student affairs and student social networks affect how students evaluate their experiences on campus, often based on their understanding of what transpires among their peers on similar campuses across the nation. In short, context matters: both the institutional context at the two institutions of this study and the national context in which "first generation" is fast becoming a commonly understood category for the college-bound.

17. National organizations such as the I'm First! Campaign provide extensive resources for students who would be the first in their family to attend college. Access their website here: https://imfirst.org/

2

Preparation

A SHIFTING SELF-ASSESSMENT

A First Generation Transition Story

I first met Jake sitting at an outdoor table of a chain restaurant below the office of his on-campus job. He had a narrow window of time between work and his next class, but he was eager to sit with me for that spare hour or so to talk about his college experiences. It was mid-fall in Cambridge, but that day was unseasonably warm and sunny. Jake wore a pale yellow button-down shirt, twill shorts, and leather boat shoes. He spoke with a southern drawl not dissimilar from my own when I was his age, and the combination of his sartorial choice and the accent transported me momentarily from Harvard Square in peak leaf season to a memory of the coastal South in the spring. With pleasantries aside, I asked Jake to tell me about his first semester in college.

First of all, being from the South, the weather is warm, and I know that sounds silly, but it was difficult getting used to the cold. I had to change my wardrobe. Also, the cultural atmosphere was huge. I've never seen so much diversity. I had no Jewish friends back home, and here people talk about the holidays all the time. And you have to know the Jewish holidays, all the different holidays. I didn't come across any situations where my not understanding a certain religion or ethnic group made me offend someone or be offended. But you're just supposed to know. Oh, and there were geographical challenges. Like people would talk about the vacations they went on, and I wouldn't know where in Europe that was. Or they would tell me where they come from in Europe, and I would think, I've heard of that country but I have no idea where it is. Or, like at home, I had Asian friends, but here there are all these subgroups, like "Oh, she's Vietnamese, she's Chinese." And people are from cities, and I'm not a city boy. Having city people here was pretty big. They know how to get around, how to be in a crowd all the time, how to navigate. I'm not used to not driving places I want to go. Those little things, they sound silly, but it was *so hard*. It was like culture shock.

Jake wished aloud that the university would hold some kind of workshop at the beginning of the year "about what to expect." How to navigate a new city, how to find your way on campus and in conversations, how to comport yourself in different settings: Jake suggested that any of these programmatic additions would have aided his transition. Not having prior experience with international travel, the different neighborhoods of New York,[1] or life at boarding school, Jake felt at sea in conversation with peers during the first weeks of school. He mused that it would be ideal if the university could host a workshop, or even a trip or evening at a nice restaurant, to acclimate students who have little prior experience with social activities associated with high socioeconomic status. Then again, he wondered, how would it look if he attended a workshop like that? By explicitly going after the skills and habits he thought he might need to comport himself so as to not stand out in this new context, would he "out" himself before he had a chance to learn how to fit in?

---

1. Despite the fact that Cambridge was a near suburb of Boston, Jake gave the impression that the city of reference was invariably New York.

Jake wished he could tell people about his background without risking their judgment, but he rarely discussed his first generation status. Instead, he quickly learned to observe the language and behavior of those in his new peer group and to either mimic or parry when conversation about pre-college experiences turned in his direction. The take-home pay from his on-campus job, which consumed more than twenty hours per week, afforded him an entirely new wardrobe at the end of his first semester. Socializing with his new friends required cash on hand as well as an appropriate look. He mused, "Everyone here is a presenter, everyone is on stage. Everyone is trying to impress. You learn to get with it."

The valedictorian of his high school, with top scores on his AP and standardized exams, and competing admissions offers from an array of prestigious universities, Jake now found himself struggling to keep up in his introductory courses while working long hours to finance a new presentation of self. In high school, he memorized impressive volumes of material, including complex mathematical formulas, in order to consistently perform well on exams. He was a darling among his teachers, a tutor to his peers. Now he struggled to concentrate. He worried that he may have undiagnosed Attention-Deficit/Hyperactivity Disorder (ADHD). Fortunately, he sought mental health counseling. His therapist explained that did not have ADHD; rather, his lack of focus resulted from high stress levels and poor time management during the transition to college.

The Disclosure Conundrum

The stress behind Jake's transition to college was in large part the result of a change in status, one that I would hear repeated among first generation students from a wide variety of backgrounds. Before college, Jake enjoyed a high status among his high school teachers and peers at least in part due to his stellar performance in classes and on standardized tests. He also attended school with students from similar backgrounds, so it would seem like an irrelevant question for someone to ask what his parents do for a living. Why should it matter whether his mother was a secretary or that his father's fingernails were caked with dirt when he was slaying the AP exams? Jake felt ready to leave his home community, to expand his horizons, and to experience the world differently than he had before. Yet entering a new learning environment dominated by students from high socioeconomic households threatened to diminish his status as a star student and expose his socioeconomic background in ways that once felt irrelevant but now threatened to define him.

Slowly, Jake would have to learn the tacit rules of achievement in this new environment, which required new ways of learning as well as new ways of dealing with the ascription of status based on parental income or high school reputation. When I asked him what advice he had to best support the academic transition for first generation students, he responded:

> That's such a tough question because personally I would love it if I had a sign on my head: "Feel sympathy for me, I'm first gen and I don't know what's going on." But at the same time, I wouldn't want to be treated badly for it. It's so tough because people assume that your parents *did* go to college and that you *did* go to a high school that prepared you well. So I think that there are professors and teaching fellows[2] who don't know that kids are here who aren't prepared from the start. I would really like more assistance from the academic side, and to not be judged for not knowing some things coming in that my high school just didn't teach.

Many first generation students in this sample spoke about the conundrum of disclosure they faced at the start of college. Top-performing students in high school, they often cultivated a sense

2. This is a term used at Harvard for graduate assistants who work for professors in their courses, sometimes grade assignments, and often host study sessions and discussion sections as part of a course.

of self associated with their personal and academic achievements. Parents, teachers, and community members played an important role, but the status they enjoyed focused on their accomplishments and potential, not their socioeconomic location within a skewed national hierarchy. As entering freshmen at Harvard and Georgetown, many first generation students were immediately confronted with questions about their parents and their high schools—questions that may be intended as innocuous conversation starters but implicitly establish a status, at least in the moment of the conversation, beyond these students' design or control. Questions like "What do your parents do?" were common conversation starters during the first few weeks. Several first generation participants felt that their peers' reactions to their response—for instance, that their mothers cleaned houses, worked for fast-food chains, or were secretaries, and their fathers were cooks, construction workers, truck drivers, or disabled from an accident on the job or years of debilitating physical labor—opened a chasm between themselves and the students asking the question. As one first generation student, Ariana, astutely put it, actually responding to the question and telling their new peers what their parents do for a living "would create this reaction that was like I was somehow so alien to them, and I felt turned into something else by their reactions, like I was an object on display." This alienation in the first weeks did not come from peers alone but also from faculty. As Ariana explained:

> I went to go meet up with an adviser about one of the concentrations[3] I was considering to talk about possible courses and possible concentrations. So I was telling her why I was passionate about neurobiology and why I was passionate about this other concentration. And she said, "Oh, I'm assuming your parents are doctors?" And I said, "No, they're not." And I tried to redirect it to why I was interested [in] the concentration but

---

3. At other universities, students would call this a "major."

she kept coming back to my parents and asking me about their job and then when I told them, she started asking all these questions, and she said "Oh, you must be a big deal in your community." And I felt really exotified in that instance. And it had already happened with some of my peers, and that struck me that it was happening with a faculty member. And it took me aback.

In the first days and weeks on campus, in the flurry of trying to forge new friendships and impress faculty, many first generation students discovered a tacit conflation between parental careers and students' academic merit that seemed not only to be a common assumption on campus but an overhaul of their own concept of academic opportunity and achievement. Questions of desert quickly followed. When faced with blank stares or misunderstanding, first generation students asked themselves, "Do I belong here?" They balanced the choice of disclosure, suspecting that some of their new peers would choose not to befriend them, or vice versa, based on their answer to deceptively innocuous icebreaker questions such as "Where are you from?" and "What do your parents do?"

For some first generation participants, this practice was symptomatic of a conflation of social class with cultural attitudes attributable to different regions of the country. In particular, it reflected an East Coast hierarchy that was unfamiliar to those coming from, say, the West Coast or the South. Here is how one first generation participant, Ashley, put it:

In California, or elsewhere, you're aware that people are rich, working class, middle class. But coming here, you see old money, new money, different levels of money, and a lot of social exclusivity. And that was something I'd never encountered before. People would ask, "What school did you go to?" Like they should recognize its name! Or, "Was it a prep school, charter school, magnet school?" "Who are your parents?" "Where did you go on vacation?" That was all off-putting because it makes you reevaluate yourself and self-worth.

Everyone who comes here were rock stars in their high schools, but coming here, not only are you average, but you are put in different classes. And you are not in control of whatever classes other people put you in. You either have to be comfortable with that or become a social climber.

At home, first generation participants sometimes had to convince their parents that the college they chose was worth the effort of moving and often disrupting complex household roles and responsibilities. One first generation participant, Eliza,[4] explained that her mother, a house cleaner, was not particularly impressed with her college plans. She was unfamiliar with any symbolic meaning or social value connected to particular colleges and was simply pleased that Eliza planned to attend a university that provided financial aid. She wondered why Eliza would cross the country for college when there were options around the corner, ones where she could live at home and work alongside her parents while taking classes. One day, one of her mother's housekeeping clients asked her whether Eliza planned to attend college. When she declared that her daughter had been accepted at Georgetown University with a shrug, the client grew palpably excited. "Are you sure?" he asked three times. His congratulatory enthusiasm on behalf of Eliza and her entire family gave her mother the impression that maybe this was a good school after all, maybe even worth the distance. Seeing Eliza's choices through the eyes of her employer helped Eliza's mother revise her view of Georgetown's merit and Eliza's decision to attend college there.

Ariana recounted a similar story. Her parents had heard of Harvard, and her father was enthusiastically in support of her pursuit of an Ivy League education, but still her mother was concerned about Ariana leaving their home state. Moreover, she was not con-

---

4. Eliza chose this pseudonym as a nod to Eliza Doolittle from Shaw's *Pygmalian* and its film adaptation, "My Fair Lady." The metaphor of education as self-fashioning will return in later parts of this book.

vinced it was any better than their state's renowned flagship or the private universities in their region. Ariana recounted:

> She had heard the name Harvard, but she didn't realize its weight until she was telling one of her bosses about it. The lady was like, "Oh, did Ariana apply to colleges this year? Where did she get in, and where is she planning to go?" And my mom said, "Oh yeah, she's going to Harvard." And it was after that that she realized what a big deal it was because the lady was shocked and so excited and my mom realized how exciting it was. After that she was very pleased. And my dad made the analogy of leaving for the US, for a better life, that they had to leave their family behind in Mexico even though they missed them very much, but it was the right thing to do to create opportunities for the next generation.

In this context where first generation families did not always automatically ascribe to the social value of Harvard or Georgetown, and continuing generation peers they met in the first weeks did not understand or give value to their home contexts, many first generation students found themselves torn and ill at ease in both contexts. Their choice of college, the status they enjoyed or endured at home, and the aptitude they demonstrated through a highly competitive admissions contest all seemed to be second guessed both at home and during the first weeks of college. For some, this came as a surprise, as they were thrust for the first time into "being the hinge on the door between two ways of life."[5] Their sense of belonging, seemingly a given by way of their letter of admission, was now in question both at home and at the university.

By senior year, many of the first generation students in this sample developed discursive strategies to avoid conversation topics that might highlight any "limbo" status, particularly questions about their parents and home communities. Age, confidence, and

---

5. Lubrano, *Limbo: Blue-Collar Roots, White-Collar Dreams*, 8.

stage in college played a role, as conversation topics focused more on future plans than past experiences. As Jake explained:

> When I made the realization that from now on people are going to judge me for what I do and not what my parents do, that made me feel more included into the Harvard community. And toward senior year, you just feel more connected and settled in what you're doing. You're not trying to find out who you are. If [I'm] at a dinner with people who come from different backgrounds from [me], then I feel okay just saying, "I don't want to go through my background with you."

That confidence is hard won, as we will see in later chapters. As for now, it bears noting that first generation students are routinely surprised by these types of questions and the discursive frame that appears to assume they are normal—that the jobs held by a student's parents plays a role in the student's academic merit and admission to an elite college.

A Continuing Generation Transition Story

Much of the qualitative research on students from first generation, low-income, or marginalized backgrounds who attend elite colleges draws comparisons between these groups of students and their more advantaged peers. Questions often frame students as "other" when they ask for descriptions of the differences between themselves and "typical" or "dominant" student types,[6] especially when comparisons are made without evidence derived from "typical" students' accounts of their own transition to college. This

---

6. Notable exceptions are Aries, *Race and Class Matters at an Elite College* and Aries and Berman, *Speaking of Race and Class*, which focus specifically on race and class at an elite college, as well as Armstrong and Hamilton, *Paying for the Party*, which focuses on women's classed experience of college, and Lee, *Class and Campus Life*, which also focuses on women's classed experience, this time at an elite women's college.

strategy of asking marginalized students to compare themselves to their nonmarginalized peers and then using that as evidence of actual difference risks concluding that differences in transition are starker than they may actually be, or that nonmarginalized students do not experience similar setbacks or turmoil in the transition to college. Campus administrators and staff may also slide into a narrative of comparing first generation students with a fictionalized "typical" student type, a strategy that both has the opposite of its intended effect, which is to encourage first generation students to seek help when they feel out of place or uncomfortable in their transition to college, *and* fails to adequately address challenges to the college transition that many students face, regardless of their family educational context.[7]

In this study, first generation and continuing generation participants were asked the same battery of questions in order to discern whether and to what extent first generation students experienced a qualitatively different transition to an elite college than their continuing generation peers. As I will expand on in the following pages, I found that continuing generation students spoke of difficult transitions at rates similar to their first generation peers, sometimes for similar and other times for different reasons. Moreover, many continuing generation participants who might otherwise appear to have experienced easy transitions nevertheless raised concerns about the "competitive" social climate at their college, calling for a widespread and honest discussion about what it would take to change the campus into a welcoming place for all. However, there was an important difference in the way that first and continuing generation students interpreted their transitions to college: if things went wrong, then first generation students were more likely to blame themselves and ask whether they deserved to be there, while continuing generation students were more apt to scrutinize the institution and ask whether it could do more to serve them.

7. Lee, *Class and Campus Life*; Wildhagen, "'Not Your Typical Student.'"

I met J.B. in the late fall of his sophomore year. He made time to meet me at a busy but convenient local café in between his rowing practice and his next extracurricular commitment. He had but slivers of available time in his otherwise packed weekly calendar, but like Jake and many of the students with whom I spoke, J.B. emphasized that it was important for him to carve out a moment to discuss his college experiences with me in the hopes that his advice could help future students.

J.B.'s path to Harvard was the result of a minor rebellion at home. A star athlete and graduate of an elite boarding school, J.B. explained that he was expected to take his place as a legacy student at a different Ivy League university where his parents and at least one grandparent were alumni. On a spring evening in his senior year, J.B. checked his email and saw that he had been accepted to Harvard as well as the university where his family claimed legacy ties. He printed out his acceptance letters, brought them to the family dinner table, and proudly ripped in half the acceptance letter where he would be a legacy admit. He chose Harvard. J.B. wanted to prove that he could gain admission without a legacy preference, and without being a recruited athlete. He would "walk on" to a team in his freshman year, and he would attend a school where he had no family ties rather than attending the expected university and worrying whether he had been admitted through a less stringent admissions standard.

J.B. grew up in a wealthy and cultured home, with long stints living abroad. His parents and grandparents had attended elite schools, and as I gathered, they expected him to follow suit with ease. So when I began the interview with the same question I asked all participants—*how prepared did he feel for Harvard compared to his peers?*—I was not surprised that J.B. felt more prepared than his peers both socially and in terms of academic preparation. Anticipating the next turn in our interview, I assumed he would describe a smooth transition to college life, success in his courses, and accomplishments in extracurricular organizations. Here I was making a predication about J.B.'s sense of success and belonging based on the narrative he gave of his parental background and prior education.[8]

However, instead of adhering to the narrative I'd assumed, J.B. described feeling overwhelmed by his coursework, falling ill early in the school year, and struggling to balance his athletic commitments and social life in addition to his academic goals. He confessed that classes and his professors intimidated him. He did not know how to use a syllabus properly; how to manage his time and energy; or when, how, and where to seek help. He explained:

> I had no preparation for the college type course and how it works, how you understand how your grade is composed and what assignments should look like. For me, freshman year, it would have been good to take three classes freshman fall and I would have been fine. . . . You suffer not necessarily because you are incapable of doing the work, but the newness of it makes it more difficult to get a handle on.

When I asked J.B. what advice he would offer administrators seeking to support students' transition to college, he proposed a course

---

8. This prediction was based on an assumption that an elite private high school would facilitate the transition to an elite college. See Jack, *Privileged Poor* (2019). An alternative hypothesis might be that parental wealth, and not private schooling, better predicts collegiate outcomes. See Pianta and Ansari, "Does Attendance in Private Schools Predict Student Outcomes at Age 15?" In Pianta and Ansari's longitudinal analysis of over a thousand children who attend selective private high schools, private school attendance was a reliable predictor of collegiate success. When the authors controlled for socioeconomic factors, private school advantages were entirely eliminated. J.B., whose transition is described in this chapter, was both a private school graduate and the son of wealthy parents, and I expected that he would describe an easy transition either based on his family wealth or his high school preparation. But I was wrong. This surprise serves as a reminder that students' personal evaluations of the college transition may yield different results than just looking at retention and GPA scores. While both types of evidence are useful when informing programmatic and policy changes, student self-reports of transition challenges may offer more nuanced guidance in recruitment and communications for new programs designed to bolster both student success and perceived belonging.

that could help all students to understand the subtleties of college-level expectations:

> Maybe in freshman fall have a required class that teaches you how to take classes. Teaching you the fundamentals, teaching you how to talk in section, how to comport yourself. The number of sections I go to where nobody speaks because they are afraid or don't feel comfortable talking in section is enormous, and it's just too bad. So the course, it could be divided into segments, like how to manage your time, how to read a syllabus and plan ahead, how to approach faculty, that kind of thing. Plus that would alleviate the stress of having four full classes in the fall. You could run it potentially Pass/Fail. I imagine it as not a performance-based class, but rather a transition class for credit.[9]

Beyond asking for an ungraded training course in how to approach college, J.B. also bemoaned the state of academic advising and the competitive extracurricular and social scenes on campus. He described advisors as clueless and unaware of how to select classes or build an appropriate schedule, advocating instead for more institutionalized peer support between upper-class and first-year students. He complained of a culture of heavy drinking, exclusionary parties, and competitive peer relations among members of private social clubs who, in his assessment, were "playing out fantasies of what state school is like."[10] As an alternative to allowing

9. Harvard, where J.B. was enrolled, offers a Freshman Seminar that is guided by similar goals to those he described. While it, too, is ungraded and counts toward one's graduation requirements, J.B. hoped for a course that more directly addressed *purpose of college* and *life purpose* questions rather than research topics developed by faculty.

10. J.B. indicated that Harvard's social clubs occasionally made reference to partying like "state schools" do, implying that "state schools" are presumed more fun. J.B. described clothing accessories, purchasable through a private website, emblazoned with a "Harvard State" logo, purportedly for donning at private social club parties. The earliest reference I could find to "Harvard State" concerned a controversial party

exclusive and unregulated social organizations to dominate the social scene on campus, J.B. advocated for more university-sponsored trips to Boston and the surrounding region, preferably encouraging first-year students to meet people outside of their current social networks and to escape the "Harvard bubble."[11]

Being and feeling prepared for Harvard did not inoculate J.B. from the bewilderment, self-doubt, and loneliness that accompanied his transition to college. His confusion, not knowing the rules—"You suffer not necessarily because you are incapable of doing the work, but the newness of it makes it more difficult to get a handle on"—was repeated when we spoke two years later, in the fall of his senior year. As with his sophomore interview, J.B. framed his high school preparation as exceptional. He was well prepared for college, both academically and socially. He built lasting and meaningful relationships with professors and peers, achieved honors and leadership positions in several extracurricular commit-

---

hosted in 2003, which was promoted with the following: "Ever wanted to party like they do at that state school you could have coasted through?" See Joshua Gottlieb, "450 Matriculate at Harvard State University," *Harvard Crimson* Nov. 12, 2003, https://www.thecrimson.com/article/2003/11/12/450-matriculate-at-harvard-state -univ/?page=2. Like nursery rhymes on playgrounds, the legacies of prior matriculants' contested cultural symbols emerge rearranged and transformed among future cohorts without acknowledgement of origin or history. These symbols signal transgression and fun within closed contexts, often alienating outsiders and demarcating stark "us" versus "them" communities. Here, the "them" is "state school" students, whose college transitions are presumed to be far easier. This is an assumption not borne out by evidence, but over time, it became a common assumption among first and continuing generation participants alike. For more in-depth cultural analysis of transgressive symbols of "fun" in collegiate contexts, see LaDousa, *House Signs and Collegiate Fun* and Moffatt, *Coming of Age in New Jersey*.

11. This term was used repeatedly by interview participants at both Harvard and Georgetown, both of which shared a convenient proximity to a city center while their student populations bemoaned feeling too busy to discover all that their city had to offer. A quick search of the Harvard College Admissions Student Blog revealed no less than forty-four blog entries, mostly written in the years of this study, decrying the "Harvard Bubble." Similarly, Georgetown students wrote of "breaking the Georgetown bubble" and in an admissions blog.

ments, and was involved in peer mental health counseling on campus. He comported himself with poise and confidence. Even so, when I asked him again what campus leaders could do to smooth the transition to college, he returned to his initial confusion and the mental strain it caused him, as well as the students whom he counseled through peer volunteering:

> Same thing I said two years ago. Freshman year either three classes or two classes pass-fail out of the four. Anything to reduce the load. Because *damn* if people aren't ready for it. . . . That's not a good set-up for the rest of the four years. You've got to be magically ready for college, and it's not realistic.

J.B.'s difficult transition would not be discernible in a review of his academic transcript or extracurricular commitments. This was true of many continuing generation participants who, like J.B. and like many of his first generation peers, criticized the social competitiveness and the lack of a clear understanding of the expectations of college. As Elizabeth Lee so astutely explains in her evaluation of low-income students at an elite women's college, the administrative act of demarcating one group of students as "disadvantaged" as compared to their peers has the effect of segmenting the student body, reifying a discourse of competence presumed on the part of the "typical" or "dominant" student, subtly labeling confusion as disfunction or deficit on the part of the now-identified *marginalized* student.[12] J.B.'s narrative serves as a rejoinder that, while first generation students may face significant challenges in the transition to college, these challenges do not impact first generation students alone. Institutional messages and policies can have an impact on an entire community while also disproportionately affecting those most vulnerable. It is not the case that continuing generation students arrive without deficits, confusion, or disenchantment of their own. While first and continuing generation students may share these sentiments, first generation stu-

12. Lee, *Class and Campus Life*, 73–77, 160.

dents like Jake often reprove themselves, while continuing generation students like J.B. scrutinize the institution for how it could
better serve them.

Self-Assessed Preparation

As we saw with J.B., self-assessed preparation does not always predict a successful college transition. However, it may play a role in
the confidence students feel upon arrival. Feeling well prepared
may boost a sense of belonging early in one's college experience.
Likewise, feeling less prepared than one's peers may cause or at
least correlate with a reduced sense of belonging, desert, and overall social value in the college context. Memoirs and personal narratives across multiple decades of first generation students suggest
that feeling poorly equipped for college can cause considerable
psychological strain in the first weeks and months of college.[13]

In this sample, first generation students were more likely than
continuing generation students to describe themselves as less prepared for college. In sophomore and senior interviews, participants were asked how prepared they felt for college in relation to
their peers. As table 2.1 shows, among the ninety-one repeat participant first generation students, forty-four percent (n = 40) described themselves as "less academically prepared" than their
peers during their sophomore interviews. This was more than
twice the rate of their continuing generation peers in the sample,
twenty percent (n = 7) of whom described themselves as less prepared. When interviewed again as seniors, the preparation gap
widened to nearly three times the rate: fifty-seven percent of first
generation seniors in the sample stated they felt less prepared

---

13. A few examples include Lubrano, *Limbo: Blue-Collar Roots, White-Collar
Dreams*; Jimenez, *Reaching Out* and *Taking Hold: From Migrant Childhood to Columbia University*; Vance, *Hillbilly Elegy: A Memoir of a Family and Culture in Crisis*; and
Westover, *Educated: A Memoir*. See also Rodriguez, *Hunger of Memory* and the rage
of misrecognition.

TABLE 2.1. Self-Reported Preparation, First and Continuing Generation
Sophomores and Seniors

	More/As (Sophomores)	Less (Sophomores)	More/As (Seniors)	Less (Seniors)
First Generation	56% (51)	44% (40)	43% (39)	57% (52)
Continuing Generation	80% (28)	20% (7)	80% (28)	20% (7)

coming into college, compared to twenty percent of continuing generation seniors.[14] While first generation participants as a group were more likely to trace a declining self-assessment of preparation with more time and increased experience in college, continuing generation participants were more likely to hold the same views of their preparation throughout college. When asked why they changed their assessment, most first generation seniors offered some version of "I just didn't know what I didn't know."

As demonstrated in table 2.2 below, when disaggregating students' responses by high school type, gender, and ethnicity, other differences in self-reported preparation also emerged. For instance, comparing first generation sophomores who attended public and private high schools, forty-six percent of public school graduates and thirty-five percent of private school graduates reported feeling overall less well prepared for college than their peers. When asked the same question as seniors, sixty-two percent of first generation public school graduates and forty percent of private vate school graduates reported feeling overall less well prepared.

14. In both instances, the difference between response types of first and continuing generation students was found to be significant. A Fisher's Exact Test, which compares first and continuing generation student self-assessed preparation (categorized as either "more/as prepared" or "less prepared"), was found to be significant: x^2 (w/Yates Correction) = 5.221, p<.05. That the difference is significant helps to understand the shape of the sample, but it should not be read as a causal claim, nor should it replace a nuanced understanding of what preparation means on the part of the participants, as described in this chapter.

TABLE 2.2. Self-Reported Preparation by High School, Gender, Race/Ethnicity

	More/As (Sophomores)	Less (Sophomores)	More/As (Seniors)	Less (Seniors)
Parental Education				
First Generation (FG)	56% (51)	44% (40)	43% (39)	57% (52)
Continuing Generation (CG)	80% (28)	20% (7)	80% (28)	20% (7)
High School				
FG Public	54% (38)	46% (33)	38% (27)	62% (44)
FG Private	65% (13)	35% (7)	60% (12)	40% (8)
CG Public	70% (16)	30% (7)	70% (16)	30% (7)
CG Private	100% (12)	0% (0)	100% (12)	0% (0)
Gender				
FG Female	52% (33)	48% (30)	40% (25)	60% (38)
FG Male	64% (18)	36% (10)	50% (14)	50% (14)
CG Female	71% (12)	29% (5)	82% (14)	18% (3)
CG Male	89% (16)	11% (2)	78% (14)	22% (4)
Race/Ethnicity				
FG African American	36% (4)	64% (7)	36% (4)	64% (7)
FG Asian	63% (12)	37% (7)	53% (10)	47% (9)
FG Latinx	47% (15)	53% (17)	28% (9)	72% (23)
FG Multiracial	40% (2)	60% (3)	40% (2)	60% (3)
FG White	75% (18)	25% (6)	58% (14)	42% (10)
CG African American	100% (3)	0% (0)	100% (3)	0% (0)
CG Asian	75% (6)	25% (2)	87.5% (7)	12.5% (1)
CG Latinx	n/a	n/a	n/a	n/a
CG Multiracial	n/a	n/a	n/a	n/a
CG White	79% (19)	21% (5)	75% (18)	25% (6)

Attending a private high school may have prepared some first generation students for the expectations of college, given that the percentage of those who reported feeling less well prepared was lower, though not significantly so, for private high school graduates than public high school graduates.[15]

15. Jack's scholarship details a distinction between the pre-college preparation and habits of low-income public and private high school graduates. See Jack, "Culture Shock Revisited," "Crisscrossing Boundaries," "(No) Harm in Asking," and *Privileged Poor.*

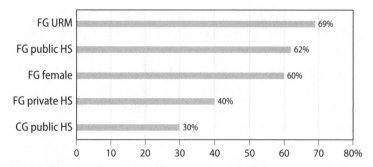

FIGURE 2.1. Percentage (in category) of senior respondents "less" prepared, by high school, gender, underrepresented minority. CG, continuing generation; FG, first generation; HS, high school; URM, underrepresented minority.

There were zero private school graduates in the continuing generation sample who felt less prepared, while thirty percent of the public school graduates did. A distinct minority of continuing generation students who attended lower resourced high schools narrated their transition to college similarly to first generation students who attended similar types of high schools. This finding suggests that, under certain conditions, high school type may matter as much or more than first generation status when students reflect on their preparation for college.

Differences emerged in response to questions about preparation based on participants' gender and ethnicity as well. First generation women were more likely to say that they felt less prepared overall for college than first generation men. First generation underrepresented minorities, who comprised slightly more than half of the overall sample, were also more likely to say they felt less prepared for college than first generation white and Asian/Asian American participants (see figure 2.1).[16]

16. However, these differences were not found to be statistically significant, and one should be cautious not to generalize from small samples. These figures help the reader to better understand the shape of the sample and to consider participant responses in relation to their peers.

As social psychologist Claude Steele and others have long pointed out, stereotype threat, or feeling at risk of performing in accordance with a negative stereotype associated with one's social group, can affect self-assessment and performance for both women and underrepresented minorities, and that effect is more significantly felt among students at more selective universities than less selective ones.[17] The difference in student responses to questions of prior preparation based on high school type, gender, and ethnicity may be the result of perceived lack of fit or a response to stereotype threat, rather than actual performance or observable objective preparation levels. As many first generation students explained to me, an initial self-estimation of lower preparation often motivated them to work harder on their academic assignments, thereby attenuating or entirely eliminating potential gaps in performance.

Kimberlé Crenshaw's intersectionality theory[18] also contributes to a deeper understanding of the variation in preparation levels both within and between first generation student groups. In her groundbreaking and highly influential 1989 law review article, Crenshaw argued that race and gender, long operationalized as mutually exclusive categories, were but single axes among many intersecting axes that can be used to define personhood. Failure to consider the collision of multiple nondominant categories in people's lived and legal experiences runs the risk of overlooking, even erasing, entire groups of people from a discourse on rights and justice. Crenshaw demonstrated how a "single axis framework" in antidiscrimination law erased the specific experiences of "double discrimination"[19] against black women in hiring practices when, after plaintiffs demonstrated a pattern of black women not

17. See Steele, *Whistling Vivaldi: How Stereotypes Affect Us and What We Can Do.* For other examples, see also Inzlicht and Schmader, *Stereotype Threat,* and Banaji and Greenwald, *Blindspot: Hidden Biases of Good People.*

18. Crenshaw, "Demarginalizing the Intersection of Race and Sex."

19. Crenshaw, 149.

being hired, the companies in three separate lawsuits succeeded in having antidiscrimination claims overruled when they pointed out that they did indeed hire "women" and "black" employees. In an argument that resembles a Venn diagram approach to categorizing the experience of status and discrimination, Crenshaw concludes: "I am suggesting that Black women can experience discrimination in ways that are both similar to and different from those experienced by white women and Black men."[20]

While's Crenshaw's argument was originally intended as a critique of the limits of then-prevailing antidiscrimination doctrine, the term she coined has since been mobilized to address conditions of structural and social inequality in a variety of contexts, including higher education.[21] How can the concept of intersectionality illuminate potential variation in first generation and continuing generation students' self-assessed preparation? A closer look at the Latina public high school graduates in this sample is instructive (see figure 2.2).[22] As mentioned above, fifty-seven percent (n = 52) of the ninety-one first generation seniors in the sample identified as less prepared than their peers for college. Seventy-one first generation seniors graduated from public high schools, sixty-two percent (n = 44) of whom described themselves as less prepared. Thirty-four participants identified as Latinx, seventy-four percent (n = 25) of whom felt less prepared. Twenty-three students in the overall first generation sample identified as both female and Latinx. As seniors, eighty-three percent (n = 19) of these female Latinx participants said that they were less

20. Crenshaw.

21. For example, see Griffin and Museus, *Using Mixed-Methods Approaches*.

22. This is the modal student category both for the sample collected from Harvard and Georgetown and for first generation students in the United States, more broadly. See Spiegler and Bednarek, "First-Generation Students: What We Ask, What We Know and What It Means." However, regional differences do matter. On the West Coast, for instance, the modal first generation student is more likely to be of Asian descent, reflecting a higher proportional representation among Asian and Asian American students than, for instance, in the US South or East Coast.

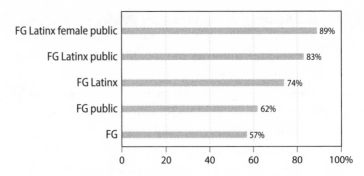

FIGURE 2.2. Percentage (in category) of senior respondents "less" prepared, by first generation, public high school, female, Latinx. FG, first generation.

prepared for college than their peers.[23] Five of these nineteen changed their self-assessment downward from "more/as" to "less" prepared between sophomore and senior year, indicating something happened during their course of college to reduce their self-evaluation of readiness for their particular college. Finally, adding the third layer of high school context, among the eighteen Latinx female public high school graduates in the sample, eighty-nine percent (n = 16) identified as "less" prepared.

Compare this pattern to the white female respondents in the sample, who, borrowing from Crenshaw's theory, may experience a single axis of marginalization as female students in a male-dominated organization. Again, fifty-seven percent of the ninety-one first generation participants felt less prepared for college. Sixty-two percent of the first generation public high school graduates felt less prepared. Among white first generation students, forty-two percent (10 out of 24) felt less prepared, while forty-four percent (7 out of 16) of white female first generation students and fifty percent (5 out of 10) of white female public high school graduates felt less prepared. These percentages indicate that, within this sample and possibly beyond, while lower levels of self-assessed

23. Among first generation Latinx male participants, the percentage who reported feeling "less" prepared was 54.5 percent (six out of eleven respondents). All but one of the Latinx male participants in this sample attended public high school.

preparation affect students from a variety of demographic backgrounds, those with multiple marginalized statuses reported feeling less prepared at higher rates than those whose marginalization fell along a single axis such as gender.

Student Interpretations of Preparation:
For Those Less Prepared

One can see from the tables and figures previously shown that first generation students were more likely than their continuing generation peers to disclose feeling less prepared for the rigorous expectations of their highly selective college. This is helpful information when considering whether and how to offer transitional support to incoming cohorts, but it may lead to injurious stereotyping or advice devoid of context. Incorporating students' own interpretations of their preparation levels helps provide a clearer picture of the conditions that commonly accompany a sense of more or less preparation.

Those students who described themselves as less prepared than their peers for college generally focused on their high school experience as a potential reason for lower preparation for college, rather than their parents or their income status. Most first generation students pointed specifically to school segregation and high school peers who were disengaged or uncurious, with well-meaning but overworked teachers and poor funding as secondary reasons.[24] They often defended their high school teachers and

24. In a recent study of state higher education systems (such as California, Texas, and Oregon) using percent plans to increase the number of students from lower socioeconomic backgrounds attending public four-year universities, researchers found that high school quality has a significant effect on academic achievement in college. Even among students who achieved top ranks in high school, those who attended lower resourced high schools were more likely to perform at lower rates than their peers in college. These effects were more pronounced for women and low-income students, and did not diminish over time. See Black et al., "Can You Leave High School Behind?"

administrators from the perceived judgement of their college faculty and peers, bristling at the suggestion that their teachers were of poor quality or incapable of preparing them for the rigors of college. First generation Ariana, who came from an urban district struggling with overpopulation, explained, "For the resources my school had, my teachers tried and did a lot. But they had fifty students to a classroom. How much individual personal attention could they reasonably be expected to give?"

Overcrowding was not the only high school challenge that first generation participants raised. Jake, who attended a small high school and described extensive teacher involvement, emphasized the lack of outward focus from his peers and teachers:

> People in my high school don't have dreams of working on Wall Street. People from my high school don't go to graduate school. Maybe some had a dream like that, but it would be very vocationally focused if they were focused on anything at all. They would have dreams of being the town doctor or accountant. Looking back at the kids who went on to technical school, they either dropped out, or maybe they are doing great, but they are stuck in their comfort zones. They have never reached beyond what they are used to, and so they have no idea what the options are out there. . . . I never thought it would affect me to leave. The way they prepared me, being in a new place or doing new things, that was not part of the preparation, and it was a real shock to come here.

Not only did Jake describe the shock of the new (new ways of talking, of doing things, of solving problems), but by the time he was a senior, he suspected that other students had been prepared to expect new and different challenges in college. He was surprised by the surprise itself, whereas he surmised that continuing generation students were prepared for the surprises to come.

When first generation participants identified a subject area where they felt well prepared, they attributed their ongoing success to a talented, dedicated high school teacher who made an effort to challenge them beyond the minimum course requirements. First generation S., for instance, explained the stark conditions of his high school context as such:

> I came from a public school that was minority dominated and predominately low income. People selling drugs on campus, police at school, metal detectors to get into school: that was what my school was like. I am trying to paint you a picture here, because on the one hand it was the best school in the district, but what does it mean to be the best school in a failing district with a population like that?
>
> We had a few AP classes offered at my school, and I am very grateful to those classes because they pushed me to think differently. In the non-AP classes, the teachers didn't care about teaching as much. It's a cyclical problem: the teachers don't respect the students and have low expectations for them, and the students respond by not working. And the teachers feel like they are legitimated in not wasting the effort on the kids because they wouldn't do the work anyway. That cycle of apathy, you know?
>
> So, lucky me, I was "smart" at a young age, so I was put in more challenging classes. And that led me down a different path. But there are plenty of kids who didn't have that experience, and they could have been provided with so much better than what they got. And it's a very bittersweet thing for me because I escaped it but I know so many kids who didn't.

Explaining why he was recommended a remedial expository writing course the first semester in college, S. excused his high school English instructor while laying the blame on his fellow classmates: "I had a great teacher but she was limited by the students. How are you going to discuss a book assignment when no one else but you and the teacher did the reading? How are you going to teach anything when none of the homework is getting done to prepare for the lesson?" When asked to specifically talk about his writing preparation, S. continued to absolve his high school instructor and blame the school environment for his lack of adequate skills:

> My English teacher was great but she couldn't spend the time challenging me, like I said. And that hits you *bam* smack dab in the face, that you're already inadequate. Afterwards, I really appreciated [taking the additional college writing course], because I am a better writer now. But that hits all sorts of insecurities right away, and I had to deal with those on top of the everyday adjustments. And that rubs off on you. If a crap-load of kids aren't reading, then yeah, you're reading more than them but what does that mean?

As with English, S. attributed his success in college math classes to the dedication of his high school calculus teacher. He also credited his mother, who reminded him of upcoming assignments and helped him to stay on top of his work in high school. In short, the blame for lack of preparation tended to lie either in less academically inclined peers or a flagging system, what might be considered the school-level ecology, but the credit for their preparation came from specific individuals such as teachers and parents, indicating a potential tension and interplay among individuals and their educational context.[25]

As noted previously, some continuing generation students reported feeling less well prepared for college in ways that were similar to their first generation peers. One in five continuing generation sophomores—and thirty percent of the continuing generation

25. Ecological systems theory, first developed by Urie Bronfenbrenner in 1979, posits overlapping ecologies that affect student learning, from the parent-child relationship to the home and school contexts, the school system's priorities and actions, and influences from broader society on student development. Human development in this model is influenced by a person's individual characteristics, the context or "ecologies," the interaction between the individual and their overlapping "ecologies," and finally, the process of time. See Bronfenbrenner, *Ecology of Human Development*. For a detailed overview of this theory and its evolution since Bronfrenbrenner first introduced it, see Ettekal and Mahoney, "Ecological Systems Theory."

sophomores who attended public high schools—stated that they felt less well prepared than their peers for college.[26] The reasons they often gave for their perceived lack of preparation echoed the first generation participants: an underresourced high school, inexperienced teachers with high staff attrition, or the absence of important pre-college courses. Several students discussed not having a math option available to them because of the precipitous firing or resignation of a key instructor, or the elimination of course funding from district budget cuts, or even teacher strikes and walkouts disrupting school. Donald, a continuing generation participant and engineering major from a small town in the American West said:

> I was less prepared. My academic background was the reason for that. . . . I attended a small school with limited resources, and I took their highest math course my junior year so had a year off math my senior year, which was not a good thing at all. Just in general not having access to academically rigorous courses, that has been the biggest adjustment.

Other continuing students from small towns or larger inner-city schools who felt less prepared for college said that they "didn't know how to study" or that their pre-college experiences were "pretty straightforward." They also argued that their high school peers did not have the same level of expectations for college. Both

26. While more continuing generation women than men claimed to feel less prepared for college, the difference is not statistically significant. Unlike with first generation students, ethnicity did not seem to be a factor in self-reported preparation for continuing generation students in this sample. Indeed, White and Asian/Asian American continuing generation students were more likely to say they felt less well prepared for college than African American students, and no Latinx continuing generation students completed two interviews to be included in this study (although there were Latinx in both sophomore and senior continuing generation samples, they were nonrepeating participants). So the hypothesis about stereotype threat does not appear to be as well supported among continuing generation students as it does for first generation students.

statements resonated with first generation descriptions of ways in which their home communities did not prepare them for the rigors of a highly selective college.[27]

One continuing generation student, Bailey, reflected on why she rated herself as less prepared for her college with the following insight: "I think it's tricky because you don't want to single people out by doing something special for first generation college students, but there are also layers to it. My parents went to 'lower tier'[28] colleges, and I'm the first one to go to an 'elite' college and there are a number of things they don't understand. There are so many things they don't know and can't help me with." She mused that a wider group of students could benefit from additional support largely targeted toward and tailored to first generation students at her college. As an African American female from the US South, she periodically felt excluded and misrecognized on her campus, and hoped that more programming could be done to convene, include, and support all students.

Another continuing generation student, Cassidy, expressed a similar concern about "singling out" first generation students for additional support when continuing generation peers also stand to benefit. As an Asian American from the East Coast, she was concerned that some may stereotype her as someone who would not need academic or social support, when in fact, she felt lost

27. One subtle geographic difference may be of interest to admissions staff: the continuing generation students who claimed to feel less prepared for college tended to hail from rural, semi-rural, or inner-city public schools, as opposed to the private and wealthy suburban public high schools of their fellow continuing generation students in the sample. However, first generation students in the sample who claimed to feel less prepared also often came from inner city high schools (both public and private) as well as the flagging inner suburbs that ring metropolitan regions across the nation, *not* rural regions, and *not* in stark contrast to their first generation peers who claimed to feel as or more prepared for college (these, too, tended to graduate from similar types of high schools from similar regions, although a higher rate of as/more prepared first generation students also attended private schools).

28. Bailey put this phrase in scare quotes with her hands during the interview.

during her transition into college and throughout her time in college. Networking, engaging in small talk, and seeking extra help from professors all felt foreign to her. When asked to compare her level of preparation for college to her peers, she ranked herself as "definitely less prepared." Cassidy explained:

> I went to a large public school. It wasn't a bad one, it's just there weren't the same opportunities. You think, "It's fine, this is the school I go to." But when you get here, you meet students who took ten APs or IBs or went to international schools. My school culture wasn't competitive. No one went to Ivies. No one applied to Ivies. One or two applied but didn't go if they did get in because of the money issue, or they never thought about it. Coming in, I was living in middle-class suburbia, and there's this whole elite community you don't have access to that you're faced with when you come here. It's a very big adjustment coming here, and thinking more deeply about it, there are serious challenges . . .
>
> People like me, you're fighting that much harder. You're not used to debating academically. You're not used to meeting so many people, not used to networking.

Cassidy and Bailey's request for additional support, which they surmised was offered exclusively to first generation students, highlights a conundrum for university administrators. By identifying a population that they suspect stands the most to gain from additional support, which can be both intensive and expensive, administrators and staff risk overlooking those students whose needs overlap with the selected population, but they do not fit the established definition or eligibility criteria for support.

Perhaps just as important as recognizing an overlap among first and continuing generation students who feel less prepared for college is the notable difference in tone between the two student groups in discussions of their pre-college expectations. First generation students who described themselves as less prepared were often surprised by this realization, framing it as a discovery they made only after spending a few weeks in college. The harsh slap in the face of a low midterm grade, especially in a subject in which they had excelled during high school, was a twice-told tale among first generation students. By contrast, continuing generation students arrived with an awareness of the challenges they expected to face performing alongside better prepared peers. For example, MacNeill, a continuing generation participant from a large urban district, characterized his public high school as "not rigorous at all." He was keenly aware in advance of matriculation that he had not developed the study habits, time management practices, content knowledge, or motivation requisite to hit the ground running. While he blamed his flagging high school for his lack of preparation, his description differed from first generation participants in his level of advance awareness of his specific academic gaps. As he put it: "Those are all a degree of transition *that you know in advance* but you still can't prepare yourself for as a high school senior in the kind of setting I came from."

The surprise—*Wait, I'm not as prepared as I thought I was*—is a common theme both in scholarly and more popular first generation literature.[29] The distinction between continuing generation

29. For example, see Stephens, Brannon et al., "Feeling at Home in College" and Stephens, Hamedani et al., "Closing the Social-Class Achievement Gap." Stephens examined surprise and "cultural mismatch" among first generation college students at elite universities for her doctoral thesis, finding that among the first generation students in her study, they were more likely to begin college with cultural ideologies informed by "interdependence," while continuing generation students began college with strong notions of "independence." While the study that is the subject of this book often found the opposite to be true—continuing generation students knew how to ask for help and work in groups, while first generation students were used to doing everything on their own and saw asking for help as a sign they didn't belong—Stephens's research is nonetheless important in discerning cultural mismatch among first and continuing generation students who may enter an elite college context with values regarding educational practice and the demonstration of merit that may not be aligned with the university's goals and norms. See Stephens, "Cultural Mismatch." The theme of surprise is crucial for understanding sensemaking among first generation students. For more about surprise and sensemaking from the lens of black male

students coming in less prepared and aware of their lack of preparation, while first generation students felt surprised, sometimes even outraged at their high schools in retrospect, is a fine but important one. It speaks to differing tacit expectations about what it means to be prepared for college. It also suggests that differentiated and ongoing messaging to incoming students could help those who "don't know what they don't know" to acclimate to college more swiftly without patronizing or fueling the anxiety of those entering college acutely aware of their relative lack of preparation.

Student Interpretations of Preparation:
For Those Well Prepared

Research studies concerning first generation college students tend to focus on the challenges that these students face when transitioning into and proceeding through college.[30] While this is an important focus of scholarship, and serves administrators and policymakers well when considering support programs to implement or augment, it nonetheless may skew the story toward a deficit narrative rather than evoke the complex reality of college-

---

undergraduates, see Harper and Newman, "Surprise, Sensemaking, and Success in the First College Year: Black Undergraduate Men's Academic Adjustment Experiences." For surprise among first generation students in terms of academic expectations, see Collier and Morgan, "'Is That Paper Really Due Today?'" For a phenomenal fictional account of surprise and sensemaking from the vantage point of a first generation Latina attending an elite liberal arts college in the Northeast, see Capó Crucet, *Make Your Home among Strangers.*

30. In their international review of research literature concerning first generation students, Spiegler and Bednarek pointed out that first generation students are often arbitrarily defined as "at risk" compared to their continuing generation peers, and that the prevailing model is one of a "deficit narrative" even in the face of abundant evidence to the contrary. See Spiegler and Bednarek, "First Generation Students: What We Ask, What We Know and What It Means," 329–30.

going, in general, and first generation college-going, in particular.[31] It may also turn a status—first generation—into a black-and-white category when the experience of being first generation may in fact be better understood in terms of intensity, location along a continuum, or the product of intersectionality. To understand more about the complexities of the first generation college-going experience, I wanted to look at those first generation students who said they had no problems transitioning to college and who felt as or more prepared than their peers coming in. While this group comprises a minority of first generation seniors, it nonetheless comprised more than forty percent of the first generation senior sample. Could they offer unique advice for campus administrators in how to connect with and best support first generation students more broadly? Do they have advice for their first generation peers about how to find a home and a solid academic footing on their highly selective campus?

I met Jason, a political science major from the West Coast, one weekday evening in the early fall of his senior year at a trendy basement restaurant, just a short walk from campus. When we were first introduced, he swung out his hand for a rigorous handshake and a winning smile. As with Jake, S., and many other first generation participants, my first impression of him was one of confidence and poise limned with an eagerness to tell me his story. When I asked him to describe his transition to college and how well he felt his high school prepared him, he responded with the following:

> My high school prepared me incredibly well for college. Because I grew up in the right area, I had extraordinary resources available. . . . My school was one of the top three high schools in [my home state]. It was public, but not really. There were some kids from disadvantaged neighborhoods there, so it was relatively normal. But it also had one of the best music pro-

31. See Horowitz, *Campus Life* and Hu, Katherine, and Kuh, "Student Typologies in Higher Education."

grams in the country. I was a bassist in the orchestra. We performed at an incredibly high level. If you didn't see who was playing, you might think you were at a professional concert.

I was around the right kind of students, parents who were in the right professions, a lot of money. I had more advantages than some of the much better off students here who went to lesser schools. The quality of my high school teachers was super high. My Model UN group was ranked #1 in the country. And that led me to an interest in international politics, which brought me to Georgetown. So yes, more prepared, I had a much easier transition to college. I had great writing skills, math skills, the works.

Jason continued his story by explaining how he achieved a 4.0 in his freshman year and retained a 3.9 throughout his time in college. He conducted his own research, coauthored a refereed publication, and was actively pursuing further research and publication opportunities. He also joined competitive extracurriculars and maintained a wide social circle. He even kept several jobs off-campus, one in which he served as the personal assistant to a wealthy businessman. Certainly there were difficult times, he explained, like when he went through a distressing breakup or struggled to understand the material for a particular class, but overall, Jason felt more prepared than his peers coming in, and this preparation carried him through his college experience. Did Jason have advice for other first generation students?

In high school I didn't need help. Subjects came easily and naturally. I could cram the night before a bio test and come in on three hours of sleep and do well. But when I got to [college] I began to spend more time studying with friends who were smarter than me or better than me at certain subjects. I made sure that I was surrounding myself with people who were generally smarter than me. It was a tactical change. It is also broadly useful: you want to be surrounded by people who are smarter than you because that's how you learn a lot more.

Jason explained his advice to other first generation peers seeking to find both academic and social success in college:

> I do think that first generation students should know this: they should surround themselves with people who are smarter and better than them because that would make them better. First generation and low-income students tend to self-segregate. I'm friends with plenty of people who could very well be trust fund babies, and they all don't really care if your family doesn't come from money. They might sometimes be oblivious, but most of my friends are generally very conscious of that kind of thing. Generally people from higher income families do not discriminate against people from lower income backgrounds. So generally telling first generation students to break out of their social circle and hang out with people who are smarter than them would [help them] be better off.

Jason qualified his remarks, stating that he did not intend to conflate "smarter" with "wealthier." Rather, if first generation students elect to form friendships only with other first generation students, they may find that they are foregoing friendships with students from different backgrounds who also have different capabilities and connections to future professional advancement.

Jason's comments were not unique among first generation students across Harvard and Georgetown who stated they felt as or more prepared for college. As sophomores, more than half, or fifty-six percent, of the first generation sample stated that they felt as or more prepared coming in. While that number decreased to forty-three percent when they were asked again as seniors, it nonetheless indicates that there is much to be learned about first generation students who arrive primed to succeed. How did they describe their transition to college? What can their perspectives offer to first generation students who may enter college feeling less prepared?

Most of the students who stated they were well prepared for college credited, first and foremost, their high schools and the school system in which they were embedded. Public high school graduates spoke of community investment to augment the minimum offerings at their schools, of dedicated teaching staff and multiple advanced academic and extracurricular opportunities. They also often, though not always, highlighted high performing peers and near-peers whose aspirations for college encouraged them to aim higher than they originally considered. Many of these first generation students attended well-resourced public, magnet, and private schools in their home towns. Stories of family sacrifice, either to move or to afford tuition, dovetailed with narratives of academic success. Some first generation participants spoke of feeling similar to their continuing generation peers in most respects. For instance, Balboa, an African American social science major, recalled:

> A lot of minority kids felt less prepared, but I took a lot of AP courses so I felt academically prepared on a national level. I felt really confident. I came here with a lot more credit from my AP classes. My grades are decent and I engage in conversation. Professors like my insight and my way of thinking. There are a lot of brilliant minds here—and different backgrounds.

Henry, an aspiring poet and professor, the son of a graphic designer and a general contractor, had this take on why he was just as prepared as his peers:

> There were never situations where I felt like I was at a disadvantage. There were kids whose parents were professors, and they were further along in their intellectual development just because of the nature of how they grew up. My impression is that Harvard is eager to take care of all of us as long as we're willing to reach out to them. So I felt like I was never at a serious disadvantage, even though my parents weren't professors.

Henry reasoned that he would experience better preparation for college only if his parents had the same career as that to which he aspired—becoming a professor and a writer—and that this was not a legitimate or useful critique of his upbringing. He considered his family and high school to have offered him a decent preparation for college. The rest was up to him to adjust and up to the college to support him in that transition.

Gretchen was another first generation student who, on reflection, felt just as prepared, if not better prepared, than her peers in college. Her private high school gave her a leg up on her choice of major, as it had offered coursework that placed her ahead of her peers in the subject at the outset of freshman year. As Gretchen put it, "I went to a prep school so I was pretty well prepared. . . . I did pretty well and I think I got better over time. . . . I already knew everything in [the introductory major course] coming in, so I was given a little leeway. I was familiar with the subject. I didn't have to go to office hours all the time. And it boosted my confidence a little because I was ahead." Moreover, she knew how to network, make friends from a variety of backgrounds, and, as she put it, "blend in well" with the dominant culture of her campus, all of which aided her transition. As she explained to me the reasons for her easy transition, I could not help but feel chagrined: when I first met Gretchen, I too mistook her for a continuing generation student.

It is important to note that economics is entwined with academic preparation due to uneven educational opportunities afforded children growing up in neighborhoods with divergent home values and education budgets linked to local real estate tax revenues.[32] However, this is not always the case: magnet schools may draw from several school districts, while open choice districts afford families from lower income neighborhoods like Jason's to send children to better resourced schools across the city. In some districts, despite high poverty rates and fewer financial resources for education compared to suburban districts, individual schools and entire school districts may beat the odds and produce well-prepared graduates.[33] Some low-income students attend schools

32. For example, see Ryan, *Five Miles Apart, A World Away*.
33. For example, see Kirp, *Improbable Scholars*.

in high-income districts, enroll in private schools on scholarships, or test into magnet programs that draw from a diverse catchment region. Likewise, middle- and high-income first generation students may attend well-resourced or underresourced high schools, depending on parental understanding of the district's offerings, their preferences for their children, and the amount of work they can afford to undertake to secure their children's place in better performing schools.

The result is that both socioeconomic background and high school experiences varied widely for first generation students who stated they felt as or more prepared for college than their peers. While this study did not ask participants to report parental income, most of the students naturally turned to social class when framing their pre-college preparation. While those first generation students who reported feeling less prepared for college were more likely to identify as low income, no similar pattern emerged for those who reported feeling as or more prepared. They identified as low income, middle income, and high income. They narrated differing histories of immigration, divergent family economic trajectories, examples of finding unforeseen educational opportunities simply by luck, and wide-ranging parental choices that impacted their educational pathways. Several first generation participants, Jason being one, even explained that while their grandparents attended college, their parents elected not to attend, making the grandchildren de facto "first generation" in college admissions files and in our study, despite a family history of college-going.

As with varying levels of economic capital, first generation students who reported feeling as or more prepared for college appeared to arrive with varying amounts of cultural capital, such as access to participation in cultural activities like the visual and performing arts; travel for educational, extracurricular, or entertainment purposes; and familiarity with social norms and behavioral expectations in different formal and informal social contexts. Again, Jason offers a telling example: although he grew up under constrained economic circumstances and was currently benefiting from a comprehensive need-based financial aid package, he considered his upbringing to be rich in cultural and social opportunities that provided him a direct advantage in college. To assume that because he was a full financial aid recipient he must also enter college with a lack of cultural or social capital would be both incorrect and potentially personally insulting. Moreover, Jason, an active mentor for other first generation students on his campus, had advice regarding the acquisition and deployment of cultural and social capital to share with his first generation peers. To downplay his personal experiences would be to ignore the potential benefit he could offer as a mentor to other first generation students.

Many of these well-prepared first generation students performed well in their first year and beyond. They emphasized that it is important to enter college motivated to succeed but also to be undeterred by initial setbacks such as poor first midterm grades. They underscored how important it was for them to meet peers from different backgrounds and to make connections with students they felt had capacities or skills that could benefit them. They emphasized that asking for help is a habit that accrues achievement rather than a symptom of its dearth. Developing friendships with students from diverse economic backgrounds could help first generation students to see that seeking tutors for challenging courses is not a sign of weakness or failure but rather a strategy for ensuring success. With this goal in mind, students like Jason tended to counsel fellow first generation students to expand their social network and to avoid self-selecting into exclusively first generation or lower income social groups.

Jason's first generation experience was quite distinct from, say, Ariana's or even Jake's. Jason's work habits, high school experiences, and accrued cultural capital, not to mention that he is a white male whose pre-college friend group included children who expected to attend selective or elite universities, all cohered to support an easy transition to college. While Jason's advice to his first generation peers to seek help early and often is well meaning and potentially salubrious, it also risks glossing over the challenges faced by first generation students who feel doubly marginalized by being first generation and a member of an underrepresented minority group on campus. Jason's story and the advice he has to offer are a reminder that the first generation student experience at highly selective universities is complex and not easily framed by straightforward narratives or generalizations based on assumptions of family life, income status, racial or ethnic identity, gender, or immigration status. One pressing question for elite universities is how to incorporate students like Jason into a discussion about supporting the college transition for first generation students. Will students like Jason be overlooked because they fail to cohere with a growing deficit narrative in the student affairs literature, or will the resourcefulness and advice that Jason has to offer be taken seriously by campus leaders seeking to improve students' social integration and sense of belonging?

3

On Academic Experiences

A Tale of Two Religion Majors

I first met Karina, an outgoing and talented applied math major, in the fall of her sophomore year. She had just declared math as her concentration.[1] As we sat adjacent to one another at a local burrito chain, she beamed as she explained, "I was more prepared in math because that was my thing, and now I'm majoring in math!" Throughout our time together, Karina gave the impression that she was proud of her multiple identities—Latina, queer, first generation, urban—but at least in that first interview the identity that seemed the most compelling to her was *math major*. Charming throughout, her face practically glowed as she discussed her academic and career plans with me. She asserted that she needed to improve her reading and writing skills, but she contextualized this gap in her education as one associated with growing up in a home where English was not the first language. "Granted, I'm an okay writer, I can get my point across and I can write an effective paper. But English is my second language and sometimes I have a difficult time with grammar. . . . I think that I am an effective writer, but it is not something I would choose to do. It is not something I want to spend a great deal of time doing." Karina's high school, a math and science specialty center, provided her with the

1. "Concentration" is Harvard's term for "major."

technical preparation to excel in her desired field of applied math. She imagined that this field would enable her to secure lucrative employment, an important priority given her family's lower income status.

When we met again in the fall of her senior year, Karina had since changed majors to religious studies. I was surprised to hear of this switch given how sophomore Karina emphasized being a "math person" rather than a "humanities person." I even recalled that during our sophomore interview, she wore a math related t-shirt from her high school and her backpack was festooned with buttons, some of which referred to algebraic expressions and witty math jokes. This time we sat opposite one another at an outdoor café on a decidedly windy spring day. Karina was warm and engaging just as she was in our sophomore interview, but the gusts that blew around us whipped her hair into her face and cast an unsettled tone to our conversation. Reflecting on her sophomore self, senior Karina explained that positioning herself as a math person was in part an effort at securing a successful future:

> I felt like anything that was what you might call "liberal arts," anything not technical or wasn't lucrative after college, it wasn't rewarded. Not just at my high school, but it felt that way at first when I came here. . . . I had a really hard time coming to terms with switching my concentration as well, but I'm really glad I switched.

When I asked her about her greatest academic accomplishment, her smile broadened as she described the process of writing a lengthy research paper for a junior-year seminar in the religion department. Completing a thirty-page paper in crisp prose was not an accomplishment she had anticipated upon entering college. Once embarrassed by her writing, she now found herself correcting her friends' grammar. Moreover, she told me that she felt empowered to engage in rigorous philosophical and moral arguments about political and social issues that mattered to her in everyday life. Her religious studies major enabled her to bridge her academic pursuits with her passion for advocacy work that enhanced diversity and inclusion on campus and in the surrounding community. Thus, she came to pride herself on becoming a well-rounded product of a liberal arts education.

I was thrilled to hear of Karina's newfound pride in her writing skills, as well as a home and a sense of self-efficacy in the religious studies department. She would never have completed such an accomplishment if she hadn't switched majors from math to religion. When I asked her what her biggest challenge in college had been, however, a cloud passed over her face. Her mood, once light and engaging, turned at first pensive and then pained. Again, she turned to the decision to switch majors. She explained that a series of infelicitous events caused her to feel alienated from the math department over the course of her sophomore year. She hit it off poorly with her first advisor, but she could not put her finger on what she had said or done to elicit his lukewarm attention. Because her university required advising appointments and physical signatures on paper plans of study called "study cards"[2] in order to register for the upcoming semester's classes, it was critical for Karina to make at least some connection with this advisor. After multiple unsuccessful attempts to reach him via email, she ultimately made the mistake of addressing him by a nickname she had heard used by others in the department. This at least caught her advisor's attention. According to Karina, he chastised her for breaking an unspoken code of etiquette in how one addresses one's professors (never by the first name, never without their title), lobbing a curt email volley: *Don't ever refer to me by my first name unless we've written a paper together or been shot at together,* as that's

2. "Study cards" are the course schedule planned for the upcoming semester that is agreed upon by the student and advisor. They ensure that a student is progressing appropriately toward a degree, and that major and general education requirements are being met in a timely fashion. Since this study concluded, paper study cards have been replaced with an online version of this process. See DiLuca, "Last Paper Study Card Day."

not how it's done around here.[3] Reeling from her gaffe, Karina tried unsuccessfully to apologize. The professor went on sabbatical at the end of the term and again was uncommunicative via email. Karina was assigned a different advisor, one outside of her concentration and unable to help her select spring courses.

Karina might have persisted in her math concentration, but she had been taking a religious studies course where she felt welcomed and at home among her peers and faculty. She explained,

> The time it dawned on me that I was in the wrong department was when I went to my religion instructor and she helped me to choose my math courses. No one in the math department would help me, and here was this religion instructor helping me select my courses. I realized then that I was in the wrong department, and I switched to religion.

Later, when I asked whether she was satisfied with her major, tears streamed down her face as she apologized, "This is difficult for me to talk about, just remembering back on how hard that time was." She explained how welcomed and cared for she felt within the religion department, but her biggest challenge was envisioning what she would do with this major upon graduation. Karina lamented:

> The hard part . . . is that I am really good at math, and when I would say I am a math concentrator, being a woman and a Latina, people would say "Wow!" And I got the impression people thought I must be really smart. Now when I say I am a religion major, people say, "Oh, and what are you planning to do with that?" They don't know that there is anything you can do vocationally with that concentration. And they don't think

3. The phrases in italics are Karina's memory of what the professor said. While these quotes are from Karina, I had no way of following up with the faculty member to verify her account. However, the significance of the event for this study lies in how Karina interpreted, responded to, and remembered her interactions with an important authority figure on campus.

it's as difficult, because it's not as highly valued as a math concentration.

As I listened to Karina, I found myself wondering whether she had ended up in the right major. While she insisted that she felt at home in the religion department, I could not help but speculate about how things could have turned out if she had experienced a better first encounter with her original academic advisor. Could better advising training help faculty understand the weight of their comments to first generation students, and could student orientation training specifically discuss what to do and who to turn to when students feel slighted or otherwise misunderstood by their advisors? Was there some way to make explicit a series of tacit norms that some (of course, not all) faculty appeared to expect their students to follow? These seem like potential solutions on the surface, but at the same time, it is not necessarily wrong that students switch majors when they find an original choice to be a poor fit, even when the experience of poor fit appears to be driven by personality and the so-called "chemistry" of interpersonal communication or lack thereof. As Daniel Chambliss and Christopher Takacs discovered in their longitudinal analysis of student experiences at a liberal arts college,[4] students often end up majoring in a professor rather than a discipline, so perhaps it should come as no surprise that the interpersonal connection between students and faculty may cause some to exit their originally intended majors when more approbative alternatives become available. As I will discuss later, first generation participants in this study were more likely to change majors than continuing generation students, and significantly more likely to exit STEM majors than their continuing generation peers.[5] Could this be the result of a higher rate

4. Chambliss and Takacs, *How College Works*.

5. One recent longitudinal mixed-methods study showed that institutional context has a significant effect on minority students' interactions with faculty, which, in turn, shapes how those students access and make use of resources to pursue science education. In this study, black students attending historically black colleges and uni-

of negative early encounters in originally more technical or perceived "practical" majors, or could the interpersonal dynamics between faculty and students also work in salutary ways, revealing to first generation students new and better alternatives to the ones they entered college assuming they would pursue?[6]

One counterexample to Karina's experience came from my encounter with Agnes, another first generation student who changed from a math-heavy major to religious studies midway through college. Similar to Karina, Agnes was a first generation American whose family had immigrated from Mexico when she was young. Excelling in school, and in particular in practical subjects like math and science, became a point of pride for this young woman who spoke no English when she first came to the United States. She arrived at Georgetown expecting to pursue a practical major that would lead to a lucrative career, but instead she found herself drawn to religious studies, with its emphasis on cultivating written and oral expression of one's moral, religious, and political views through the lens of well-crafted argument and exposition. Before college, she worried that she would never be a great writer, having spent much of her youth mastering the mechanics of the English language to the detriment of learning to craft an argument. Her religion professors took the time to work with her on her written

---

versities (HBCUs) reported having more support and frequent interactions with faculty, while minority students attending more selective institutions "have less frequent, less personal interactions with faculty." See Hurtado et al., "'We Do Science Here.'"

6. And not incidentally, could an electronic signature system help students who do not hit it off well with their first academic advisors to stay on course with their intended major? Harvard switched to digital submissions of student "study cards" in 2015 (see DiLuca, "Last Paper Study Card Day"). It may now be easier for students performing well in their courses to request digital signatures without visiting their advisors in person. There are of course pros and cons to making this kind of in-person advising effectively optional (even when it may remain an official requirement), but one advantage would be to minimize the potential for unnecessarily negative encounters as well as the anxiety produced when advisors become difficult to track down for an appointment.

arguments, and this, in turn, gave her courage to declare a religion major despite her original concern that it would lead to a less remunerative career. When I asked Agnes about her proudest academic accomplishment in college, she responded without hesitation: "Finding my own niche within the academic world. Finding my academic passion, and not conforming to a pattern. Just to find what I wanted to study—mostly Catholic studies—and being okay with that."

Agnes's story speaks to the promises and perils that first generation students perceive in choosing among majors that, on the surface, appear more or less likely to lead to a lucrative career. At highly selective universities like Harvard and Georgetown, first generation participants expressed concern that pursuing certain majors may lead to less lucrative careers—say in the arts, education, or community development and advocacy work—and that these choices may "waste" the value of an elite education. I will return to Agnes and her academic choices later in this chapter. For now, let Agnes and Karina's stories of how they came to choose religious studies serve as a reminder that some mid-program changes in major may be the result of finding the courage to take risks and make authentic choices, while others result from constraint or unwelcoming experiences.[7]

For the remainder of this chapter, I explore the similarities and differences in the ways that first generation and continuing generation students talk about their academic experiences in college over time. The choices they make, the ways in which they respond to critique or outright failure, and the bonds they form with faculty (or the fractures they experience) are all interrogated with reference to how first and continuing generation students experience

7. The idea that some students were able to make "authentic choices" in their courses and majors, while others settled for "constrained choices," due in large part to the combination of high school quality and individual preparation, circulated among senior administrators at Harvard during the course of this study. See Rosenberg, "'Authentic' Versus 'Constrained' Choices in the Classroom."

and interpret the academic core of college. This chapter addresses a perennial higher education question—What is the purpose and value of college for various demographics?—with a specific data set, a comparative look at first and continuing generation students at two legacy institutions.

First generation students more commonly framed their academic experiences through descriptions of motivation and overcoming hardship. They tended to narrate academic successes in the context of turbulence: as slow or even false starts, meteoric rises, and, at times, savage disappointments. By contrast, continuing generation students did not describe their academics as exhilarating peaks or petrifying cliffs. Instead, they described their faculty as coaches and their coursework as incremental exercises designed to help them achieve external goals such as internships and, later, prestigious jobs or graduate programs. Their figurative language for success implied that higher education was a continuation of prior habits, while first generation students underscored the emotional turmoil associated with unfamiliarity in all its excitement and terror. In addition, first and continuing generation participants wrangle with the perceived "value" of different academic majors in distinctive ways, leading to choices that impact how they reflect on the overall "worth" of their college experiences. I explore why these academic narratives diverge when they do, and how they may indicate a relationship between familial experience with college and individual expectations for what college can and should do for the person.[8]

Academic Choices

The first and continuing generation participants in this sample, and students at Harvard and Georgetown more generally, graduated at very high rates compared to college students in general and

8. For a compelling and lyrical case for what higher education can and should do for the development of the person, both as an individual and as a citizen, see Delbanco, *College: What It Was, Is, and Should Be.*

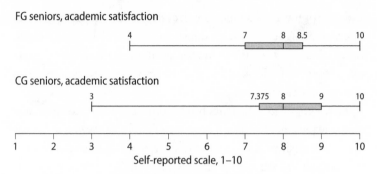

FIGURE 3.1. First and continuing generation academic satisfaction. CG, continuing generation; FG, first generation.

first generation college students in particular across the United States.[9] In the years of this study, 2012–2016, the six-year graduation rate for Harvard and Georgetown undergraduates approached ninety-seven percent and ninety-five percent, respectively, and with virtually no difference in those rates for first and continuing generation students.[10] Similarly, the overwhelming majority of participants in this sample were on track to graduate within eight semesters. When asked to rate their satisfaction with their general academic experiences on a scale of 1 to 10, (where 1 is completely unacceptable and 10 is outstanding), first and continuing generation participants shared a similar range of responses, with a median of 8 for each group and a range of 4 to 10 among first generation participants and 3 to 10 among continuing generation participants (see figure 3.1).

9. Shortly after this study concluded, the National Center for Education Statistics published a comparative study of first and continuing generation students in the United States, tracing their high school outcomes, college enrollment and persistence patterns, and college completion rates. The six-year graduation rates for first generation students who were high school sophomores in 2002 were twenty percent for first generation students and more than double this rate at forty-two percent for continuing generation students. See Redford and Hoyer, "First-Generation and Continuing-Generation College Students."

10. Graduation rates among first generation students at Harvard were ninety-six percent and at Georgetown were ninety-four percent during the time of this study.

Likewise, first and continuing generation students appeared to hold similar opinions of their academic major experience. Asked to rate their major experience from very dissatisfied to very satisfied, eighty-seven percent of first generation seniors and ninety-four percent of continuing generation seniors across both schools in this sample were either satisfied or very satisfied with their overall experiences within their chosen majors. However, thirty-six percent of first generation and twelve percent of continuing generation participants switched majors sometime between sophomore and senior year. Those who changed majors rated their satisfaction with their final choice high, but they were likely to be less satisfied with their original major selection. This figure, combined with the thirteen percent of first generation seniors who reported feeling "neutral" or "dissatisfied" with their major by their senior year interview, indicates that close to fifty percent of first generation participants either started out or ended up with a less than satisfactory academic fit. This number was closer to twenty percent for continuing generation students. In open-ended responses, first generation seniors spoke less often of academic awards than their continuing generation peers and were less likely to complete a capstone project or senior thesis.[11] These figures indicate that first generation students were more likely to face difficulty in their chosen major, or to switch majors and potentially deal with the challenge of "catching up" in their new field.

These differences matter. University administrations strive to ensure similar levels of satisfaction with academic experiences and outcomes for all of their students, regardless of background. However, in the past decade there has been a growing concern that doing so may require more attention to differential supports based

11. At Harvard, the senior thesis rate was thirty-six percent for first generation seniors and 54.5 percent for continuing generation seniors. At Georgetown, the overall numbers were lower for both first and continuing generation seniors due to different capstone requirements in the School of Nursing and Health Studies and the Business School. Both of these schools require their seniors to complete a capstone course, but a written thesis is not always required.

on individual students' prior academic experiences as well as their career goals. Charles Deacon, the dean of admissions at Georgetown at the time of this study and the key administrator in the founding, funding, and continued support of the Georgetown Scholarship Program (GSP), explained:

> The point is not to see whether first generation students graduate at equally high rates. They all graduate at the same rates at elite schools. Sometimes first generation students even graduate at higher rates, like our GSP kids. So the point is not whether they graduate. The point is to ensure that our low-income and first generation students thrive here. That they feel equally that they are included and have the same opportunities afforded them through their education that continuing generation students do.[12]

A close look at first generation students' academic choices and their satisfaction with those choices can help campus leaders discern the extent to which first generation students participate in and benefit from the academic core of college compared to their continuing generation peers.[13]

The choice of academic majors is one piece of this puzzle. In the United States, first generation students are more likely to graduate with vocational or professional degrees rather than traditional liberal arts degrees.[14] Their major selections also tend to

12. Charles Deacon (dean of admissions, Georgetown University), in discussion with author, September 24, 2015.

13. When I refer to the academic core of college, I mean not only students' choices of courses and majors but also the proacademic activities that are offered by the university and expected of its students. These include practices such as attending office hours, asking questions to faculty and graduate assistants, participating in class, attending tutorials, studying in groups, using library resources, and generally "showing up" to perform the role of an intellectually curious person.

14. This is true also for continuing generation students. In fact, a large-scale survey of college graduates in 2016 found that first generation students were slightly more likely than their continuing generation peers to major in social sciences or the humanities, two traditional "liberal arts" fields. See Eismann, "First-Generation Students and Job Success."

be interpreted as "less risk averse" than their continuing generation peers.[15] At highly selective colleges like Harvard and Georgetown, however, a common adage is that the college conferring the
degree matters as much if not more than the selection of academic
major. Even so, first generation students still enter Harvard and
Georgetown often without prior knowledge of the range of majors
available and may be more inclined to seek a professional degree
than one they deem less useful in terms of transferable skills in the
workplace.

When I asked first generation students at Harvard and Georgetown why they selected their majors, they frequently explained
that they were unaware of the academic choices available to them
when they first matriculated, and so their choices were made in
the context of limited information. They selected classes based on
their level of familiarity with the subject in high school and so
often began their collegiate academic trajectories as a continuation of high school choices—math, science, social studies,
English—regardless of their personal talents and interests. Over
time, either through serendipity or purposeful exploration
through general education requirements, many first generation
participants described finding their academic home outside their
original or intended major. This contributed to a higher proportion of first generation participants changing their major at some
point during the course of college.

In this sample, the most popular type of major for first and continuing generation students was social science, with sixty-two
percent of first generation and forty-three percent of continuing
generation seniors graduating with a social science degree (see
figure 3.2). These majors included economics, political science or
government, sociology, psychology, and anthropology. The second most popular major was natural science, at twenty-four
percent for first generation and twenty-six percent for continuing
generation graduates. Often these students indicated an interest
in pursuing graduate work in medicine or the health professions.

15. For example, see Trejo, "Econometric Analysis of the Major Choice."

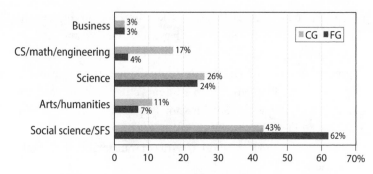

FIGURE 3.2. Academic majors, first and continuing generation.
CG, continuing generation; CS, computer science; FG, first generation;
SFS, School of Foreign Service.

Continuing generation students were more represented in the arts and humanities at eleven percent compared to seven percent for first generation graduates. The starkest contrast in major selection, however, was with the nonmedical STEM majors like math, engineering, and computer science. Seventeen percent of continuing generation students and only four percent of first generation participants in this sample graduated with a math, engineering, or computer science degree.[16] Finally, first and continuing generation participants from Georgetown, which offers an undergraduate degree in business, majored in business at similarly low rates of three percent.

When asked how they came to select their majors, many first generation participants explained that they began with that subject in which they excelled and with which they were familiar in high school. They had little knowledge of the diversity of academic choices that awaited them in college. First generation S. explained:

I didn't know half the names of these subjects or anything. Through the course search, I looked at the disciplines I already knew I liked. I wasn't looking for things that were different. I

16. For more on the role of race in the experience of racial and ethnic minorities in STEM, see Museus et al., "Racial and Ethnic Minority Students' Success in STEM Education."

never looked for things I'd never heard of, of course. I had this ignorance of how the system works.

First generation seniors were also apt to make their choice of major because they hoped it would lead to a remunerative career. They were more likely than their continuing generation peers to double major or hold a "secondary" in a concentration that they desired purely for themselves, with their first major being a pragmatic choice either to please their parents or to gain skills for an intended career path (e.g., accounting, finance, natural sciences, etc.).

Some first generation participants ruminated during their interviews on the major they would have selected if they felt free to choose without consequence. As one first generation senior put it, "I felt like I would get a lot more out of my college career if I took classes that I enjoyed, like psychology or film, instead of classes that were strictly career focused." This student, who chose the pseudonym "Alien" to emphasize his stranger-in-a-strange-land experiences, described pressure from his family to secure a well-paying job so that he could support them after graduation. At the same time, he also commented on how the university's academic climate fostered his personal development beyond professional training: "Georgetown has ... taught me to pursue a life I want to live, and taught me how to balance that." Alien mused:

> I'm proud that Georgetown has taught me to pursue what I want and not just something that's good for my future. I'm an accounting major and that's very practical. I'm also taking Japanese. I'm not getting a minor or certificate out of it, but it's something I enjoy. I wish I had the courage to take it sooner. Because I get so much out of it personally.

Similar ruminations were quite common among first generation participants, but not at all among continuing generation students. Instead, most continuing generation participants spoke of pursuing their academic interests without overly worrying whether these scholarly pursuits would relate directly to their future employment. They treated their academic majors as personal preferences, considering the overall degree itself rather than their choice of major as the signal of academic value. In some extreme instances, the degree and major merely signaled their intelligence or "merit" while something else entirely would signal their work-ready skills.[17] In lieu of viewing academics as the locus of skill building, many continuing generation participants honed work-ready skills outside of coursework through extensive, time-consuming extracurricular commitments. For instance, Paul, a continuing generation participant who described his academic pursuits as a history major as "pretty obscure," explained that as an upperclassman, he focused more of his time and efforts on developing managerial skills through a campus organization leadership position:

> My emphasis now has been a lot less academic in focus, but rather [on building skills like] communication or developing the responsibility of managing others, or working on a project, or working on a team. I'm interested in cultivating those skills more. Areas which aren't strictly academically focused but have challenged me to learn and become a more concrete person, not just an academic.

An important difference between Paul and his first generation peers is that Paul firmly believed his extracurricular experiences would equip him with transferrable work-ready skills, while his academic experiences were more about his personal and even quirky interests. Most first generation participants believed the opposite to be true: their majors offered skills that would open doors to future careers while their extracurriculars were where

17. For an in-depth argument about college as signaling, see economist Bryan Caplan's *The Case against College*. In particular, Caplan argues that a college degree signals intelligence, work ethic, and conformity over any other job-ready skill or specific content knowledge.

they went to relieve stress, find a home, and fulfill personal needs such as faith, fun, or service to others.

In short, first generation participants deliberated on their academic majors differently than continuing generation participants did, often relinquishing their passion for a more practical choice, or if they embraced their passion like Agnes, then they predicted a rocky financial road ahead. By contrast, continuing generation participants did not articulate a connection between declaring a religious studies major and a predicted reduction in potential lifetime earnings.[18]

On Academic Successes and Challenges

During the senior year interview, first and continuing generation participants were asked to identify and describe their greatest successes and challenges in terms of college academics. They were encouraged to reflect on aspects of their academic experiences that were the most rewarding and the most difficult for them, as they would likely return to these moments as alumni reflecting on how college shaped their life outcomes.

Knowing whether first and continuing generation students describe their greatest academic successes and challenges differently could help predict diverging relationships with their college over time, especially as young alumni who go on to forge adult lives. Understanding differences in these evaluations could then assist

18. Much has been written about the economic value of different major selections. For instance, in their 2015 Center on Education and the Workforce publication, *The Economic Value of College Majors*, Carnevale, Cheah, and Hanson detail early and mid-career earnings of more than one hundred majors and compare major groups by postgraduate earnings. A 2018 report produced by the American Academy of Arts and Sciences, "The State of the Humanities 2018: Graduates in the Workforce and Beyond," argues that while humanities majors may earn less than their STEM majoring peers, their job satisfaction and well-being are similar to other majors. This report argues that postgraduate earnings should be considered as one among many factors in evaluating the "worth" of an individual major for undergraduate degree seekers.

campus leaders as they reflect on and seek improvements in campus inclusivity and accessibility.

Academic Successes

When speaking of their academic successes, first and continuing generation students tended to offer similar narrative content, with a few notable exceptions. When asked to describe their greatest academic successes, the most common themes among both groups included: forming meaningful relationships with faculty or experiencing a transformative moment in a particular class, success on specific assignments or in especially challenging courses, external indicators of achievement (GPA, academic awards and nominations), integration of different interests into a coherent academic structure, and finding their passion. They also pointed to experiences known by education scholars as "high impact practices":[19] studying abroad, conducting research or working in a laboratory with a faculty mentor, completing time-intensive independent research projects, and writing analytical or creative papers at least twenty pages in length.

Both first and continuing generation participants spoke of these experiences as transformative at similar rates, while first generation students were more likely to frame these experiences as surprise outcomes of their educational trajectories. This was particularly true with study abroad. Many of the first generation stu-

---

19. For detailed descriptions of "high impact practices," see Kuh, *High-Impact Educational Practices.* Considering how high impact practices may have an outsized effect on collegiate success for first generation students, Pascarella et al. found that when first generation students were deeply engaged in both academic and extracurricular activities, they experienced greater gains in areas like critical thinking and writing skills than their continuing generation peers. First generation students gained significant social and cultural capital from their extracurricular and peer involvement in college, but, in comparison to their continuing generation peers, they were significantly less likely to be engaged in these activities due to factors like the need to work to alleviate financial burdens. See Pascarella et al., "First-Generation College Students."

dents interviewed did not anticipate studying abroad before college, but, often through circuitous routes and after convincing wary parents of its value, it became one of the highlights of their college experience. It often led to a deepened commitment toward a major or academic path, reduced stress upon return to campus after a semester, summer, or year abroad, and an expansion of the sense of possibilities for their future careers and how they wished to balance their personal and professional lives. Agnes, for instance, described studying abroad as one of her greatest academic successes at Georgetown:

> I went abroad and that was a great experience. I spent seven months abroad, spring semester through the summer. And experiencing a different educational system and applying what Georgetown had built me up to, and living and breathing a completely different reality, that was really transformative. The small details of living abroad, from riding on the buses in the city where I lived to volunteering there and just seeing the way other people live, that changed my life.

Likewise, first generation Tolu explained that studying abroad allowed her to shake "this whole 'I don't belong here' feeling." As a first generation American from a low-income background and an underresourced public high school, she felt intimidated by her professors despite her objective academic accomplishments in college. She also found the well-off, private school educated *Joe and Jane Hoya*[20] "a bit unapproachable." While studying abroad, she began to reexamine her interactions with professors and peers back at Georgetown. "Now I'm studying abroad, I'm trying to see if that was just my impression of them. If I approach them differ-

20. Taken from the Georgetown college cheer, "hoya saxa," a Hoya is a member of the Georgetown community. Students, staff, faculty, alumni, and athletic teams from Georgetown are endearingly dubbed Hoyas. For a description of the corrosive *Joe and Jane Hoya* stereotype and its misrepresentation of what Georgetown is and should stand for, see Williams, "Joe and Jane Hoya Must Go."

ently, maybe my experience would be different." Moreover, when abroad, she represented Georgetown to the world, and this made her feel more a part of the overall Georgetown community rather than a niche. As Tolu explained, "I didn't feel like I fit the culture. But now that I'm away, I feel better about it. When I'm far away, I feel part of Georgetown. But when I'm there I don't really feel it."

Another first generation senior, Anthony, recalled that studying abroad changed his approach to how he spent his time on Harvard's campus:

> I feel like, here, there has been a culture established where you have to be involved in X, Y, and Z. I know my first two years I felt that pressure. Not so much anymore. Going abroad changed that for me. When I got back, I chose to participate in activities that I found truly fulfilling.

Descriptions of academic success were comparable across the first and continuing generation samples, though there was a different tone to the first generation students' descriptions of academic success that included overcoming their initial feelings of intimidation about the academic process. Particularly anxiety provoking were the scholarly performances of class participation and general interaction with professors. S. recalled feeling inadequate in class discussions and office hours, counting one of his greatest successes as "proving to myself that I'm not dumb." Anthony, who felt empowered by his study abroad experience, described the anxiety of classroom participation:

> Participation in section is a huge hurdle. I struggled to keep up and to say even one sentence in my sections. I felt there was a language I needed to learn in order to properly express any idea I had. I remember struggling the first couple of years, and now I definitely see an improvement in being able to speak up in class, but it took some time. And also, in high school it was rote memorization, not being challenged to critically analyze different topics or engage in these discussions.

Even though Anthony was considering pursuing an academic career, he suspected that what was expected of him in class discussions was some kind of ritualized speech performance, the rules of which he failed to grasp. Likewise, first generation Henry, who also aspired to become a professor, felt remiss in class discussions: "Talking in class is challenging; it's very scary and a lot of how you are perceived in courses affects your overall grades. You have to participate and I feel intimidated to do so." Very few continuing generation students spoke of feeling intimidated by their professors or the academic process, while this was a significant theme among at least one-third of first generation students interviewed, many—though by no means all—of whom came from high schools where content memorization was favored over class discussion and oral argument.[21]

Generally speaking, however, first and continuing generation students alike pointed to moments when they achieved clarity or integration, completed a challenging assignment, or developed capabilities they did not have prior to college as their greatest successes in college. Yet while the content of first and continuing generation student descriptions of their academic successes were often similar, the overall tone was quite different. First generation students described their academic successes in terms that underscored their fears of failure as much as their pride in success. This difference may be due to the practice of performed success that sociologists like Shamus Khan underscore with students from elite high schools: continuing generation students' practice of

21. The development and then deployment of a glib tongue and an impromptu—seemingly, if not actually, well-informed—response to any question is a cliché among scholars who study elite schooling and memoirists who describe its rituals. Sociologist Shamus Khan explores this theme extensively in his ethnography of St. Paul's School. He sees a racial divide. Black students view learning how to speak up in class, among other academic expectations of the "hidden curriculum" at an elite school, as learning to "bullshit their way through," while working- and middle-class students "were some of the firmest believers in the school." See Khan, *Privilege*, 101–113, esp. 103 and 108.

achievement may be conducted in the context of demonstrating "ease" with academic pursuits.[22] Nonetheless, there is a distinct attitudinal difference between those who narrate academic success as evidence of ongoing achievement and those who couch success within a broader discussion of striving or struggle. In this manner, the general tone of the two groups—first generation and continuing generation—may be best described as contrastive despite similar content. The unpacking of personal narratives offered by two students, Agnes and Emily, both "A" students who at the time of our follow-up senior interview were considering futures in graduate school, underscore this point.

As described at the start of this chapter, when asked which accomplishment she was most proud of, first generation Agnes responded without hesitation: "Finding my own niche within the academic world, finding my academic passion and not conforming to a pattern." However, Agnes described her greatest academic success as also her greatest challenge:

> Every semester is a challenge. But I think I really enjoyed my junior year, because I did really well and took challenging courses. I took a human development course, and I learned so much from it. I still talk to my professor from my human development course, and he was genuinely interested in me and my success as a student. He said to me, "Agnes, your ideas are phenomenal, it's just the way you present them that needs work." This course proved to be my greatest challenge but also the greatest success. My professor pointed out that I made a transformative improvement from the first paper to the final, and that recognition, and that it's going to take a lot of work . . . it's not just about the grade, but the way I approach material, my future career, and how I live my life, that really changed me.

Agnes worked indefatigably in this and in her other courses. As she explained, it was emotionally taxing for her because she

22. Khan, *Privilege*, 77–113.

wanted to do well in her courses, but she also desired the opportunity to fully engage with the material without fear of performing poorly. She longed for a deep engagement with the material, but worried that she could not make the leap expected of her in terms of her writing abilities. The refrain, "*Am I good enough?*" repeated noxiously in her mind.

Agnes offered her backstory to put in context her current concerns. She and her mother had arrived in the United States from Mexico when she was in elementary school. They spoke little English, and most of her public schooling thenceforth revolved around Agnes learning to read, write, and speak English fluently. Her mother, who did not speak English at first, could not help her with the technical aspects of her American schooling, although she provided something else essential: unflagging emotional support, encouragement, and a safe haven to which Agnes could return when her academic challenges grew overwhelming. Agnes performed in the highest percentiles on her state's standardized exams and graduated at the top of her class, but was dogged by fears that she lagged behind her peers because of the content loss (history, science, math) due to the time taken over by learning English. As Agnes described her background and experiences to date, she showed herself to be a passionate, articulate, goal-oriented young woman. But it took a couple of years in college for her to gain the confidence she needed to fully embrace her academic pathway:

My freshman year I was intimidated by the academic process. . . . I was afraid to go to office hours. Now I go in to talk about all sorts of things, their work, how much I enjoyed the lecture, specific questions I had about the readings. At first I was intimidated by these formidable figures with PhD's. In my family the maximum level of education was high school. So I felt I was getting intimidated by the difference between the reality I grew up with and the reality that I was meeting. And going from that intimidated and cautious and trembling all the time person to become less intimidated with a person with a PhD and filled with courage, that was the major change. For me to know more about the world and dialogue with the world, that was a change.

Let us compare Agnes with another passionate, articulate, goal-driven young woman, Emily, who was not only a continuing generation student but a legacy with multiple family ties to her university. Emily graduated from a well-resourced, project-based public high school. Before high school, she participated in a Spanish immersion program in her public school and spent much of her instructional time mastering specific language skills related to learning academic content in one's nonnative language. In some ways, her experience mirrored Agnes's for its focus on technical language acquisition over general content knowledge. Emily arrived in college concerned that because of these alternative schooling experiences she may not have the tools to excel in certain aspects of college: specifically, she suffered from test anxiety and was afraid she would perform poorly in large lecture-format courses. When asked how well she felt her high school prepared her for college, she confessed that she felt less prepared than her peers, explaining that her math and science preparation were lower than she had hoped, and that she arrived in college "less intellectually curious" than she was by the end of freshman year. Like Agnes, by the time we sat down together for a second time during her senior year, Emily had found that she grew immensely during her four years of college. When asked about her greatest academic successes, Emily noted:

> Junior year for me was really transformational from an academic and intellectual perspective. I did the junior tutorial in both the fall and spring, and in both semesters I was told that I turned in the strongest thirty-five-page research paper of my peers. And that meant so much. I'd been told that in other classes, but that meant even more to me because it was among peers [in my major]. I think [my major] attracts the most inter-

esting and intelligent people in the social sciences, and for me that meant even more because I was so impressed with the people around me.

Also I developed a personal relationship with the professor. . . . I've been good at developing personal relationships with faculty. It's typical, you don't know how to navigate that when you first get here. Being able to engage with faculty on a personal level, to be able to talk about what they're working on and not just what you're working on is really unique.

In many respects, Emily's concerns about her academic preparation mirrored Agnes's, despite their disparate backgrounds. One difference between the two, however, was that Emily could reach out to multiple family members when she needed academic advice, whereas Agnes felt as though she was on her own in learning to navigate college. Agnes sought the assistance she needed from her peers, her professors, and the Georgetown Scholars Program (more about this program in the next chapter), of which she was a member. Both Agnes and Emily described an initial fear of approaching professors, but there is a subtle and significant difference in the tone of Emily's narrative. Both students used the word "transformation" in their narrative, but Agnes's narrative underscores the path from "intimidation" to "courage" as a core feature of her transformation. Indeed, the word "intimidated" came up no less than five times in that one paragraph transcribed from our interview. By contrast, Emily described becoming the best at something and feeling both humbled and inspired by this experience in the context of such excellent peers and faculty.[23] The story of success—and the "A's"

23. Again, this distinction mirrors Khan's finding among elite high school students: those who embody "ease" do so as a way to instantiate their success as a form of meritocracy, while those who describe or enact a struggle to achieve (sometimes even the scholarship students in Khan's ethnography) are not doing it "right" according to their peers. See Khan, *Privilege*, 145. Not incidentally, according to sociologist Lauren Rivera, the embodiment of "ease"—and the expectation of it on the part of

that attended them—may be similar in content, but their tone is distinctive. One may be regarded as *academic turnaround*, and the other as *ongoing academic achievement*.[24]

---

employers seeking an appropriate fit in a new hire—also smooths the transition to elite professions. See Rivera, *Pedigree: How Elite Students Get Elite Jobs*.

24. This way of articulating the difference between first and continuing generation students is echoed in the informal analysis of university administrators. In informal conversation, it is often assumed that students from lower performing high schools may take time to "catch up" with their peers from better resourced high schools, but that their academic transformation will be secured through their course of college. One senior university administrator was said to have told the following story to his colleagues as his rationale for supporting the recruitment and ongoing support of students from underresourced high schools: *Say you are a baseball recruiter and you attend a high school pick-up game. One player has somewhat poor form but hits the ball hard. His arms may flail as he runs around the bases, but he gets to home plate and scores for his team. Another player has perfect form, hits a home run, and confidently glides over the bases to home. Which player are you going to recruit?* In this scenario, you pick the less polished player, assuming that with a little guidance he will perform even better than his well-trained peers. In reality, college admissions officers are concerned with a host of issues, among them creating a balanced class that includes full-paying students from well-heeled backgrounds as well as promising strivers. See Stevens, *Creating A Class*; Steinberg, *Gatekeepers*; Duffy and Goldberg, *Crafting a Class*; and Soares, *Power of Privilege*. For more on "strivers" and how they may be supported, see Kahlenberg, *Rewarding Strivers*. The scenario above assumes two young men of unidentified ethnicity are vying for the same academic slot, while in practice admissions officers must balance gender, race, ethnicity, and geographical representation in their classes without adhering to illegal quotas or questionable recruitment techniques. And as higher education scholars have pointed out numerous times, students from low-income backgrounds, who often attend lower resourced high schools, do not even consider applying to elite colleges. See Radford, *Top Student, Top School?*; Hoxby and Avery, "Missing 'One-Offs'"; and Hoxby and Turner, "Expanding College Opportunities." For those that do and who ultimately enroll, the difference in experiences between those low-income students who attended elite high schools on scholarship and those who enter college without prior exposure to elite educational settings is stark. Clearly, what we might call "academic turnaround" or, as is described by sociologists Jenny Stuber and Ashley Rondini as "catching up," is a complex set of processes begun long before college despite its continued usefulness as a simple distinction between those who enter college pre-

First generation students, especially those from lower resourced backgrounds, were more likely to speak about overcoming challenging beginnings, learning how to achieve academic success over time, and coming around to believing in their own desert. *Academic turnaround* was a key theme as they reflected on the arc of college. Many specifically spoke of beginning with "D's" or "F's" in a course and ending with an "A." First generation Marie, for instance, explained that her biggest success was "British poetry class freshman year. First assignment I got a D and it was terrifying, and I ended up finishing out the class with an A–. I was pretty proud of that freshman year." Similarly, first generation Stephanie said:

> The most tangible success is my success in one professional class with [professor's name]. He is phenomenal. I took a writing class with him because I needed to make my writing better. Our initial assessment, it would have been a D for that paper, and each paper kept getting better until I ended up getting an A in his class. I was one of the few to manage to get an A. My dean told me that. That was the most tangible success, when I felt like I could keep my head above water.

Notice how earning an A, and being one of few to do so, was described as equivalent to simply keeping one's head above water. That sense of needing to prove oneself perfect to feel normal was repeated in multiple contexts throughout the first generation interviews.

Some first generation participants did not apply the *academic turnaround* theme to a single course but rather holistically to their approach to coursework in college. For instance, S. offered this assessment:

> Sophomore slump was super real for me. I had to choose a major, figure out what I'm trying to do here. There was a lot of

---

pared and those who do not. See Stuber, *Inside the College Gates* and Rondini, "Negotiating Identity."

pressure because I didn't understand myself enough and what I wanted outside of college. My entire life was spent on figuring out how to get to college. College was the final goal. So I didn't see myself beyond college. I come from a low-income community, one where not a lot of people go to college. And it was like, "I did it, but now what?" I was very lost and didn't know what to do with myself . . .

And then I read this book about how to get A's in college. I found it surfing the internet. I literally Googled how to do better in college, and this book came up. So I got the book. And implementing these strategies, it began working. And then realizing this wasn't so hard.

But you know what? Maybe if someone told me what I needed to do in order to succeed in college, I wouldn't have done it. I needed to go through the experience of sucking—develop moral fiber, character, whatever—and then decide I wanted to do better for myself, and looking [sic] for a solution.

S. realized that he "needed to get [his] mindset right" in order to tackle his coursework and define his vocational pathway. At first, he did not put enough time into his coursework, skipped classes, and turned assignments in late. He explained that he did so out of a lack of direction. Once he succeeded in the college admissions competition, he had no idea what to do in order to succeed in college, let alone how to discover his passions and purpose while in college. Peers, especially S.'s roommates and friends who came from two all-male, ethnically affiliated social organizations encouraged him to work harder, put in longer hours studying, and adapt his habits to prove his potential.

When I came here I felt like I wasn't smart enough . . . but then I realized you don't get through stuff like that by thinking it away. You need to put yourself into action. Once I put myself into action I realized, "Oh, this isn't so hard. I can do this."

A how-to manual discovered on the internet, coupled with supportive friends and a renewed motivation to succeed, helped S.

pivot from a struggling first- and second-year student to a mostly "A" student whose academic adviser "was begging me to write [a senior thesis]." Echoing psychologist Carol Dweck's decades of research on fixed versus growth mindsets and Angela Duckworth's widely cited research on grit,[25] S. framed his problem as one of switching from a fixed mindset—thinking he was not smart enough—to a growth one—taking action to learn new techniques for success. This led him to an *academic turnaround* and renewed confidence both in his merit and his capabilities.

Whereas S. and other first generation students adroitly narrated the *academic turnaround*, often accomplished with an enormous amount of work and the will to succeed, most continuing generation students told their stories of academic success as *ongoing academic achievement*. No significant turnaround to create a dramatic arc, and often no single achievement in particular, was offered as a compelling story of academic success. Instead, many continuing generation students made general statements about academic integration or reminisced briefly on a particular course without underscoring the effort it took to succeed. They sometimes spoke of academic outcomes in the form of grades as less important than deep learning, preprofessional planning, or a robust extracurricular resume. Whether they indicated that they cared about their grades or not, continuing generation students were less likely to narrate their academic successes in the context of turmoil but instead more like an extension of prior experiences. Continuing generation Lawrence's description provides a typical example:

> There haven't been courses where I walked out and thought "Wow, I completely nailed that course." I've insisted on taking five courses every semester, and I've been very busy. I didn't make too many solid "A's" but I kept busy and these were really interesting courses. It's less important to me now to get perfect grades than to have the opportunity to take as many courses as

25. Dweck, *Mindset: The New Psychology of Success*; Duckworth, *Grit: The Power of Passion and Perseverance*.

I want to. It still stings when I see a 3.6 on my overall GPA, but it's less important to me now. Just being able to be where I am now, being able to take these grad-level courses, especially taking a lot more physics and a lot *harder* physics, more than I needed to, that's been reward enough.

A few continuing generation students spoke of initial doubt and subsequently proving to themselves that they were capable of the work expected of them. This way of talking about their academic success was more aligned with first generation responses than it was with the modal response of their continuing generation peers. For instance, continuing generation senior Raphael said of his biggest success: "To give myself the chance to try a lot of things and to work through a lot of potential passions to come through the other side with a solid set of goals and the feeling that I'm moving on the path towards them." However, his success was shadowed by a nagging concern with belonging, much like many first generation students:

> The biggest [challenge] has been self-doubt and the things that come with that, like procrastination, poor time management, and adjusting from the feeling of being natural at everything to the feeling of reaching your limits and really start working hard and pushing through things that are less comfortable to sustain yourself academically.

Raphael, who attended a well-resourced high school and had parents who were college graduates, echoed many of the concerns that his first generation peer S. raised. Despite pre-college advantages, he still felt as though he had been too slow to seek help, especially in terms of academic and mental health assistance. As with S., Raphael explained that it took time to realize he needed help:

> I've more recently begun visiting [an academic counseling center on campus] for more general counseling that also pertains to academic stuff as well. I know I would have benefited from receiving this kind of counseling sooner. There were definitely

times when I could have sought help instead of burying myself in frustration alone. Academic trouble began sophomore year. I went to office hours, and it helped somewhat. It was better than nothing for sure.

This might be relevant, relating to the whole "did high school prepare you for things" [question]: I wasn't prepared to be bad at something. I definitely had times when I had to work hard to turn things around and I did, but I didn't feel ready to do it in college. But it might be my own hang-ups [more] than my own lack of training.

Raphael interpreted his own self-doubt and poor performance as evidence of a mental health problem, one that required counseling and stress-reducing techniques. While many first generation students also asked for improved on-campus counseling and campus-wide discussions around mental health, they often described their academic struggles in terms of not knowing what was expected of them before arriving on campus rather than in psychological terms.

Raphael's advocacy for destigmatizing mental health issues around academic and social pressure was shared by first and continuing generation students alike. For example, J.B., who in an earlier chapter explained that his high school did an excellent job at preparing him for college, and who had Ivy-educated parents who were available to help him navigate academic life, emphatically advised that the university lower the academic pressure to succeed for entering freshmen by reducing the course load to three courses or two pass-fail out of four, "because damn if people aren't ready for it!" J.B. and other students in the sample advocated for improved mental health services and underscored that the convergence of academics and mental health is something that affects students regardless of their parental background. Given the culture of "success" on elite campuses, this issue is too little attended to on such campuses at present. For continuing generation students like Raphael, they blame themselves for their own "hang-ups"; for first generation students like S., they blame their lack of preparation. Either way, the fear of failure fosters unhealthy academic habits: procrastination, poor time management, failure to concentrate on assignments. Finding a way to reduce academic stress in the first two years of college would benefit first and continuing generation students alike.

Academic Challenges

First and continuing generation participants often described their greatest academic challenges in the context of their successes: mastering challenging course material, academic turnaround, learning how they learn best, and applying these findings to their daily practices. Many students identified specific challenges related to academic habits: time management, seeking academic assistance early and often, going directly to the professor with a question rather than an indirect route, or learning to speak up in class. But there were also specific challenges that first generation students discussed that did not arise in interviews with continuing generation students. These were either directly related to their experiences of being first in their family to attend college, or they were compounded by their status as low-income and/or underrepresented minorities in historically predominantly white universities. No continuing generation student in this sample addressed "catching up" as their greatest academic challenge, while this was a common theme among approximately fifty percent of the first generation participants.

First generation Erik explained how his high school experiences affected his college choices, and how those choices ultimately led to a feeling of alienation from the university and his peers in class. Erik's underresourced rural high school was fairly weak in math and science, with young and inexperienced teachers mostly in charge of those courses. He gravitated toward English when he arrived in college, simply because his best high school teachers had been in the English department, but he still felt underprepared:

There is definitely a level of knowledge that teachers and fellow students expect you to have. If you don't have that knowledge, it feels alienating. For example, knowledge of the classics or reading in the original language. Once you're in the class, the way the classes are structured, there is very little time to have an interaction, and not knowing what this thing is about, you're not going to raise your hand to stop a lecture. In section, if you raise your hand, you're one of a dozen, and you look like the kid who doesn't know that [topic]. The next alternative is to go to office hours and have that alone time. But it's such a myth. Academics here are awkward. You need a question, but you don't have a question.

Having never experienced the formality of office hours in high school, Erik did not know how to formulate an "office hour question." It seemed to him that he was expected to know the linguistic codes of a ritual performance when it came to the practice of office hours, and that his classmates were already well versed in the ritual, its expectations, and cadences, whereas Erik had no idea how to even begin to try. His professors seemed distanced, their book-lined offices from an altogether different plane.

Erik spoke about the disconnect he experienced between himself and the faculty in his department. He lamented, "The lack of professors that 'get it' makes everything a little more difficult." When I asked him to explain, he replied:

There is definitely a lack of diversity in academia here. Even with professors of color, there's still this sort of roadblock to get to them. It's the same thing as with any professor. What do I talk to them about? They're not from the same background as I am. A third generation immigrant is not the same as me, maybe he doesn't really know what I'm talking about when I talk about my immigrant status. Maybe he's never had to deal with the problems I have dealing with immigration. There aren't a lot of professors here who have dealt with poverty or who came from rural backgrounds as I have.

Erik had difficulty connecting with faculty when he arrived on campus, and this was something that affected his overall experiences in college. Eventually, he made meaningful academic connections with faculty and peers through an on-campus job in the computer science department, but he never felt fully comfortable in his own major. If he had found a mentor early, an adult in his department who shared or at least understood his background, he might have been more satisfied with his overall academic experiences.

While Erik faced challenges making connections to faculty, Ariana, whose challenges with the transition to college are discussed in the previous chapter, struggled with stereotype threat and a fear of seeking assistance in the classroom. Ariana described the corrosive effects of self-doubt coupled with peers' ignorance of and insensitivity toward her background.

My first two years, I struggled a lot in my classes mostly because I didn't speak up, or try to talk to my [teaching assistant] or professor. Especially freshman year. I was used to in high school, you only asked if you needed help, and if you needed help then you weren't good enough, strong enough. During the first midterm season, I got two "D's" in a row. I remember sitting in the dining hall with my friend, and he noticed I was upset. And I started crying, telling him, "I shouldn't be here. I don't belong here. I'm not good enough." There are various reasons for why that happened. Later on, you realize that everyone goes through that. But the degree to which it affects someone depends on these variables. I went through my first year thinking, "Why am I here?" But I also felt like I couldn't complain.

Even fall semester my sophomore year, I struggled through that as well. I remember taking a [general education course]. It was a class on the intersections of race, gender, and class. My peers' perspectives on my identity were shocking. They were theorizing a lot of experiences that they don't know about. I know they won't say those things to a person, but it's easy to say when they're theoretical. Here's an example: we were talking about the education of low-income families of color. And students in the classroom were blaming parents or teachers for students' failure. They said things like, "the parents don't care," or "the teachers are apathetic." That couldn't be farther from the truth. And they refused to consider any institutional or structural reasons why students from low-income minority communities weren't succeeding. It was shocking.

Ariana's example highlights that talking about race, class, and gender in class is a potentially fraught and volatile exercise, especially when some students speak from a position of authority on conditions that they are personally foreign to them.[26] For Ariana, the experiences in this class exacerbated her feelings of inadequacy. Only when she found mentors in her residence hall and in her science major during her junior year was she able to reclaim her sense of belonging and gain the confidence she lost in her first two years of college. Junior year was the year of her *academic turnaround*, and like many other first generation students, a combination of study abroad, finding an academic home, and building connections with peers and mentors helped Ariana reframe her experiences. She went from struggling in a perceived hostile environment to thriving and envisioning a successful future.

Ariana and Erik both pointed to their sophomore year as the nadir in their college experiences, as did continuing generation Raphael. They were not alone. At least half of the first generation students in this sample, and roughly one-quarter of the continuing generation students, identified sophomore year as particularly challenging for academic and personal integration. Many alluded to "sophomore slump" and the so-called "struggle bus," which referred to the low feelings of satisfaction during sophomore year that came from the combination of committing to a major but not yet feeling at home in that department, the lack of attention from university administrators, and the sometimes challenging aspects

26. See de Novais and Warikoo, "Colour-Blindness and Diversity."

of moving into new residential settings with different roommates from the previous year.[27]

University administrators have long understood the value of intentional diversity and inclusion efforts and transitional support for students during freshman year, but ongoing programming and support has not been institutionalized for sophomores until recently. At Georgetown University, the Georgetown Scholarship Program launched an event in 2014 entitled "Sophomore Strong Summit" based on findings from this study and recommendations from first generation undergraduates in their program. In 2018, the university offered a standalone course entitled "The Hidden Curriculum" designed to equip first generation and other interested students with the language and tools to unpack "unspoken rules" of academia, including how to approach office hours and what to say during class discussions, as well as how to reframe potential academic setbacks as opportunities for growth. It remains to be seen whether these and other sophomore-focused initiatives change the arc of college-going earlier for first generation students, but they promise, at the very least, to validate a dialogue begun years before by first generation students and alumni seeking to improve the college-going experience.

Evolving Approach to Academics

First generation participants described an evolving approach to academics, including the way they interacted with faculty and approached class participation, as a stark shift between high school

27. Some researchers have posited that the so-called "sophomore slump" affects first generation students' sense of self-efficacy more dramatically than it does for their continuing generation peers, leading to disproportionate attrition rates among first generation sophomores. See Vuong, Brown-Welty, and Tracz, "The Effects of Self-Efficacy on Academic Success of First-Generation College Sophomore Students." Sophomore slump has long been identified as a typical problem among college students. A perfunctory Google Scholar search yielded 1,280 hits for the term, with the earliest date for a publication addressing "sophomore slump" in 1933.

and college—one they presumed to be a less significant leap for their continuing generation peers. Continuing generation students generally spoke of their approach to academics and interactions with faculty as a continuation of habits learned before college. However, continuing generation participants were also less likely to describe strong relationships with faculty, or even the desire to forge such relationships. They also did not consider class participation as a form of empowerment or opportunity to find their voice, which was a common theme among first generation seniors. While first generation students appeared to have more difficulty adjusting to academic expectations such as speaking up in class and building connections with faculty mentors, their desire to do so and the rewards of successful faculty-student relationships seemed much greater than for their continuing generation peers.[28]

When asked whether their approach to academics changed between freshman and senior year, most continuing generation participants either demurred or spoke vaguely of time management and balancing their extracurricular commitments with their coursework. First generation participants would often openly laugh at this question, followed up with an emphatic affirmation of the sea change in their approach to learning. Some of this was due to experiencing a different pedagogical approach in college than they were used to from high school. First generation Alien explained, "For me, it was a huge difference in the style of teaching. So in high school, the teacher would introduce a new topic and you would go home and do the homework for the topic. In college it's different. You do the homework on a topic before the teacher introduces it."

Approaches to homework changed as well. Instead of simply completing a reading assignment to prepare for class, they now read the assignment and all around the assignment by searching on the internet for critical analyses, synopses, and exegeses of the topic. This was something they had not done in high school, and

28. See Pascarella et al., "First-Generation College Students."

some even came to college believing that it was a form of cheating to conduct outside research on a topic beyond the assigned reading. Some first generation participants had never worked in groups before, also believing it was like cheating to study or review assigned readings in group contexts. Now they found themselves foundering when they tried to work alone. As first generation Daniel explained,

> It's been a lot more group work, [and] realizing people can help you was the big difference. Especially going to office hours and getting to know the professors. Freshman year was a lot of big classes. Now I have friends in my classes, and we help each other get through courses. Instead of having to struggle alone and hope everyone else is, too, we work together and support each other.

Similarly, learning to ask for help aided first generation participants' changing approach to academics. First generation Elizabeth explained,

> I have a rather *I can do everything by myself* kind of streak. So I have difficulty asking for help. I have a friend who is in my major who really influenced my behavior. She literally asked questions all the time. Her willingness to ask for advice was something I learned from.

First generation Amy shared a similar reflection when asked whether her approach to coursework changed between freshman and senior year in college:

> Classes here are a measure not of how much you learn but of how you approach the material. I did not ask for help at first. If I had asked for a tutor sooner, it would have been easier for me. After learning that the hard way, in later semesters I would get a tutor early on even if I didn't need it. I always had a tutor, even if I was doing well. Also, I went to all of the TF[29] sessions and

---

29. TFs, or teaching fellows, are graduate students assigned to provide academic and grading support in certain (particularly large, introductory level, or especially challenging) undergraduate courses.

asked the TFs to clarify concepts. They are often better teachers than the professors at explaining concepts. Also, I learned that it is important to prepare before lecture. That really helps. Earlier I tried to do p-sets[30] by myself. I changed that and found a friend who was reliable and had the same work schedule as myself.

So I learned from my early mistakes. I work with friends. I go over past exams from classes, because there is a huge disparity often between what is taught and what is tested. And having past exams is really helpful.

Amy described an evolution in her approach to coursework, learned in part through trial and error and in part through mimicry of peers whom she considered better prepared for college, which also signaled how much she had revised her sense of appropriate study habits and the demarcation line between good study habits and cheating. Some may argue that using prior exams to study for current semester tests is a form of cheating, but Amy's unvarnished description of learning to do this alongside completing homework with peers and asking questions of faculty and graduate assistants as a better approach to coursework signals a tectonic shift in both an ethical and pragmatic evaluation of how learning happens.

Learning from peers to ask questions, seek tutoring, and take advantage of professors' time (and teaching fellows/assistants in those courses that included them) challenged first generation students in their first two years of college. Having been the tutors in their high schools, they arrived in college with the false but firm belief that one could not be both smart and need a tutor in college. By contrast, many continuing generation participants disclosed securing tutors or going to their professors with lists of questions as a preventative measure or when they sought to master particu-

---

30. P-sets, or "problem sets," are homework assignments. It was common for Harvard undergraduates to call their homework "p-sets" predominantly in courses heavy in math and science content, but there were occasions when this term would be applied to any type of homework assignment.

larly difficult material. For them, seeking help was a habit of success rather than a sign of weakness. In addition, it was difficult for some first generation students to believe they "had a right to the professor's time" or "deserved" their professor's attention, while continuing generation students assumed their professors would welcome their questions and office hour visits. First generation Henry's reflection on his evolution to believing he had a right to his professors' time sums up this general sentiment:

> I think the biggest difficulty is feeling like you have a right to take advantage of certain things on campus. First generation students are sometimes scared of asserting their position, taking what they need. The idea of taking a professor's time made me very uncomfortable. Now as a senior, I understand how this place works and that's what you do, but as a freshman it was very scary. In this place, you have to think you are more important than you might think you are.
>
> It's not that I didn't feel that there were resources for me. I just needed to learn myself how this place works. You can't diagram it. You can't be told something, because in theory I understood it. You have to go through it.
>
> I forced myself to go talk to professors, and I learned the hard way. I guess a boot camp forcing me to go talk to professors might have been a good idea. It wouldn't be less painful, but it would be quicker. My counter to that is that I was more stupid freshman year. I had less to say to professors freshman year, regardless of how entitled I was.

In reflecting on a changing approach to interacting with professors, Henry identified the gap between what the mid-twentieth century philosopher Michael Polanyi dubbed "personal knowledge" and a given understanding of how something—a scientific process, a social interaction—works.[31] The development of personal knowledge takes time, a good deal of trial and error, and

---

31. Polanyi, *Personal Knowledge*.

ample opportunity to learn from and alter one's habits. College, with its cyclical calendar and multiple chances for do-overs, provides the time and space for this kind of personal development.[32]

In addition to learning to ask for help from faculty and tutors, to work in groups, and to take ownership of initiating the learning process, many first generation seniors reflected on the power of developing relationships with faculty to give them confidence about their own academic journey. Agnes's example of going from an intimidated and trembling freshman to someone who confidently dialogued with her professors dovetails with her sense of academic empowerment: "My freshman year I was intimidated by the academic process, and I was feeling like the world was crumbling apart. And now looking back, I guess it's a challenge and the world *is* crumbling apart, but how am I going to help put it back together?"

Agnes's emphasis on "dialogue" was echoed by another first generation senior, Eliza. She pointed out that the rewards come from the interaction—even the mutual teaching and learning— that can occur between mentors and their mentees:

> Forming relationships with my professors is really awesome. . . . I think finding those professors and having them motivate me, wanting to do well, is so important. You're able to question them and they question you, and it's very satisfying to have those kinds of experiences. When they come back to you after class about something you said and they want to continue it, that's so rewarding.

For first generation Francis, his relationships with a few key faculty made all the difference in an overall challenging college experience. After having sought help from other resources on campus, such as the writing center and the academic resource center, Francis felt defeated by the dearth of authentic support and the feeling that he was anonymous to campus officials until a few

---

32. See Cuba et al., *Practice for Life: Making Decisions in College.*

faculty in his courses reached out when he thought he had no-
where else to turn. "Professors you form relationships with, they
offer that support when you're feeling helpless. People who make
an impact on you and it's like, '*Wow!*'" Of course, not every faculty-
student relationship evolved this way. As Francis explained,

> Last year I had two professors I was really close to. And I would
> visit them constantly. With the professors who made an effort
> to know their students, I would learn better. Initially you would
> seek assistance with the material, and then it becomes personal.
> You go from there. You feel more comfortable, feel like you can
> participate in class, you get engaged. If I don't want to let that
> professor down, then I feel more motivated. But those are the
> professors who really cared about the students. With other pro-
> fessors, office hours wasn't as welcoming, and I didn't interact
> as much with them.

Ultimately, a different approach to the purpose of learning, as well
as guidance from faculty mentors, ushered in an evolution in the
way that many first generation students came to understand their
college experience. As Francis further explained:

> When you go to college, it's not about a diploma. It's about an
> education. I'm not proud of my transcript. I would argue that
> I've had a phenomenal education at Georgetown in terms of
> opening my mind and in acting the values that Georgetown
> institutes. I can't tell you about what I learned freshman year in
> my classes but I can tell you about how my experiences in col-
> lege educated me. You have to be able to separate those two to
> be able to prepare for the real world and what's to come.

Similarly, Eliza came to conceive of college as a "very precious
time in which you challenge yourself." She distinguished the degree from the experience entailed in earning it:

> [I'm] not thinking of it as a piece of paper that will make me
> wealthier or better off than my parents. It's still a privilege and

something that was fun and cool and something that I will cherish. I'll get a job some day, and I'll be able to look back on this as a special time when this was something that was mine, and not forced on me.

The first generation participants in this sample described various ways in which their approach to academics evolved, though their statements showed that they all came to see their academic experiences as more social than transactional, more interconnected than individual, which may have been a stark difference from high school. If the experiences went well, their fond academic recollections were invariably closely associated with relationships they forged in college—with peers and friends, with faculty mentors, and with the academic material itself. When it happened, being able to connect deeply with faculty, and to teach as well as to learn, was transformational.

One first generation senior, Jackie, spoke of taking several courses with a famous philosopher. When asked about her proudest academic moment, she described how she felt leading a presentation in this philosopher's seminar on social mobility and the American Dream. This renowned professor, whose work on ethics and market systems had taught Jackie so much over the course of several semesters, was now visibly moved and thanked her for such a powerful presentation. She explained, "I was speaking about poverty and issues that we had discussed in class that I experienced but others only read in scholarly articles. It is something different to speak to a person who goes through those things." Jackie's proudest moment? She beamed: providing a personal, riveting example of how the issues described in their readings impacted people in real life, and thereby "making [Professor X] cry."

Jackie signaled that she was one of only two minority students in that seminar course and that her experiences growing up in poverty appeared alien to everyone else in the room. For some first generation participants, the burden of choice to disclose their life experiences or stay silent when class discussions addressed social inequality or mobility proved a heavy toll. Listening to peers discuss issues with which they had no personal experience could be infuriating. However, some, like Jackie, felt empowered by telling her story and bringing what appears to be abstract discussion into concrete focus. Anthony, who earlier described how his study abroad experience helped him to develop a more confident approach to college, also described feeling empowered to tell his peers when he thought they were off base on a topic about which they had little personal experience:

> This is very simple but it means a lot to me: I now speak up in class or section. I no longer fear that requirement. I was very timid freshman and sophomore year. Junior year I began to branch out more. Senior year I now feel like I deserve to share my opinion. I now feel like I can add to the conversation, and I don't feel that my opinion is wrong. That's something that matters to me.

Anthony and Jackie's evolving sense of empowerment to speak from a position of authority on issues that matter to them is just one among many examples of the evolving approach to academics underscored by first generation participants in this study. It is an evolution that enables them to own their education, and to forge the academic experiences they wish to have. Not all first generation participants felt that empowerment, either due to the inability to overcome initial feelings of intimidation, better prepared peers, and the tacit classroom norms and expectations, or due to challenges related to lack of preparation, or the experience of implicit bias or stereotype threat. Universities invested in improving all students' academic experiences, and those of first generation students in particular, are wise to seek an understanding of the range of their successes and challenges to forge a nuanced approach to supporting their diverse educational needs, interests, and goals.

4

Mapping Social Life

My greatest social successes? Picking an awesome group of people to live with freshman year. That was luck. These are the greatest guys I've ever met in my life. There's so much depth to their experiences, and what I can offer them. I know it sounds corny, but as different as we are, we are also very similar. So my success has been picking great friends.

Biggest social challenges? Everyday life. Getting around, taking care of myself. How do you talk with people in public? Nobody tells you how to do these things. You just do them.

—S., FIRST GENERATION

On Social Satisfaction

Given that a higher proportion of first generation than continuing generation participants in this study felt less prepared for college than their peers, would there be a similar disparity in terms of satisfaction with social life or a sense of belonging on campus? When first generation students who felt less prepared for college described early academic upsets, they often asked themselves, *"Why am I here?"* Did this moment of self-doubt extend beyond those initial moments, and did it have an effect on their social lives on campus? What could be done to encourage social integration for first generation students on these "legacy" campuses?

To address these questions, all participants were first asked to describe how satisfied they were with their social lives in college. They were asked about their greatest achievements and challenges

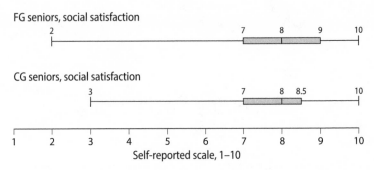

FIGURE 4.1. First and continuing generation social satisfaction. CG, continuing generation; FG, first generation.

in terms of social life in college, their extracurricular involvement, their friend groups, and the extent to which they felt they belonged on campus. When asked to rate their satisfaction with their social experiences in college on a scale from 1 to 10, where 10 was "terrific" and 1 was "truly disappointing," the first and continuing generation groups shared a similar range of responses, with a median for each group hovering round an 8 and a range of 2 to 10 (see figure 4.1). This pattern held consistent between the participants' sophomore and senior interviews.

While the pattern of responses was similar across the two groups, first generation seniors were more likely to describe peaks and valleys in their social experiences on campus, revising their sophomore assessments up or down more dramatically than their continuing generation peers. This meant that a continuing generation participant was more likely to stick with their original assessment, say, a 4, while first generation participants might reverse from 2 to 10 or 8 to 2, essentially swapping places along an imaginary number line with other first generation peers.

Both first and continuing generation participants explained that their self-assessed social ratings were based on a combination of personal, social, and institutional factors. The more likely they were to have found a tight-knit group of friends or extracurricular colleagues on campus, the higher their reported satisfaction for both first and continuing generation students. Those who reported wide variation between sophomore and senior year—again, a more common response from first generation than continuing generation participants—were also less likely to report having close friends or participating in an extracurricular group that mattered to them.

While first and continuing generation participants may have reported similar rates of satisfaction with their overall social experiences on campus, content and thematic analysis of their response to interview questions asking them to describe their "greatest successes and challenges in terms of social life" indicates important patterns revealing both overlap and divergence among first and continuing generation participants. First and continuing generation students highlighted certain social experiences as similarly important: joining extracurriculars, making friends, taking on leadership roles, and developing community within their residence halls. Likewise, first and continuing generation participants were equally likely to discuss the need for improved "safe spaces" on campus as well as a more comprehensive effort to reduce stress and bolster mental health across the student population. First and continuing generation participants also tended to frame these experiences differently, as described in greater detail in the following pages. In addition, first generation participants were much more likely to describe specific instances of financial hardship, both on campus and at home, while also experiencing pressure to engage in a lifestyle that they perceived as the norm on campus, which also required a higher spending budget. While not all first generation students were low income, nor were all low-income students in this sample first generation, the first generation participants were more likely to assume that the overwhelming majority of their peers were wealthy, conspicuous consumers, unaware of the everyday struggles and choices of most Americans.[1]

---

1. Chetty and his colleagues' research, which strives to disentangle parental income data among students attending hundreds of colleges in the United States,

First and continuing generation students similarly described their "greatest successes" in their social life in college as making friends, finding community, and taking leadership positions in extracurricular activities. Their reported "greatest challenges," however, were different. The most common first generation responses included experiencing "culture shock" over an abrupt change from public high school to an elite private college and their new participation in a world of "privilege;" dealing with quotidian challenges regarding financing social life and managing social class differences; finding ways to speak to peers in class who talk "in the abstract" about social conditions that relate to them directly and personally but that do not relate to the speakers; finding or cultivating spaces on campus where they feel they belong and are validated; and finally, overcoming homesickness and negotiating family ties from afar. Commonly reported "greatest challenges" for continuing generation students included finding welcoming and open social spaces on campus; tackling the scourge of sexual assault on campus; and dealing with the contested role of exclusive, often unrecognized, social clubs, either through their efforts to make these social clubs more inclusive or through their critique of these institutions as corrosive to social life. In the following pages, I explore how first and continuing generation students describe two key factors related to social satisfaction with their college experiences: friendships and extracurricular involvement. In the next chapter, I focus on related themes—demographic transitions, money matters, and belonging—that, in addition to friendship and extracurricular participation, organize how first and continuing generation students framed their social experiences in college.

----

indicates that students' perceptions of many of their peers as financially well off may indeed be true. See their Opportunity Insights database here: https://opportunity insights.org/education/. Their College Mobility interactive tool on the *New York Times* website (https://www.nytimes.com/interactive/projects/college-mobility/) indicates that fifteen percent of students at Harvard and twenty-one percent of students at Georgetown come from families in the top one percent, while fifty-three percent and sixty-one percent come from families in the top ten percent, respectively.

Friendships

By far the most important aspect of first and continuing generation participants' social lives entailed the new friendships they
forged in college. As sophomores, both first and continuing generation participants spoke of making friends early in the first
weeks and months of college, sometimes even before classes
began. As seniors, many of these students reflected fondly on their
sophomore selves, pointing out that they were still close friends
with the same people they spoke about in the sophomore interviews. Moreover, these friendships shaped how they felt about the
college experience overall: if they and their friends felt integrated
into campus life, then they rated the entire campus as welcoming;
if they and their friends felt isolated or excluded from certain social circles, particularly by race or ethnicity, then they were more
likely to view the entire campus as unwelcoming and unsafe.[2]
These peer effects reverberated in all aspects of social life on campus; as such, an understanding of how and with whom first and
continuing generation students made friends cannot be underes-
timated by university officials who strive to cultivate a safe and
inclusive campus for all.

While it was true that first and continuing generation students,
as a group, emphasized their on-campus friendships as generically
important, first generation participants, especially as seniors, were
more likely to underscore their friendships as the most important
feature of their social lives in college. A consistent two-thirds of
the first generation sample, across Harvard and Georgetown and
in both cohorts, specifically named making good friends on campus as their greatest social achievement. "Friends for life" was one
of the commonest phrases they used. This was true even among
first generation students who expressed a lack of social fit or belonging with the larger campus. That number was lower among

2. For an in-depth longitudinal analysis of how friendships affect academic and
social success in college, see McCabe, *Connecting in College*.

continuing generation participants, with slightly less than fifty percent mentioning their friend groups as their greatest social achievement. Continuing generation participants were more likely than their first generation peers to say that they were too busy for friends or to complain that they had to visit other universities or return to their hometowns to make or renew friendships while in college.

The way first and continuing generation students described their friend groups reveals variation both within and between the two groups of students. In general, descriptions of friend groups in both samples indicated variability in students' personal choices as well as how they chose to define "friends." There were participants from each group who spoke of being proud of their few close friends, or their many friends from different groups across campus, or their deep friendships with peers who shared interests, or their surprising connections with people different from themselves. Some underscored the diversity of their friend group, while others mentioned sticking closer to people like themselves, whether that meant fellow "music people," social studies concentrators, teammates in a sport, or friends from the Filipino Students Association.

The majority of first and continuing generation participants explained that their friend groups comprised fellow students from a wide variety of backgrounds, representing the ethnic and social class diversity of the university as a whole.[3] They met their closest friends either in their residence halls (the most commonly reported way), their extracurriculars (a close second), through other friends, or, to a lesser extent, in their courses and majors. First and continuing generation students who spoke of having diverse friend groups were also more likely to say they felt connected to

3. For a nuanced comparative analysis of how white and nonwhite students at three elite universities talk about race and racial diversity on campus, including the value of racially diverse friend groups, see Warikoo, *Diversity Bargain.* See also Light, *Making the Most of College,* 129–89.

many aspects of the campus and to express greater confidence in their social lives by senior year. As first generation David put it,

I feel a part of Harvard. I have lots of friends from all over. I don't just stick with First Gen or Hispanic students. At the start, I was a bit lonely, especially sophomore year. As I got more involved in my concentration, I got more comfortable and felt my confidence growing. There's really no way to categorize my friends. I have, though, stuck with my freshman roommates in [my residence hall]. Terrific pairings!

A minority of first generation participants reported that their friend groups were comprised almost entirely of students whose backgrounds were similar to theirs, either in terms of social class or ethnic identity. Those said that they met their close friends early in college, either during their preorientation programs or through ethnic identity organizations they joined in their freshman year. Some of these students reported "branching out" toward the end of their junior or early senior year in an attempt to make friends with people from different backgrounds, but those efforts were often less successful than for those who sought to make friends with a diverse group of students early during their time in college. Those students whose friend groups were more homogenous were also more likely to express regret in their senior interviews. One first generation senior, Lucy, provided this example:

I wish I had broken out of my social circle more. At George-town I would say I ended up sticking with people from my own culture, my own identity or social class level compared to what the overall Georgetown community has to offer, like, students, and I wish I would have gotten to know more people in that sense.

I think it's because when I came in to Georgetown I came in as a [Community Scholar],[4] and that's where I met most of my

4. The Community Scholars Program (CSP) at Georgetown is a highly regarded and long-standing five-week academic summer program managed by the university's

friends from the beginning. So I didn't put too much effort when I got here in August and September. I kind of already had friends that I knew, and that was comfortable so I kind of stayed there, and we all just stuck together all four years rather than getting to know more people.

When first generation participants spoke of having diverse friend groups, their definition of "diverse" often differed. They sometimes spoke of diversity as making friends with students from ethnic, racial, religious, political, and socioeconomic backgrounds, with whom they would never have interacted or even met in their hometowns. They pointed out that home communities were often far less diverse than highly selective college campuses that draw people from all over the nation and the world. Additionally, they would never have met the friends they now cherished had they stayed closer to home. High school context played a role in how they cast the diversity of their college friends; some first generation students spoke of always having sought diversity among friend groups, while others considered it a sign of personal growth that they now cultivated friends from disparate backgrounds.

Continuing generation seniors described their friend groups differently than their first generation peers. They were more likely to speak of one or two close friends rather than the friend group typically described by first generation students, and they were less likely to cast their social relationships as friendships in the interview context. Continuing generation students were more likely to

---

Center for Multicultural Equity and Access (CMEA). Established in the late 1960s to recruit African American and other ethnic minorities from the Washington, DC, area, its mission is to expand social justice, equity, and opportunity for those who had been previously excluded from Georgetown. In addition to offering for-credit coursework in advance of matriculation, it provides workshops, extended interaction and mentorship pairing with faculty, and social events on and around campus to orient its participants to Georgetown. In addition to the pre-college summer program, the CSP also supports its participants throughout their time in college with exclusive academic advising, mentoring, personal counseling, study groups, workshops, and seminars.

say that they had few close friends or even no friends from their university. They wondered aloud whether anyone had time for one another in college and suggested that their busy schedules hindered true companionship. In lieu of describing friendships, they discussed their leadership roles and output in extracurricular organizations. This is not to say that continuing generation students valued friendships less than first generation students; rather, in the context of describing social successes and challenges, they were less apt to discuss friendships in language beyond abstractions or generalizations. While both first and continuing generation students commented that it could be challenging to forge meaningful friendships in a competitive academic or extracurricular environment—either people were "too busy" or "too work oriented" to meaningfully connect with one another—nonetheless it appears that for first generation students more explicitly than continuing generation students, meaningful and lasting friendships were expected and achieved in college. That is, friendships were part of the assumed curriculum.

Extracurricular Involvement

Extracurricular involvement—and for many, leadership in at least one organization by senior year—was also a critical source of social satisfaction for first and continuing generation students alike. Close to one-quarter of the first generation participants described leadership or significant achievement in an extracurricular organization as their greatest social success in college. For continuing generation participants, that percentage rose to over one-third of the sample.

Types of extracurricular involvement varied between first and continuing generation participants (see figure 4.2). One in five first generation participants joined an ethnic organization and were three times as likely to do so than their continuing generation peers. The ethnic organizations they joined did not exclusively match their personal identity. Indeed, many first generation

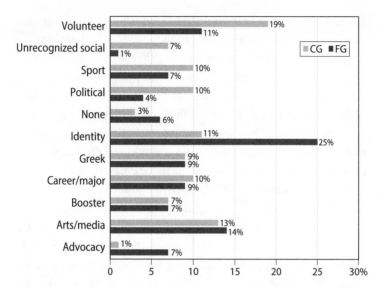

FIGURE 4.2. Extracurricular involvement, first and continuing generation. CG, continuing generation; FG, first generation.

participants stated that they were curious to learn about other people and cultures, and so joined organizations based on that curiosity rather than racial or ethnic identity. They joined the Filipino Students Association or the Black Men's Forum because they felt welcomed and found community there, even though they were not always Filipino or black. First generation students also participated in and became leaders of ethnic organizations affiliated with their personal racial or ethnic identity at higher rates than continuing generation students. Overall, they joined identity-based organizations—inclusive of ethnic-, religious-, gender-, and sexuality-based social organizations—at more than twice the rate of their continuing generation peers. One-quarter of all named extracurricular involvements listed by first generation participants were identity-based social groups. They were also more likely to engage in advocacy work or to have no extracurricular affiliation.

Continuing generation participants were more likely to join volunteer organizations, competitive political or debate-focused groups, or exclusive social clubs unrecognized by the university. First and continuing generation participants joined preprofessional organizations, groups that aligned with their major, arts or performance clubs, sports (including club), Greek organizations, and college booster groups, such as the new student organization, campus ambassadors, or residence hall "house" committees at similar rates.

Both first and continuing generation participants took their extracurricular involvement very seriously and considered them imperative to forming the networks that sustained them in college and would likely support them upon graduation. Both first and continuing generation students considered extracurricular organizations as a primary context for making "friends for life." Anthony, a first generation senior, stated:

> My biggest success was the scope of different social circles I've been able to branch out to. I feel like I've met a lot of individuals through different organizations, by taking part in different programs, and not restricting myself to my [residence hall] or something like that. That's a success, being able to meet a ton of people.

Likewise, Elizabeth stated, "Successes were . . . getting involved in organizations and having multiple cohorts of people I am involved with." Robert Lee, who joined multiple extracurricular groups during college, explained:

> I've made what I hope to be lasting friendships with a group of people, and that's a really big social success. These are people I trust, people I've told about me and my life that I don't try to hide from. I pride myself on trying to engage a lot of different social groups at Georgetown, and I've at least dabbled in a lot of social settings that Georgetown has to offer.

For these and many other first generation participants, having multiple groups of friends, forged through extracurricular involvement, signaled deep engagement with the college and afforded them social networks that they believed would serve them well upon graduation.

It was not always easy to maintain diverse friend groups, as not everyone was understanding of circumstantial difference. Mikel, whose "greatest [social] success was integrating myself into various different things on campus," also pointed out that his greatest challenge was getting his friends to understand his circumstances.

> In terms of students with very different backgrounds, sometimes they can clash in a way. I met a lot of people who were really offensive but didn't know they were. Or people who didn't know how to deal with people from different cultural or economic backgrounds. That was the biggest challenge, to interact with and hold relationships with people from all different backgrounds. It was also really fun. I definitely enjoyed getting to know peers from very different backgrounds, like those of privilege.

Mikel explained that while studying abroad, he would often demur when a costly meal or beverages out was suggested among friends, and that they would think he was "stingy" when he simply did not have the money to pay for the activity. In his estimation, this was the problem of calling a financial condition an identity attribute: "A lot of students who have never interacted with people from lower income backgrounds see that as a characteristic of a person and not a matter of circumstance."

For students who rated their social satisfaction low, like Rosemary, who as a senior rated her social experience a lukewarm 6 out of 10, one reason they felt disconnected from the college was because of their lack of commitment to a meaningful extracurricular early during their time in college. Rosemary reflected, "I feel like I didn't get involved in extracurriculars to the extent that I wanted." When asked why that was the case, she responded, "I don't think I branched out enough or tried new things, not only out of my comfort zone but outside of my people comfort zone. A lot of things I do involve people I already know." She lamented not taking risks and trying new social organizations early in college, but as a senior she worked to rectify her perceived lack of social connections. Joining an ethnic organization was a meaningful first step:

> I also came into school very adamant [about] not wanting to find friends in my racial group, and now I think I missed out on having those kinds of networks and support systems. I joined the Chinese Student Association this year as a senior, and I wish I'd joined as a freshman. Some of the new recruits were surprised that I joined so late. They asked, "Why are you joining as a senior and not as a freshman?" I said, "Well, I didn't want to join then, but I do now."

Rosemary's point about not wanting to join an ethnic group, but changing her mind when she realized the kind of support structures these organizations offer, raises another common issue among first generation students. For many of our first generation participants, ethnic organizations were important sources of social connection and comfort in the often unfamiliar terrain of a college campus. Many participants believed that other first generation students were more likely to participate in ethnic organizations, and so they joined these groups assuming that they would meet "other students like me," not just ethnically but who had similar familial backgrounds or childhood upbringing. While this assumption did not always bear out, in many cases, first generation participants felt confirmed in their belief that ethnic associations operated as safe spaces and places where they did not have to "explain themselves" or their prior life experiences to others, in part because they believed other first generation students populated these groups at higher rates than other social organizations.

Beyond safe spaces, ethnic organizations also offered near-peer mentors eager to guide younger students in transitioning into and navigating the college experience. For older members, having younger students look up to them gave them a heightened sense of purpose and motivation. Older members coached junior members in social and academic behaviors that would optimize positive outcomes: they strategized responses to insensitive remarks that could be made by classmates in a seminar or discussion context; they role-played scenarios and methods to avoid challenges prior members had identified; and they provided invaluable advice about approaching faculty and teaching assistants regularly throughout courses, finding and cultivating faculty mentors, improving time management, and creating study groups. They were also sources of fun and a release from the competitive extracurricular environment. As these groups were open to all students, they operated their initiation processes on the apprenticeship model, and accommodated varying levels of involvement and opportunities for leadership.

Based on their statements, the level of extracurricular involvement determined the level of satisfaction both first and continuing generation students felt toward their overall social life in college. The general pattern among both groups suggested that students with a strong commitment to one or two extracurricular organizations, plus a loose connection with a third group (or alternatively, involvement in residence hall activities), were most satisfied with their social experiences in college. The opportunity to hold at least one leadership role between sophomore and senior year was also essential.

While both cohorts of students deemed extracurricular involvement critical to social satisfaction, there were challenges to access and participation among certain types of extracurricular groups. For instance, first generation senior Ironman complained about "applying for every position worth having" at his university:

> You have to apply for anything if you want to be a part of it, and your social life is based on the organizations you are a part of. I wasn't aware of that at first. So it's definitely challenging breaking in if you don't know that going in.

During his first semester in college, Ironman attempted to sign up for organizations he considered interesting, only to discover that an application deadline had passed or that he did not meet the selection criteria. He spoke of the sting associated with working so hard in high school to achieve the reward of admission to an elite college, only to discover that admission did not confer access to the social life promised in glossy brochures. He would have to apply, compete, and prove himself all over again. This became a source of considerable frustration, but he overcame these obstacles by researching application deadlines and applying early in subsequent rounds. While relevant information about extracurricular timelines was not readily available or centrally located, he redoubled his efforts and eventually navigated the process. Others were less fortunate.

Of course, not all extracurricular activities require an application, but the application or "comping" process, as it is called at Harvard, can feel daunting and at times exclusionary, even when application criteria and deadlines are widely available and accessible. Some participants recounted that they refused to join clubs that required an application, but admitted that many of those clubs appeared more socially exciting and potentially more powerful in terms of the social and preprofessional networks they offered. Several participants argued that thinking of extracurriculars in terms of their economic value proposition served to corrode the relationships they sought by joining these extracurriculars in the first place. As first generation Elizabeth explained:

> Sometimes I feel that people are too work-oriented. You get this sense that people here try to do too many things and are not committed to any one thing. Relationships didn't feel genuine with those people.

Another first generation senior, Fay, who served as a leader in organizations ranging from club sports to a volunteer organization and a preorientation program, framed her relationship to extracurriculars as such:

> I think freshman year, it's a competitive campus, so the second semester everyone is a leader of some group, and sometimes

that can feel isolating if you don't know your place yet. First semester, I joined a bunch of things trying to find my place. I was also trying to balance what I want and climbing the ladder, and just being in a competitive place all the time is a challenge.

Incidentally, Fay, Elizabeth, and Ironman all rated their social experience a very satisfied 9 out of 10. While they found their extracurricular involvement challenging in nuanced ways, they were nonetheless quite pleased with the social outcomes this participation conferred—friendship, belonging, and opportunities for leadership development.

Both first and continuing generation participants spoke ambivalently about competitive extracurricular organizations. Competitive, or application-based, extracurriculars ranged from a cappella groups to fraternities and sororities to the college newspaper and artistic societies. Students considered the application or "comp" process as salutary when it operated like an apprenticeship— where you learned valuable skills along the way even if the process ultimately did not lead to full membership—but deleterious when near-peers judged students' worthiness, merit, or relative value to the organization without offering much in the way of guidance or skills building. For instance, continuing generation senior Mac-Neill pointed out that "comping" for the college radio entailed enduring other students' interrogations of his music taste and choice of arrangements when he was hoping to join a community of music lovers. As he put it,

I have been so turned off by the comping process. I can't even join a radio show here without comping. Everything is about comping. It's very pedantic. I don't want to comp for things that shouldn't be stressful or competitive, it's just a huge turnoff, especially for older students like me.

Even continuing generation Emily, whose sister warned her about "comping" and guided her through the process, nonetheless bemoaned the anxiety-provoking sense that "you need approval from somebody else to do what you want to do." She underscored the psychological toll of constantly having to prove one's abilities among peers:

> It can be really discouraging for a lot of people to have to "comp" for a lot of the worthwhile activities. Just comping for everything can get so draining, especially if you get rejected for things you know you can do. And it's hard because you don't always get to do everything you want to do once you get here. I think the big thing is somehow leveling the extracurricular field.

First generation senior Eliza echoed MacNeill and Emily's sentiments about social exclusion, adding a practical concern about the unanticipated and otherwise unremarked financial costs to club leadership:

> It would be great to break down the really competitive nature of clubs, where you have to apply to everything. Georgetown feels like the only place in the world left where you apply to your social life. Some clubs brag that they have an acceptance rate of ten percent. These clubs serve to exclude just as much as the way fraternities and sororities supposedly do, and they are extracurriculars!
>
> And leadership costs money. You have to throw parties and keep people happy. So no wonder all of the leaders of the major extracurricular groups are well off. They can afford to spend some of their own money. Or they know how to get extra money to manage the social requirements of being that leader.

Certain competitive organizations, such as the secretive "final clubs" at Harvard and the student-run food service chain "The Corp" at Georgetown, were singled out as populated almost exclusively by the campuses' well-heeled students. They were also considered more white than other organizations, although it was universally acknowledged that their exclusionary nature was not solely based on race or even on class, but on comportment and appropriateness of "fit." While this assumption may not be factually true, this was the guiding frame of discourse around these organizations' merits and sins. Continuing generation participants were their primary defenders, although more than half of these participants also complained about the exclusionary tone and practices of these organizations and others, especially clubs that owned their own private property and thus are not under the purview of the college administration. One continuing generation member of a final club confessed that it was challenging to belong to a club that "is viewed negatively by the college, for the most part." She stressed that her participation advanced her opportunities as a female leader and "as someone who wants to see women socially at the same level as men on this campus," a goal she assumed the college's administrators would support.

> The reason I joined this particular club was that as a first year student when I looked at upper-class women who I admired, not just socially but who have done really incredible things—those who go on to become Rhodes Scholars and go to incredible law schools and medical schools—they are there. The alumnae hav[e] a network of women who have graduated from Harvard and who want to see you succeed and want to help you. For example, later today I will be sending my resume and other information to an alumna to look over my application materials for a particular job because she works in a similar position I'd like to get into. So having that is tremendous.

Other continuing generation participants would disagree with this student, arguing that the entire system must be overhauled or dismantled before equality of opportunity can be achieved. As someone who already benefitted from a system of privilege, the benefits she accrued as a member of an organization that promotes and supports women as future leaders simply serve to widen opportunity gaps between her and less well-connected peers, men and women alike. This debate largely existed among continuing generation participants, as first generation participants were near unanimous in their distaste for the school's secret societies.

When the scope was broadened to all competitive social organizations and not just the secret societies, there was much more nuanced parsing between the good and the bad versions of selective social institutions. Fraternities and sororities, for instance, were often attractive to first generation participants, largely because they were viewed as more inclusive than the private-property-owning secret societies. They entailed open membership rules and comprised a more diverse membership than Harvard's final clubs or Georgetown's "The Corp." When they did not find social organizations that aligned with their values and goals, first generation participants founded chapters of fraternities and sororities they considered more inclusive and values-driven. They launched and led chapters of service organizations, some selective and some with open membership, to provide models of positive social organization. Likewise, some continuing generation participants gravitated toward such organizations because they set a better example of behavior for men and women seeking companionship through shared vision and group activities. They often held fraternities and sororities up as a counterpoint to the secretive final clubs. This narrative was confirmed by equal participation rates among both cohorts of students: slightly less than ten percent of both samples spoke of membership in a Greek organization. Of course, not all fraternities and sororities modeled inclusive and values-based practices, but those that did presented a stark dividing line between toxic and palatable selective organizations on campus.

Continuing generation participants were not only divided in their level of support for competitive social organizations, in general, and specific types, in particular, they also sometimes offered views that included conflicting statements. One continuing generation senior, Z. explained to me: "I don't participate in extracurriculars. I go to events but don't participate. I'm not a joiner." He admitted to feeling exasperated by the ongoing discussion about exclusivity on campus when it felt to him that not much concrete action by officials at the university or students was being taken to effect real change. He realized that he, too, participated in the problem. It was so easy to become siloed in one's social circle when external authorities appear to legitimize or look the other way. Z. described his internal conflict as such:

> One of the biggest [social] challenges is how fractured social life is here. Being frustrated by seeing the same people over and over again even though this place is so big. Also knowing that there are people I'd like to get to know better but I just haven't been able to.
>
> And conversations about spaces and exclusivity and all that stuff are mind numbing, and you can't escape them. I am extremely bored by them. Talking about it is another stress and drain.
>
> I am in [an exclusive social club]. As of this week I'm getting the hell out of there. You've caught me at a very unusual moment. I had very intense feelings about social life and decided to make a radical shift in how I will spend the rest of my time here.
>
> It all started with a party at [another exclusive social club]. A member invited me. Once you're a senior, you're allowed to go there as a guest. The aesthetic of meaninglessness and denying the value in life was overwhelming and horrible. And I couldn't believe I was participating in this completely nihilistic ritual. I didn't understand how hypocritical people are until that night. I know [this social club] has an aesthetic of meaninglessness. They parody all things. But seeing it up close was revolting. How they trash valuable things. For example, there is this very valuable piece of furniture that there are only two existing and the other one is in a museum, they use it to mix drinks on top of. Like none of it matters. And it was really disorienting to see that people I know clearly don't believe in that would participate in that. I don't know why, maybe for the thrill

or the experience of being in an exclusive place. It's not easy to escape it. But after that party, I did feel like it's time not to participate in those types of organizations here. To speak to the real challenge at Harvard for the whole community, [this] place, I can't put it any more simply than this: the problem is that there are buildings on Mt. Auburn St.[5] that some people have an ID card that lets them in and that won't let others in, no matter what. That's not fair. Even if it's legitimate. . . . The administration feels like they can't do anything about it. They're worried about the donors. They follow the money. . . . But they could, for once, dip into their endowment to stop this. That's what's angering. The problems with social issues are beaten to death. No one has solutions, and it's up to the school. [Administrators] throw their hands up in the air as often as we do. I know they care, that doesn't mean they understand the problem.

Z.'s frustration with the exclusionary nature and excessive behaviors of the property-owning selective organizations—ranging from conspicuous consumption to potlatch-style rituals of destruction—only serves to highlight the corrosive power of these social groups on campus as well as the value of more salubrious community organizations. That they comprise such a small proportion of the overall college-going population does not seem to matter when they come up time and again in student reflections on what is wrong with social life on campus.

5. Z. is referring to the property on Mt. Auburn Street in Cambridge, Massachusetts, owned by the Harvard final clubs. The final clubs have endured much controversy in recent years, with the university administration attempting to shut down their influence by barring student leaders from their membership. The following op-ed piece, "Equality on Mt. Auburn Street," published in the *Harvard Crimson* on February 6, 2017, offers a glimpse into the parameters of the debate: https://www.thecrimson.com/article/2017/2/6/rhodes-marshall-club-sanctions/.

First-Generation-Specific Organizations

Student organizations focused specifically on the identity, interests, and needs of first generation students were sparse when this study began in 2012, but they took hold on campuses across the country and are now somewhat commonplace. They emerged as an important, if potentially controversial, extracurricular organization among the first generation participants in this study. Their importance to some participants' lives, contrasted with the reticence of others to officially join or participate in their activities, underscores a complicated set of choices first generation students make about whether and how to disclose their parental educational status, and whether they find this status relevant to their social lives in college.

The two campuses in this study exemplified different organizational structures for first generation student groups on campus. At the risk of simplifying a complicated set of motives and practices, one might argue that Georgetown's approach operated from a multiculturalist frame, where some students were valued and even prioritized over others according to their different needs and backgrounds. Harvard's approach was more classically liberal, where all students, regardless of background, were given access to available resources in an opt-in, optional disclosure model.

Georgetown's approach to first generation support modeled the one-stop shop with centralized programming and networked ties to other units across campus. As a staffed program with its own office, the Georgetown Scholarship Program (GSP) hosted events proposed and run by administrators, alumni donors, and community partners, as well as activities devised and carried out by students with the blessing and support of the office staff and its student advisory board. The GSP office suite, housed in the garden level of the admissions building, was a warm and welcoming venue with comfortable seating, small rooms for private conversations, and a larger conference room for student planning meetings, trainings, and workshops. Any given day one might find administrators from different units, alumni volunteers, community partners, and students discussing upcoming programs, ongoing initiatives, or personal matters with the GSP staff. From an outsider's perspective, the GSP office appeared to be the hub for all things first generation at Georgetown.

A student could conceivably seek services at the GSP and not be first generation, but students recognized that this office and its programs were designed with first generations students in mind. The GSP used its limited resources to uphold its mission to serve those who might otherwise be overlooked in the general Georgetown population, making low-income first generation students the primary targets for all GSP initiatives. A proportion of first generation students at Georgetown did not have full access to the GSP because their families earned too much for them to qualify for its scholarship. They were offered affiliate status, while non first generation students could participate in selected activities as "friends" and "allies." In practice, this meant that the GSP was generally considered around campus to be a resource for low-income first generation students, and not a place to turn if a student who was not first generation needed financial, social, or academic support.

By contrast, Harvard modeled a distributed and more classically liberal approach to first generation support and programming. Students launched and led a First Generation Student Union (FGSU) to provide social support and a locus of student activity, while different administrative units across the campus operated programs designed to assist first generation students with issues ranging from study skills and time management to dealing with roommate conflicts and resolving financial strains. In addition, a first generation alumni group formed in 2012 to provide mentorship and advocacy for current first generation students. The design and operation of the programs and activities supporting first generation students was not controlled or organized by a single unit or office at Harvard but rather was incorporated into administrative programming based on the type of service offered rather than the type of student served. Other than financial support, there were no programs or initiatives that served only first generation students, and no obligations that required first generation student participation. Even the FGSU was required to admit non first generation students into its membership in compliance with the university's nondiscrimination policy. As such, while there were pockets of first generation representation and support available all over campus, in practice, there was no single dedicated space for first generation students at Harvard.

A Closer Look at Georgetown's Institutional Organization: Georgetown Scholars Program

At Georgetown, most of the events and programs designed to support first generation students fell under the purview of the GSP, which had its own staff and a director as well as ties to other administrative offices across the university. The GSP, which was launched in 2005, conducted weekly and monthly gatherings, issued a newsletter, cosponsored campus-wide events throughout the year, hosted office hours, and assisted students on a variety of personal, social, preprofessional, and academic matters. The GSP was well known among first generation students who needed advice and concrete assistance dealing with expensive course materials, an emergency at home, or a surprise dental bill. Its staff also coached students in how to seek mentors and talk with professors. Via the encouragement of "scavenger hunt" style initiatives, they pulled disparate partners in the campus community—faculty, career services, the wellness center—into a networked campaign to provide a stronger sense of inclusion for first generation students in their program.

Beyond the on-campus support, the GSP also sought to provide resources for students seeking internships and off-campus employment. For example, they partnered with the clothing retailers Ann Taylor Loft and Joseph A. Banks to hold interview attire programs for first generation juniors. Young men were awarded gift cards to Joseph A. Banks. Young women were treated to a private shopping party and a free consultation on the appropriate wardrobe for different types of professional interviews. At the annual Ann Taylor Loft event, the local Loft store near campus closed early on the evening of the event and brought in sales clerks, career service professionals, executives from the clothier's headquarters, and donor alumni to assist first generation junior women as they perused the racks. They discussed mix and matching while eating chocolate dipped strawberries and finger sandwiches, drinking sparkling wine, and ultimately each of the participating young women left the store with $600 worth of merchandise at no charge to them.

GSP staff, alumni supporters, and community partners who identified specific needs among GSP members designed and executed the professional attire initiative and many other GSP programs. This does not mean, however, that the GSP operated with a top-down approach to programming. GSP Director Missy Foy regularly consulted students on what kind of programming they would like to see, reevaluating and revising events based on student feedback. In addition, a peer-elected student advisory board was selected each year and tasked with planning a slate of programs for the new academic year to ensure that the activities and approaches for building community in the GSP represented the current students' desires and needs rather than ones established by prior cohorts. As several alumni from the earliest GSP cohorts explained in personal interviews, there was a considerable evolution of the GSP between its earliest iteration and what students experienced during the time of this study. What began as a scholarship, a pizza party at the start of their freshman year, and a hearty "congratulations and good luck" quickly transformed, under the directorship of Missy Foy and the support of Dean of Admissions Charles Deacon, into a program office that understood creating the conditions under which first generation students could thrive required more than just a scholarship and a congratulatory meal. It required mentoring, guidance, ongoing proacademic initiative, occasional emergency financial support, and robust advocacy both on and off campus.

The GSP at Georgetown was widely known and generally respected among first generation and continuing generation students alike. The overwhelming majority of first generation participants who were enrolled at Georgetown were familiar with the GSP, even those (approximately 10% of this study) who did not qualify as official members. There was a clear tone of appreciation for the GSP and its staff. As several first generation participants explained, GSP staff routinely went "above and beyond." First generation senior, Q., reflected many of her peers' sentiments:

> [GSP staff members] are amazing. You know you can go to that office with a range of issues, and one, they've heard it before, so it's okay. And they can give you an action plan and help you solve the problem, whatever it is. Sometimes you need adults who can say, "We can take care of this."

Students dealing with serious personal and family crises turned to the GSP for support, and were not disappointed. When asked if there was ever a time when she needed help for a personal matter in college, first generation Reyna reflected, "Yes, pretty much all of college!" She listed emergencies at home, dealing with painful mental health challenges among family members, and a debilitating sports injury.

> And through all of it GSP helped. My GSP mentor called me all summer, whenever I needed anything. When I tore my ACL, at one point I was in a wheelchair and [GSP staff member] came and wheeled me to class and bought me breakfast. Just above and beyond!
>
> I don't think I would have ever excelled the way I have without that mental health support. My back home is really intense, and it's hard to concentrate on a paper when real life things are happening. It's great that GSP has funds to back up that sup-

port. They got me into counseling when I needed it, and they pay for my sessions.

Even for students who were wary of joining ethnic organizations or expressed concern about appearing as "victims," the GSP provided a welcome refuge in times of stress. First generation Francis, who avoided the campus's multicultural center because he thought it cordoned off ethnic minorities from the rest of campus, stated, "GSP, though, does a really good job. They bring students from different backgrounds, different races, different ethnicities and sexual orientations. I go there to hang out. They can be white, black, Chinese, whatever." While it was not generally the first extracurricular that students discussed when describing their extracurricular involvements, students framed it as a place to turn in times of crisis, when they wanted to get ahead or when they needed a place to relax and call home.

A Closer Look at Harvard's Student-Led Organization: First Generation Student Union

For Harvard students, the primary source of first generation specific extracurricular involvement was the FGSU, a student-led club founded during the course of this research study. The FGSU had a loose faculty sponsorship, an operating budget provided by the university's student organization fund, and a program agenda to raise awareness, foster pride, and administer peer support. The club hosted campus events such as study breaks, community meetings, student speakers, a peer mentorship program, and a first generation parents' reception during Junior Parents Weekend. It also sponsored a national event, the 2016 IvyG Conference, a well-attended inter-Ivy first generation student conference featuring nationally renowned speakers.[6] Other extracurricular groups and

---

6. For a review of the inaugural IvyG Conference and its goals, see Kahlenberg, "How Low-Income Students Are Fitting in at Elite Colleges." Since this time, the

administrative offices on Harvard's campus offered programmatic activities in line with the mission of Georgetown's GSP, but their services were spread throughout the university in capillary fashion, rather than centralized in one office. Unlike GSP, which evolved over the course of more than a decade between its inception and the time of this study, the FGSU was a new program, and the level of campus visibility, as well as the depth and breadth of its programming, may also change as it establishes itself.

During sophomore and senior interviews, first and continuing generation participants were asked to list their extracurricular involvement and describe their level of participation in each. At Harvard, only a handful of first generation participants reported participating in the FGSU. Those who did were enthusiastic about its message, and several included their own leadership in the FGSU as an important achievement in college. Many who did not participate were either suspicious of its purpose or considered it irrelevant to their experiences. Some stated that they were unaware of its existence before our interviews and asked for more information about how to join. Several participants joined the group but stopped attending because they found it "cliquey" or "complaining."

Fear of Stigma in First Generation Student Groups

Some first generation participants described a difficult choice in electing to participate in Georgetown's GSP or Harvard's FGSU. By seeking valuable support and services, they outed themselves in ways that seemed unfair compared to their continuing generation peers. Some worried they would be seen as "needy" in a context demanding an image of effortless competence. First generation Gretchen, for instance, hesitated to join the first generation group because "I don't want to go there just to cry about our bad

---

organizers of IvyG have hosted multiple annual conferences under the names IvyG and EdMobilizer. See: https://www.edmobilizer.org/

experiences. The problems that I have are very personal. I don't want to broadcast them." Similarly, S. explained, "I stay away from those groups because there's such a propensity to place yourself as a victim." Others believed that membership in one of these organizations did or should also correlate with racial or ethnic minority status or lower socioeconomic status, and when they did not self-identify as such, they described those organizations as "not for me." Ironman confessed that, after attending GSP events in his freshman and sophomore year, he stopped showing up in his junior year. "I didn't find community there." When asked why, he responded: "I don't want to sound weird, but I'm one of the few white people there. Sometimes I feel awkward like I don't belong there. I know that's not true, and I don't want to appear racist, I'm not racist, but there aren't many people like me hanging out there and it feels like it's not for me."

Marie, an economics major with a rural and conservative upbringing, explained that she did not feel like she belonged among fellow first generation students, largely because they held a narrow view of how a first generation student should look and act. When she told fellow students that she was first generation, they often did not believe her. In our interview, she said she was unaware of the activities of the first generation group on campus, but she shared the following personal insight:

There seems to be a perception of first generation students that isn't always true. People imagine minority, alternative, or they look poor. . . . I've had people say to me, "I don't believe you're a first gen." I've had people call me elitist, which I think is hilarious. I don't fit the stereotypical first gen mold. I'm also Republican. I've been accused of being wealthy. Someone once trying to insult me said, "You've never cooked food in your life and you're an elitist Republican."

I don't know if there's a way that we could change the perception of what first gen students are. When you see a white girl wearing business clothes, because I'm on an internship, you think, "Oh, that girl is in the business school and her parents have money." And for me at least, that's not true.

Jake, who preferred to keep his identity cards very close to his chest, pointed out:

> You know there is a first gen college student group on campus. I joined that last year. I got on their mailing list and became a member. I haven't been to any of the events because they're kind of cliquey, I feel, but I also don't want to be part of that culture sometimes. I talked to one of the founders last year and was like, "Don't you just get together and cry about where you come from?" I feel like I might not feel better about myself if I went into that group and talked about my background.

With the GSP, there was an additional layer of concern over disclosure because it served as both a social organization and a scholarship program. Some first generation students were grateful for the scholarship, but did not want to associate with the social organization, or were conflicted about attending the events designed to build community for the scholarship recipients. First generation senior Veronica, who called the GSP "a great support" and "economically . . . really helpful," explained:

> There is a stigma that comes with being in that program. You can spot "us" because we look different. We don't look like we come from a privileged background. For some people that was embarrassing. There are other people who thrive in that support. I found the support in the faculty and staff, not with the other students as much, and not with identifying with the program. It can be overwhelming to have all these communities, all these networks you could juggle. Especially when you feel like you could belong.
>
> I speak Italian, Spanish, French. I've always had the more international focus in my studies. I was always interested in studying abroad. And because I felt like I could pass as white and meld into that larger group, I wanted to do that and not stick

out with the GSP. I'm thankful for the support, but it's not this nice loving kind of thing, you know? I'm not always there, I don't go to the events. I'm thankful for what they've done.

First generation students were able to opt in and out of both the GSP and the FGSU as they deemed appropriate. The level of commitment and use of services could be fluid, and that worked well for those first generation participants who were reticent to wear that label in public or who preferred to be known for other features of their identity—say, their academic major, their professional goals, their ethnicity, or their views on religion or politics. Some, like Eliza, who identified more as a budding journalist and member of the Latinx community than a first generation college student, explained that despite her hesitance to become involved in the GSP "[the director] was there for me" during a challenging sophomore year. While the GSP was not on her list of important extracurriculars, it nonetheless provided her invaluable support when she needed it most.

The opportunities and challenges concerning participation and membership in first generation specific organizations, as described by students in this study, underscore a dilemma in student programming that has no easy answer. By offering a safe space and central location for emotional support, pride development, and network building, the institution risks excluding some students who might otherwise benefit from these services but who do not match the selection criteria. Even student organizations that have open membership due to nondiscrimination policies may be perceived as exclusionary by those who do not fit the modal student type. Other students may be cordoned off, outed, or otherwise typecast by their peers on campus due to their association with the organization. However, simply offering support services and activities for an underrepresented or marginalized student group at different locations and offices across campus—what might be called an à la carte or add-on approach to inclusion—risks suppressing minority perspectives, decentralizing and losing sight of the whole-person needs of the student, and potentially encouraging an assimilationist view of what success in college looks like. The educational benefit of diversity assumes that students learn from and respect one another's differences, not hierarchize and judge their peers on the basis of those differences. As the students in this study can attest, both the one-stop shop and the decentralized programming approach have their benefits and drawbacks, and students will reject either one for personal reasons or if the support looks like it is just not there. Nonetheless, student groups and student-serving support offices play a significant role in the overall climate of inclusion or exclusion on a campus and thus warrant ongoing deliberation about whom they serve and how they deliver those services to optimize student growth in college.

5

Negotiating Belonging
and Critique

THE CONDITIONS and extent to which students chose to disclose
their first generation status, and the identities they chose to highlight in different contexts, underscore a complicated negotiation
of status and role within the larger campus community. First generation students narrated their identities on campus through
themes of belonging, recognition, assimilation, and social critique.
First generation students were no more likely to express conflict
about their personal identity or a sense of mismatch between
themselves and their college than were their continuing generation peers. They did, however, consider their first generation status
to be a reason for conflict when it arose. Some first generation
students chose to "pass" as continuing generation students, while
others expressed pride in their first generation status, and still
others critiqued the university for their sense of isolation and lack
of fit on campus. The complicated negotiations of identity disclosure underscore the liminality[1] of the first generation status, one

1. Anthropologists Arnold van Gennep and later Victor Turner defined liminality
as that ambiguous and confusing interval in a ritual context where the persons involved have already shed their pre-ritual status but have not yet been accepted into
a post-ritual world. It is the betwixt and between, where rules are overturned, identities are fluid, and participants must consign themselves to vulnerability and risk. See
Turner, "Betwixt and Between." College has often been considered a rite of passage

that is intergenerationally unstable and largely a result of a cultural association in the United States that conflates education with merit.

In the following pages, I describe three themes first generation participants identified as crucial to understanding their social lives on campus. Demographic transitions, financial concerns, and an overall sense of belonging were essential factors associated with positive or negative social satisfaction in college. Each of these topical themes intersected with how first generation participants elected to disclose or conceal their first generation status and whether they assimilated into or critiqued the perceived unspoken norms of campus life.

Demographic Transitions

First and continuing generation participants spoke of loneliness and the fear of not fitting in at similar rates in this study. However, first generation participants were more likely to describe feelings of shock over demographic differences between their home communities and the makeup of the campus, particularly in their first year of college. This tended to trigger two layers of bewilderment: not recognizing one's surroundings, while feeling apprehension over misrecognition by others in the new space.[2]

---

in the United States. Vincent Tinto famously revised van Gennep's framework of the rite of passage in his student attrition model. See Tinto, "Stages of Student Departure" and *Leaving College*.

2. When Bailey spoke of feeling "misrecognized" on campus, she referred to times when university administrators, faculty, or her undergraduate peers assumed habits or qualities about her that she rejected. Throughout our interviews together, she described being asked questions about her hair, being told she was surprisingly smart (why should this ever be a surprise at an Ivy League institution?), or being told that her accent was (or was not) a tell-tale sign of her Southern origins. She felt pinned to a fictional identity—a skewed but recognizable facsimile—that other people, most often white students, created for her. This fictional identity cast her as either a privileged minority, one with wealthy parents and a private school education, or as a poor minority, one with a heroic story of escaping poverty, violence, or neglect.

Sam, a biology major on the pre-med track and a first generation college student, explained to me that he felt unrepresented in
his student newspaper's freshman survey. He worried that other
students would believe he was "from the projects" simply because
his family's income put him in the survey's lowest reported socioeconomic bracket. His family had immigrated to the United States
from Ethiopia, and while his parents worked in tenuous and low-
paying jobs, they placed a high value on education for Sam and his
brother. He felt supported at home, but confused by his new collegiate surroundings, especially the discourse of "liberal arts education" with its seeming nonchalance about the connection between learning and career. He suspected that there was a
demographic link between the language of educational transformation and the obvious affluence of his new surroundings. Sam
felt very confused by the people he met: "Coming here felt really
foreign." His campus had hosted a visitation weekend for accepted
students in the spring, but, for financial reasons, Sam had been
unable to attend. So, he explained, arriving for the first time in the
fall of his freshman year, "I had no idea what the school was going
to be like. I had no idea what to expect." He wished he had some
form of advance preparation, perhaps a primer on this new "liberal
arts" concept he kept reading about in the letters home or hearing
in the recruitment videos. Sam wished he had prior warning about
what the college expected of him, and likewise, felt "there should
be more opportunities for you to be able to frame what you expect
the experience of college should be like."

Neither of these were true for Bailey, who described her family as staunchly middle
class and her public school background as decent though not stellar. She also happened to be an excellent student, a star athlete, a leader among her peers, and an
altogether charming person. Bailey fought against "misrecognition" through a media
campaign called "I, too, am Harvard," which sought to deepen and complicate a
conversation about blackness at Harvard (see https://itooamharvard.tumblr.com/).
This use of "misrecognition" by students is related to, though not the same as Bourdieu's use of the term, which refers to the denial or repression of an objective truth
in favor of a common-knowledge fiction. See Bourdieu, *Practical Reason*, 121.

For Sam, the demographic disconnect was influenced by his family's socioeconomic and immigrant statuses, and the way these statuses informed their expectation of what formal education should be and do. That he was a racial minority did not help with this challenge, but he did not foreground that in the interview, either. For Reyna, also a child of African immigrants, the demographic disconnect was all about race and how it intersected with her immigrant and socioeconomic status. Reyna described growing up in a segregated urban neighborhood and school district. Before college, she had never before been in a setting where she was a minority. Now there were routinely times when she was the only black student in a social group or a classroom. She characterized her experiences as such:

> I was in a racial and socioeconomic bubble that I didn't realize would cause such a crisis when I got here. I wish I understood more about racial and socioeconomic issues when I got here. The experience of being the only person of color in your class. And language, not having a huge vocabulary or not knowing a lot of different things. I didn't really have the language that some people here have. Being comfortable about my identity. I wish I at least knew I was going to have to deal with that.

Reyna attended a preorientation program hoping to make friends before college. Instead, she found that she "didn't relate to a lot of people there," that is, Republicans of color, black students from the American South, students who did not know or care about the cultural and social distinctions among different immigrant black communities:

> It made me feel like blackness is way different than what you know growing up. If I can relate to a white student who grew up in a poor area more than a black student who grew up wealthy, that's just different. There was all this emphasis on class respectability and coded language that I did not fit into.

Reyna expressed a demographic shock that called into question her prior ideas about race and how it intersected with social class and immigration status. She was disturbed that she related less to her African American peers who came from wealthy backgrounds than she did to other low-income white students.

Other first generation students pointed directly to race as their initial barrier to belonging. First generation participants who were also underrepresented minorities were more likely to describe feeling overwhelmed by their white peers if they attended majority minority high schools. Rocket, who identified as Southeast Asian, described the dissonance he felt between his home community, where being first generation was "normal," and therefore invisible, and his college experience, where he felt like an outlier. He explained:

> I'm from L.A., from a nonwhite community. My high school was eighty percent Hispanic and fifteen to twenty percent Asian. Not many white students. Coming to a place where everyone is white, at the time I didn't think about it as a thing, but there is like a cultural barrier that exists, I would say. And learning, figuring out my own identity while interacting with everyone, figuring out my values and my identity in this new context has been challenging. Getting to reflect on my own upbringing has been a process.

Francis, who also came from Southern California, described the culture shock of West to East Coast social norms and feeling as though he was never "white enough" nor "Latino enough" to seamlessly adapt to either community on campus. He was also frequently homesick. Francis recalled:

> Freshman year I would cry myself to bed. My roommate freshman year was also a minority student who came from the inner city. Even in the winter freshman year, we would sleep with the windows open just to hear the noises outside, the sirens, the helicopters. You miss home. You miss the helicopters, the

screeching tires, the sirens. It's where you come from. So you miss it, no matter what others think.

Tolu, who expressed conflicted emotions about finding her place on campus, and who only began to feel like she belonged while studying abroad for a semester, pointed to her experience as a female black student and an immigrant on a predominately white campus:

> Race and gender matter. It's not the same if you're first gen who's white or black or international. We have a lot of similarities, but there are a lot of differences that need to be addressed. We need to be multidimensional about it. And I feel like it's an important part of our academic and social life. For example, the reason I felt excluded was not because I was first generation, but because I was black in a PWI [predominantly white institution] or female in a predominantly male department. Those kinds of stereotype threat experiences inhibited my ability to succeed, but I don't know the full extent of the impact of those experiences.

As with Reyna, Rocket, Francis, and Tolu, many nonwhite first generation participants who also attended high schools that were demographically dissimilar from Harvard or Georgetown spoke of the additional adjustment challenges of navigating sociocultural spaces that were different than those in which they were raised. What other students appeared to value, what they considered appropriate to talk about, and the opinions they expressed all led some nonwhite first generation students to feel that they did not belong. First generation Skylar explained that she struggled to adjust in her first months and years at Georgetown. She pointed to cartoons in her campus newspaper featuring women and underrepresented minorities running for student government on diversity and inclusion platforms as "dead horses" to be beaten. She described her exasperation:

> You'll be dealing with struggles about your identity, how you fit in, and any other things that happen on campus. We've been

talking about race and privilege on campus, and if you're a student of color, feeling literally like you don't belong here. A normal human being can't be successful because you're dealing with all these things at once.

Often embedded in ideas about race, privilege, and belonging are social norms that took first generation participants by surprise. Paola, who confessed that her university "was not anything I expected it to be at all" explained:

There were social norms and expectations that I didn't know and I had to learn. The ways that people engage in conversation, the ways that people interact with each other, the way that they know about each other and this entire culture, the way people dress, the places they shop, the things that they do for leisure. It was this whole culture that I had no experience with, and the expectation was that you acted that way or you missed out on opportunities to meet people and become part of these networks that people were building.

Some nonwhite first generation students from predominantly nonwhite or low-income communities embraced their matriculation into a historically predominantly white and wealthy university as a new experience and opportunity to grow. They explained that they chose to attend an elite private university far from home instead of selecting their public flagship or local college because they wanted to experience new and different opportunities that they thought would not otherwise be available to them. Salama, who was raised in a rural black community in one of the lowest income regions of the country, shared that she relished the opportunities her university afforded her as well as the chance to explore a different life than what was expected of her at home. She characterized her greatest social success as "getting out of my comfort zone" and "making friends with different kinds of people" in college. She savored the solitude of the library, snatches of alone time in her residence hall, social events with her new best friends, who were all Latinx, and rigorous discussions in her linguistics classes.

Chris, another first generation student who, like Salama, was an African American from the Deep South, also viewed his collegiate experience as an unparalleled opportunity for growth. He, too, savored his university experiences, beaming over his achievements in his senior year: "only one B in college, in music theory my first semester." Chris shared that he made the time to engage in intimate and introspective conversations with new friends in college while also maintaining deep connections with family and friends at home. His greatest social success and challenge were one and the same: building lasting friendships in this new context while taking the time to honor and nourish his relationships at home. Extracurricular participation took a back seat for Chris, but his few close friends at school, family and friendship connections at home, and stellar grades all cohered to give him the feeling that this was a good choice, despite the challenges. Chris and Salama's satisfaction with the new experiences that their campus had to offer is not one that all first generation students share. We learn a crucial lesson from them, however, that deep and intimate friendships, rather than superficial connections, combined with positive academic experiences and the ability to choose how one spends one's time in college, are important factors for overall social satisfaction with the college experience.

Money Matters

When asked to identify their greatest challenges in terms of social life on campus, first and continuing generation students alike spoke of battling loneliness, feeling misrecognized, and struggling to balance social life and academics. First generation participants, however, described additional financial concerns that most continuing generation students did not raise. These financial concerns were complex, and not limited to paying bills or delivering on family obligations. Many first generation participants were initially overwhelmed by the economic gulf between their home communities and the well-endowed campuses they were expected to inhabit. In addition, their peers often hailed from the highest economic brackets, their habits included spending money at rates and on items hitherto unheard of by most first generation participants, followed by seeming not to appreciate or value those purchases after the money was spent.[3] First generation students described trying not to appear surprised by their new friends' or roommates' expensive proclivities. They described the routine of mental calculations behind poker faces: a single night out with friends compared to their entire family's monthly grocery bill; a peer's suggestion to load a metro card with fifty dollars when a single ride cost two dollars; a roommate leaving for class and returning with new boots and a four hundred dollar receipt. The neighborhoods around their campus were no help: the restaurants and cafés catered to tourists and wealthy consumers, and there were few bargains to be had within walking distance. With family members often calling on them for financial support, many first generation participants spoke of the dissonance they felt between their friends' habits of calling home for money and their own tendency to send money home whenever they could.

One first generation participant described the shock she felt at her roommate's habit of "blowing through a sixteen thousand dollar a month budget." For many, this kind of shock quickly translated into anxiety over fitting in, sometimes coupled with the harmful coping mechanism of maxing out new credit cards in an attempt to blend in. Many first generation participants worried that they would be judged as out of place at their university based on how they dressed, where they ate, or what they chose to do on

3. Thorstein Veblen's concepts of *conspicuous consumption* and *conspicuous leisure* as the competitive and inflationary wastefulness of upper-class lifestyles—that the goal is to demonstrate how little one values such objects and experiences to demonstrate one's economic status—is apt here. See Thorstein Veblen, *Theory of the Leisure Class* (1899), http://www.gutenberg.org/files/833/833-h/833-h .htm#link2HCH0004.

the weekends. They drew the conclusion that student success was correlated with parental wealth, which could be verified publicly, though nonverbally, through the age-old practices of conspicuous consumption, namely: elaborate and wasteful clothing conventions, opting for restaurant meals instead of the campus dining hall, and planning weekend excursions off campus rather than socializing through institutionally planned channels. Veronica, who worried about being "outed as one of the poor girls on campus," divulged her experiences as such:

> I maxed out so many credit cards buying really expensive things trying to fit in. My parents needed to help me with the bills, all just because of my insecurities, and I didn't know how to deal with it and keep this image for as long as I could. No one would say anything bad about me, but I was always worried anyway. It wasn't until I went abroad that I realized none of that mattered.

Like Veronica, Anthony spoke of his concern that he should look the part, namely by mimicking a particular clothing style of his peers, and then his realization that this concern was ill placed when he, too, studied abroad:

> I definitely thought I had to fit this certain type of profile, especially in terms of how I should be dressing, etcetera, like having to have this name brand jacket or boot. But over time, I realized it's just not like that. The reason why it felt like that was because there were a lot of people like that coming from backgrounds not like mine. But when I went abroad I met students from other colleges, and I realized that this group of college students . . . is not representative of the general college-going population. So I realized I didn't have to follow that pattern.

Skylar described her greatest social challenge as the initial shock of freshman year when she discovered her peers' expensive tastes and then felt she had to replicate that in order to look and fit in appropriately with the image of her elite college:

When I first came to Georgetown, this is so embarrassing but I have to tell it, convocation was really shocking because I had never seen so many blonde people in one room. I was overwhelmed by how different I looked from all of these people. I started hanging out with the Korean immigrant group, which was largely an international group. A lot of immigrants are incredibly rich, and I got sucked into that very quickly. I was walking down the street with one friend, who said she wanted to pop into a local boutique to pick up a dress for a party that weekend, and she went in and dropped eight hundred dollars on a cocktail dress like it was nothing.

And when I first got to Georgetown, I didn't know about J. Crew or Vineyard Vines or boat shoes, or anything like that. And here everyone is wearing all of that. And you think, "Oh my god, I'm not Georgetown enough!" So you end up going to J. Crew and end up buying all this stuff. You think, "I have to at least look like I can dress the part."

I ended up telling my mom this, and when I would come home she would surprise me because she would have piles of clothes from these companies for me. She didn't know anything about them before—we always shopped at Marshall's or whatever. But she would come home with all these things she bought on clearance from these stores. Like she cleared the entire clearance rack out at J. Crew for me.

My mom's sacrifice made me cry. I felt so bad, because one Christmas she got nothing for herself and piles of clothes for me. I felt awful. It shows you how stupid you are, but that social pressure of fitting in, and feeling like you're already an outsider. Georgetown is telling you that you are amazing and you are Georgetown, so you want to look that part. I spent a lot of money freshman year, buying clothes and eating out with friends. My mom still talks about it, jokingly, but not really joking.

Some students coped with the social pressure to spend by pretending to be ill while their friends planned meals or evenings out.

Others volunteered at ticketed social events so they could participate for free. Still others resisted or delayed confronting sartorial
conventions they considered ubiquitous but unnecessary. Francis,
who lamented that "so much of social life is driven by money around
here," explained, "I refused to buy boat shoes until my junior year.
Someone bought me a pair as a gift, and then I bought another pair.
But everyone has them here. I held off until junior year." Ironman,
whose friends came from wealthier backgrounds, said:

> I wished I had known etiquette issues, like how much a meal
> costs, and that people want to go out and spend money. It's not
> like they're trying to be mean, it's just that they don't know this
> is not normal—not for most people—to spend this kind of
> money on a meal. I would have appreciated more heads up. And
> also, someone to tell me early on, "Don't take it personally."
> And the same for people from wealthier backgrounds, "Don't
> take it personally if I say 'no I can't do that.'" Now I tell my
> friends, "I can't do that," and they're cool with it. And if they do
> feel bad or angry about it, they're not people you should be
> with anyway.

A few continuing generation students raised financial concerns
in their interviews, but the reference tended to be about a campus
climate warped by socioeconomic inequality rather than stories of
personal dilemmas when navigating fraught social and financial
situations. They described their peers through the lens of financial
haves and have nots, and drew the connection—without
evidence—that wealthier students would also have higher grades.
Continuing generation Sarah, for instance, described people she
met whom she assumed were hurt by having to compete academically and make friends socially with wealthier peers:

> Something that really bothers me is basically the . . . amount of
> socioeconomic diversity on campus. It's a great thing to have
> people from so many different backgrounds here, but you have
> to understand that it is that much harder for students from low-

income backgrounds to succeed here, and there should be support for that. I have a friend whose G.P.A. would be a lot higher if she didn't have three jobs. It's really unfair that some kids don't have to work while others have to work to send money home, and they get graded on the same scale. We need to equalize the playing field. It's not fair. I'm very privileged. But part of me recognizes that this is not fair that I have access to resources and others do not. That I do not have to work while others do. That I had the education prior to coming here that set me up well for academics at Harvard. . . . You can maybe try to equalize it somehow.

First and continuing generation students agreed that their campus should provide cheaper alternatives to socializing off campus. Such requests often included remarks about alcohol policies on campus and rules about parties in the residence halls. But when asked what the institution could do to promote better social experiences on campus, most first and continuing generation students pointed out that the problems were among peers, not with university policies or programs. They tended to emphatically retort that the administration should not be in the business of engineering or surveilling their social lives. Greater socioeconomic diversity among students, as well as more explicit conversations about socioeconomic inequality and the pernicious effects of conspicuous consumption, might shift the social norms on campus more than university-sponsored social events or tweaks to rules governing student parties in the residence halls. In addition, no one spoke of the middle class. One was either poor or privileged, and there was an assumption—perhaps true, but untested in this study—that the children of the American middle class, say, the second to fourth economic quintiles, either did not exist on campuses such as Georgetown or Harvard or existed in such paltry numbers as to have no influence on consumption habits or social norms.[4]

4. While extensive in public discussions about American society and democracy, there is very little public discussion of the role of the American middle class at elite

Not all first generation participants' financial concerns revolved around socializing or sartorial assimilation. Some described working part-time jobs to send money home to support family members, particularly when younger siblings were still at home. Others, like Veronica and Skylar, divulged their guilt in asking for money from parents they knew were already making personal sacrifices to support their education. In addition, travel home was often prohibitively expensive for first generation students, so family ties were tested by the distance and a sense that these students were habituating to lives radically different from home. Both Georgetown and Harvard created funds to send students home for their first Thanksgiving or Spring Break, but not everyone who qualified knew these resources existed, and the additional requirement to request and justify these expenditures was sometimes reason enough for first generation students not to ask. Returning home also meant reacclimatizing to lifestyles that grew more distant as they advanced in college. As first generation Jake once put it, "Going home is so hard sometimes." A few continuing generation participants described not being able to travel home for holidays, or navigating an increasing cognitive dissonance when shuttling between home and campus, but it was a far less common concern than it was for first generation participants.[5]

---

institutions. Children of families earning in the middle of the American income distribution—from the second to the fourth quintile—are often overlooked in discussions of class on campus or are categorized as part of the "lower class." Indeed, families earning $65,000 per year in 2016, a figure more than thirteen percent higher than the national median family income in the same year, were considered "low-income" at Harvard and Georgetown.

5. Beginning in the fall 2016 term, Harvard initiated a startup fund of $2000 for incoming freshmen from families whose incomes fell below $65,000. A no-strings-attached fund, automatically sent without the need for paperwork or request, may alleviate some of the initial financial burden that first generation participants described.

Campus Belonging

In the wake of campus uprisings against racial injustice, institutional racism, and universities' current and historical roles in the perpetuation of social inequality across the country,[6] many universities have recently made or redoubled efforts to increase inclusion and a sense of belonging among all their students. Task forces, centers, and initiatives for diversity and inclusion have been charged with, among other things, cultivating a culture, processes, policies, and programs to support inclusion and success among all students, with a particular focus on those identified as historically marginalized, underrepresented, or excluded on their campus. These initiatives look different at every institution, given that they must address issues in the local or regional context as well as the particular demographic mix of the student bodies they serve. First generation students as a group cut across many demographics. They transect multiple marginalizations: they may be ethnically minoritized, international, immigrant, undocumented, low income, from an underresourced high school, or from an underresourced zip code. Sometimes, none of these categories pertain to them. As a whole, they do not have parents with a college degree, but even this identifying feature is complicated by the fact that some have college graduate relatives such as siblings or grandparents, or their parents started but did not finish college and have some college-going advice to offer. Given the complexities of how

6. This study began one year after the Occupy Wall Street Movement, but many participants were freshman during the Occupy Movement and several incorporated their views on it into their interviews. The Black Lives Matter movement, founded in 2013, and later the unrest in Ferguson, Missouri, in 2014 after the police killing of Michael Brown, had a profound effect on campuses across the country, sparking numerous protests and conversations about racism and racially motivated institutional violence, racial injustice, and systemic inequality. At the same time, elite universities like Georgetown and Harvard began publicly examining their historical involvement with slavery, eugenics, and systems of racial oppression and exploitation.

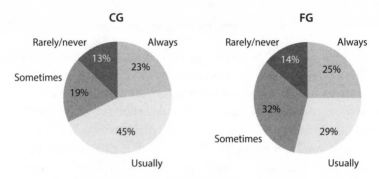

FIGURE 5.1. Belonging, first and continuing generation seniors. CG, continuing generation; FG, first generation.

this group may experience inclusion and belonging on campus, it is worth exploring and comparing how first generation participants discussed belonging in comparison with their continuing generation peers.

When asked to rate their belonging from "never" to "always" feeling like a part of the campus community, first and continuing generation students responded at similar rates at the two ends of the spectrum (see figure 5.1). Fourteen percent of first generation and thirteen percent of continuing generation seniors reported they "never" or "rarely" felt a part of the campus community during their time in college. At the other end, twenty-five percent of first generation and twenty-three percent of continuing generation seniors reported "always" feeling a part of the campus community. Two-thirds of the first and continuing generation respondents landed somewhere in the middle of this spectrum, where "sometimes" and "usually" were the available selections for describing their sense of belonging on campus. First generation respondents were roughly evenly split between these two categories, while continuing generation participants were more likely to say they were "usually" part of the campus community.

These differences were not statistically significant, but they helped clarify nuanced distinctions that emerged when first and continuing generation students spoke about their feelings of belonging on campus.

Most first generation participants and a handful of continuing generation participants tended to critique the whole-campus concept of belonging, pointing out that there were multiple communities on any given college campus, and that not all were equally accessible or welcoming. First and continuing generation seniors alike described feeling like a party or other important social activity was always going on behind a secret set of doors, without their knowledge or invitation. More than party invitations, though, there was a sense that important relationships were forged and decisions made that would impact later careers. First generation seniors chose to deal with that sense that they might be missing out on critical events in different ways. Some, like Ileana, emphatically declared that they belonged no matter what anyone else might say: "I am a part of the Harvard community. I feel like some people feel isolated, but I think that I am Harvard because I go to Harvard. If they want to distance themselves from the institution, then fine. But I feel like I am Harvard because I go to Harvard, and no one can tell me otherwise." Others shrugged off the pressure to socialize, pointing out that being a member of a club or attending parties and large social gatherings was not the only way to experience community. Chris, for instance, who cast himself as an introvert and very connected to his family back home, considered his social life in college to be a success even though he did not participate in extracurriculars and preferred quiet socializing to off-campus parties. "I've started thinking more critically about what the Harvard community means," he explained. "It isn't one thing. It's pretty fragmented. Just because I haven't had some of the experiences that some people have had here, it doesn't mean I'm not part of the Harvard community." Still others pointed out that they were satisfied with their social life even while knowing that other students' experiences may reveal a very different college than the one they came to know. Rocket, for instance, reflected,

I feel like Georgetown. I feel like I know a lot of people in my grade. Georgetown has a small campus and it's pretty central. . . . There are multiple Georgetowns, though. There's one where everyone's in the court and white, and the other one that's all about diversity, inclusion, social justice. There are so many spheres of Georgetown. I've managed to become pretty integrated into the overall Georgetown, but within those different versions of Georgetown, maybe not all of them. But that's fine because I don't want to be part of them.

Rocket's concept of "multiple Georgetowns" was a common refrain on both campuses. First generation Paola referred to "parallel Harvards" and, like Rocket and others, considered herself well integrated into the version of campus she inhabited while understanding that other "Harvards" not only existed beyond her experience but may even be hostile to her version of Harvard. First generation Amy, who worked off campus twenty-five hours a week and made closer friendships with her work colleagues than in her residence or through extracurriculars, echoed Rocket and Paola's point: "It is not a unified community. There are many communities. I feel like I fall out and in all the time."

Still others, like first generation Ashleigh, admitted that campus life could be "a bit of a social jungle," but thought that administrators should not be held responsible for providing a sense of belonging among first generation students. When asked what campus officials could do to help, she responded: "It's not up to anybody to 'do one specific thing' to help first generation students. You need to do it yourself." She bristled at the idea that campus officials should involve themselves in her social life. Instead, she claimed, "I feel there are many communities at Harvard, and it's somewhat up to me to be part of them. For instance, choosing to attend morning prayers makes me feel part of the intellectual community here."

Many first generation participants critiqued the campus social scene through lenses of openness and exclusion, and tied the sense of individual belonging to how open they felt the overall campus to be. Alex thought that too many people on campus were over-scheduled and career-oriented even in their social lives. He bemoaned the habit of putting lunch dates on calendars and never having time to engage in unstructured and serendipitous socializing. Paola explained her lack of a sense of belonging as "I haven't developed deep relationships with people I would consider a part of the Harvard community." Even Ileana, who at first declared, "I am Harvard," walked that declaration back a bit when asked to rate her overall social experiences. Rating them a middling 6, she explained:

It's harder to find yourself socially in the greater community. Academically you can prove yourself through your merit, but socially there are a lot of different facets that are out of your control. How incorporated you are into the community might have to do with your looks, background, money, your parents' work. Having these positions is going to affect what sorts of opportunities you have over the weekend or social opportunities, overall. . . . That can be a problem, and I have definitely found it problematic over time here.

The concept of campus belonging, while embraced, critiqued, or modified at similar rates among first and continuing generation participants, did raise a concern among some first generation participants that was not addressed by continuing generation students in this sample. That is, the challenge to one's identity and the pressure to assimilate or "pass" as one type of person on campus and behave as another type at home or in other contexts. First generation Jake, for instance, worried that he would be "outed" by his parents and sister when they visited for one of the university's family weekends. He coached his family to embellish their work and school to appear more polished to his friends' parents in the event that careers entered the conversation. Fortunately, he explained, his parents and his friends' parents got along just fine without any awkwardness: "Parents are going to know how to talk to each other regardless of background." For first generation Gretchen, a similar concern about "outing" meant that she starkly separated her home life from her campus life. While her mother was unflaggingly supportive of her education and career aspirations, not everyone in her family was. She felt misunderstood and frequently attacked in public by some of her relatives for attending an elite college and planning a career in the technology industry. She mused:

> Sometimes I don't know where I fit in. If I weren't thinking about all these other things I just mentioned, it would be really high. I would say a 9 [out of 10]. But thinking about it makes it different. Lots of my friends don't know that I'm first generation. Most people I interact with don't realize it. People don't look at me and realize. If I tell people, then they are surprised when I say that I'm on full financial aid. I'm aware that I blend in well. The clothes I wear. No one knows. But there is a tension. I still believe I am a full part of the Harvard community. But part of my personal identity is tough. When I have my Harvard hat on, I'm fully fine. But is this me?

First and continuing generation participants often spoke of the challenge of "fitting in" in such a complex and often hierarchical social milieu, but first generation students were singular in that they drew a connection between "fitting in" socially and exploring, evaluating, embracing, or bifurcating their personal identity. They echoed Gretchen's concern, *"When I have my Harvard hat on, I'm fully fine. But is this me?"* First generation students repeatedly spoke of having to deconstruct the persons they thought they were before coming to college while also experiencing significant changes in their thoughts, values, and tastes due to their collegiate experiences. This happened in the classroom as much as it did on the weekends and in the residence halls. The Bourdieusian sense that first generation students identified—that they were shifting positions along a social field—was a common trope in the first generation interviews and rare to nonexistent among continuing generation participants. In addition, many first generation participants who identified this experience and disclosed that they tried to hide their first generation status from others also expressed significant loneliness back home, on campus, or both. When asked whether she felt a part of her campus community, first generation Veronica knitted several related themes together in her response:

> I was kind of bitter about it. I'd see my roommates calling home and talking about papers with their moms, having their moms read through a paper, and *I* would have to figure things out all on my own. I would get angry with my parents because they couldn't help. And just feeling so alone here. I think overall it motivated me more, helped me find things for myself, be more independent.
>
> I am really proud of my parents for the obstacles they faced, they still face. But there were little things, like seeing the workers on campus, I'd feel so guilty and feel like they were invisible to everyone else, and I saw them being so helpful. And feeling this privilege here that I'd never felt before. I could be like those workers.
>
> And there were issues of identity. I was perceived as white because people couldn't tell about my background because of my looks. And I would want to fit into the community, but I felt guilty all the time. I wasn't used to the privilege we have here, and it wasn't comfortable. You would think that it was, but it wasn't. I didn't want any attention. I didn't want any special treatment. I just wanted to fit in.

These themes that Veronica addressed cohere around a sense of identity inextricably linked with parental relationships, social class, work, racial categorization, and racial identity. They highlighted the gap between what Khan calls "ease" among those students raised in the context of privilege and the uncomfortable feelings of those experiencing such privilege for the first time.[7] They provide a stark reminder that "belonging" while in college does not simply mean "belonging" *to*, *in*, or *at* an institution. It is a sense of place and an order of things that shifts when the

7. Khan, *Privilege*; see also Jack, *Privileged Poor*.

imagined context is conjured. That context can foreground or submerge multiple loyalties, histories, and tethers: family, race, home, identity, aspiration, work, mind, image, performance, aesthetics, time, experience. While first and continuing generation students may categorize their sense of belonging at similar rates, first generation participants were far more likely to question their identity based on how they were received by peers and the larger campus ecosystem. Veronica and other first generation participants shared stories of ambivalence and conflicting loyalties that offer a reminder to campus leaders seeking to improve inclusion at their institutions: the lessons they receive, the changes in their lives they seek to assimilate and make meaning of, are often far more complex, tacit, potentially ubiquitous, and connected to identities and experiences beyond any official curriculum or explicit intentions of a university campaign.

6

The External Influences on
Alma Mater

SO FAR I have explored the varied and interrelated factors associated with the college-going experience that either fostered or hindered first generation students' achievement, feelings of inclusion, and sense of agency in defining their identities and determining their futures on and beyond an elite college campus. Now I consider factors outside of the college realm that affect how first generation students perceive and evaluate their collegiate experiences. Administrators might overlook these external factors, or at least not fully appreciate them, in their attempts to improve the overall college-going experience for their first generation students. While this is by no means an exhaustive list, the three factors I explore here—parents' interactions with the college, pre-college connections, and post-college plans—were the most commonly articulated as those first generation students said affected their college experience.

Parents' Interactions with Their Children's College

When speaking about the roles their parents and other family members played in their choices in college, there were several initial distinctions that indicated different parental roles between first and continuing generation students. As sophomores and again as seniors, first generation participants overwhelmingly described their parents as providing no specific academic advice or assistance, while closer to half of the continuing generation participants spoke of parents assisting with course selection, helping their children prepare or edit course assignments, advising on curricular pathways to maximize career opportunities, and, in one or two instances, even tutoring their children in a particular subject. While rare, a few continuing generation participants spoke of their parents' personal connections with specific faculty members. More common was the admission by legacy students that their parents helped them navigate academic choices based on their own experiences as undergraduates at the same institution.

The distinction in academic support behaviors between parents who attended college—in some instances, the same college—and those who did not should come as no surprise.[1] For parents who have no or little experience with college, there is not much they can do to provide specific academic guidance or firsthand advice; by contrast, parents with undergraduate and even advanced de-

---

1. Sociologists have long been concerned with how parents confer advantages to their offspring, including specific academic and social advice during the college years. One recent example is Hamilton's *Parenting to a Degree*. In this longitudinal qualitative analysis, Hamilton carefully disentangles four distinct parenting styles— which she dubs professional helicopters, pink helicopters, bystander parents, and paramedic parents—among upper-income, middle-income, and lower-income parents of female college students, as well as the postgraduate outcomes for daughters shepherded under different parenting styles. Earlier examples include Lareau's investigations of social class and parenting styles in *Unequal Childhoods* and *Home Advantage*, and Roksa and Potter's "Parenting and Academic Achievement." In addition, Lareau and Cox delineate the processes by which well-resourced parents "foresee and forestall problems" by "untying knots" to assist in their children's relations with institutions like colleges and universities. See Lareau and Cox, "Social Class and the Transition to Adulthood." Putnam's *Our Kids: The American Dream in Crisis* and Reeves's *Dream Hoarders: How the American Upper Middle Class Is Leaving Everyone Else in the Dust* examine the threat to democracy and the American social fabric when parents and communities hoard opportunities for their own offspring to the detriment of communities, school districts, and our country.

grees have experiential knowledge they believe translates into support that could smooth their children's transition to college. First and continuing generation students spoke of these differences extensively. First generation students often underscored that their parents stopped helping them with schoolwork long before college, while continuing generation students routinely took for granted the procedural and content-specific guidance their parents continued to provide.[2]

At first glance, the stark distinction between many first and continuing generation students' descriptions of parental academic support appears to uncover a crucial disadvantage for first generation students. However, many of these participants were quick to point out that the mentors they found on campus—especially when those mentors were tenure-line faculty members—served as more than adequate guides to support their academic growth. They indicated that because their parents could not help with their academic development, they were used to cultivating mentor relationships with teachers and other adults who showed an interest in their development. Moreover, continuing generation participants were divided in their views of parental academic support. Some found their parents' advice stifling or outmoded, and specifically asked university administrators to help keep their parents at arm's length, while others relied on their parents to the detriment of cultivating mentor relationships on campus. Indeed, stories of deep and abiding mentorships came from first generation

2. One taboo subject, however, entailed the extent to which parents hired college consultants for their children. While continuing generation students openly discussed the advantages conferred to them by parents and other family members, they never spoke of hiring private admissions coaches. During this study, I spoke with several admissions counselors and first-year deans who suspected, but had no way of confirming, that private tutors and consultants were hired at scandalously high rates among the wealthier matriculants. They complained of this unfair advantage, but, short of overhauling the admissions process, they had no specific ideas to curtail this legal but dubious practice.

participants far more often than from their continuing generation peers.

While parents of first generation students rarely offered specific academic advice to their children, they were not uninvolved in that aspect of their children's college experience. Most first generation participants pointed out that their parents loved hearing about what they were learning in their classes and often expressed a desire to learn more about their children's academic experiences. They were enthusiastic about meeting their professors, seeing inside the libraries and study spaces on campus, and knowing where and how their children accessed opportunities that could lead to remunerative careers. In short, they desired a more intimate knowledge of the campus and its academic resources. However, parents of first generation participants rarely came to campus in large part because the cost and time required to visit their children in college was prohibitive unless those parents lived within driving distance and could get away from other family and work obligations on a weekend.

By contrast, most parents of continuing generation participants visited their children in college. Some came to campus on a routine basis, while others visited only once or twice. Some continuing generation participants spoke of the burdens of cost and time associated with these trips, but most simply took it for granted that their parents would be able to afford the time and travel. Several continuing generation participants discussed extended parental visits, for instance, when a student needed surgery or was recovering from an injury or illness. Parents, usually mothers, would rent apartments near campus and spend their days tending to their recovering children. This was nearly unheard of among first generation parents, who were more likely to work seven days a week than to have access to paid leave time.

During this study, both Harvard and Georgetown sought to provide families of low-income students with the resources to attend at least one campus visit during college as well as funding to bring them to campus for graduation. Many of the first generation students in this sample qualified for these benefits. While the idea and effort were deeply appreciated among those first generation students who qualified, the execution of these programs could be improved. For instance, parents of first generation students often felt overwhelmed, overlooked, or excluded by the tacit and explicit messages at such events as homecoming or Junior Parents Weekend. For those who were from immigrant backgrounds, they may not have the English language facility to sit through and follow long presentations without the aid of translators or translated materials. Many campus events on those weekends were ticketed and charged additional fees that essentially excluded lower income families from participation. Booster groups sought to fundraise for a variety of campus initiatives during these family weekends, but fundraising activities at such symbolically marked times served to further alienate families who could not donate and whose children were the recipients of the university's largesse. While these weekends were intended to create a sense of community among families, students, and university officials, their focus on fundraising and ticketed access to special events served to rank, segregate, and even alienate those families attending on scholarship funds.

Homecoming events and Junior Parents Weekends were not only occasions where university representatives may have accidentally alienated parents of first generation college students. As sophomores, first generation participants pointed out several alienating acts committed by university officials or college boosters. In particular, students criticized the common practice at top-tier universities of allowing area alumni chapters to host yield events and welcome parties for recently admitted students and their parents at country clubs or the private residences of wealthy alums. With American public high schools experiencing the highest rates of segregation since *Brown v. Board of Education*, students who graduated from highly segregated high schools commonly had very little prior interaction with wealthy peers, their parents, and older alumni.[3] The setting, the dress code, the catered food, the conversational topics and "small talk" performances were new and excruciatingly uncomfortable. For some first generation participants, these "welcome" events only served to alienate them, or worse, to alienate their parents and potentially drive a class-based wedge between new students and their families. They spoke of managing their parents' hurt feelings at these parties, or dealing with the shame of their parents' discomfort, early departures, and whispered arrangements to await their newly privileged children in idling vehicles—*text me when it's over and I'll come pick you up*. A simple fix could make these welcome events far more inclusive. One could organize a party at a public park or a local museum grounds, or plan an outing such as a day at the beach, a hike, a game, or a picnic at a local park.

Yield and welcome events are intended to foster bonding among an imagined community of university affiliates across multiple generations. There is no reason why they should be associated so strongly with wealth and privilege. While it is currently true that many students at elite American colleges are from wealthy family backgrounds, it is neither a positive nor a necessary fact, but rather a contingent outcome of how Americans use merit and education as a class weapon rather than an end in itself.[4] Hosting events at country clubs or inside the homes of wealthy alumni only serves to reify one type of lifestyle above all others and to conflate it with an education promised in the letter of admission. There is no necessary correlation between a country club lifestyle and a Harvard or Georgetown degree, and as an initial

3. The scholarship on this subject is broad and deep. I would point the reader to one stellar example from UCLA's *Center for Education and Civil Rights* in its recent publication Orfield et al., "Harming Our Common Future: America's Segregated Schools Sixty-five Years After Brown."

4. Veblen was the first to identify education as a form of conspicuous leisure (a term he coined) and a tool to separate the upper classes from everyone else. See also Weis, Cipollone, and Jenkins, *Class Warfare: Class, Race, and College Admissions in Top-Tier Secondary Schools*.

welcome to a community, these alumni groups should be more mindful of the messages they send to the newly admitted students in their regions.

As seniors, first generation participants pointed to fundraising materials, development events at family weekends, and the excessive cost of graduation as sources of consternation and exclusion both they and their parents experienced. Francis pointed out the hypocrisy in conflating the explicit institutional values of truth seeking and civic virtues with crass fundraising rituals of "donate this, buy that, spend, spend, spend!" Continuing generation participants occasionally complained of their parents feeling bombarded by requests for donations, but first generation students connected these requests with their feeling of belonging, or lack thereof. As a senior, Gaby thought back to her first glimpse of the college where she would be for the next four years:

> My mom dropped me off for college. It was eighteen hours on Greyhound buses to get here. And she went to the orientation stuff and stopped and said, "I don't understand what they're saying." So she left the orientation and traveled around DC instead. And whenever we get mail sent home to parents, they wait until I get back and show me the letters. The school always calls asking for donations, and they don't understand we don't have money to donate. If you're going to have people calling, have people who can speak in that language, so parents feel included, because they don't understand. My parents, they felt not included.

One common trope among administrators at these universities was the notion that first generation students would experience a greater disconnect between their on-campus experiences and their families than continuing generation students, and would thereby avoid talking to their parents out of fears of misunderstanding, alienation, or causing concern. It was also often suggested that continuing generation students would seek and receive more advice than their first generation peers about choice of majors, preprofessional planning, and social interactions.

Sophomore and senior interviews generally supported these views regarding differences in the role of parents between first and continuing generation participants. First generation participants commonly responded that they received no specific advice from their parents in academic matters and that the social advice they received was either generic or unhelpful in their new context. Rosemary echoed many other first generation seniors' reflections:

> I think some of my experiences were the way they were because I was first gen. I felt like I had to blend in, and that I should be able to blend in. I had to be able to get through this experience on my own because other people weren't there to help me. My parents weren't there to help me. Non first gen students who struggle turn to their parents more, and I thought I had to do all of that on my own. And I didn't realize how much guidance people got from their parents and from other people. And had I realized that, I would have reached out more. I also think a lot of my experiences have to do with not being close to my family. I feel like I'm closer now, but not as close as other people are. I think that if I were closer to them, then these times when I needed help, I would have seen them as an outlet for that. And that would have made things better here on campus.

In contrast to Rosemary and others, most continuing generation participants spoke of receiving periodic to regular advice, though not always appreciated or followed.

Parents of first generation students were by no means absent in their children's college journey. Even though they may not be able to provide specific academic advice, they still tended to be involved in their children's academic development. Interviews revealed that most first generation participants spoke regularly, even daily or multiple times per day, about their college lives with their parents, often sharing concepts and facts they learned in their courses with their parents and using them as soundboards and sources of academic encouragement. Some parents of first generation students reveled in the learning opportunities their children described, while others expressed initial fear or confusion, but nonetheless desired to know. At the same time, first generation participants desired that their parents have more opportunities to become involved in their college lives and wanted the university to include their parents in the collegiate experience through outreach, newsletters, and increased formal and informal interactions unrelated to financing college or fundraising. They expressed a strong desire to bring their parents along for the educational journey. As a senior, Agnes pointed out that regular information from the institution, particularly if translated in a few key languages, would demonstrate to the parents of first generation students that they, too, are part of "the Hoya family." She advised this information not be appended by a request for donation but rather a simple offer of engagement, one made in earnest by communicating in the common languages spoken in first generation students' homes. Agnes was clear in her assertion that the university owed a certain recognition to these families as members of the larger university community. She emphasized, "These, too, are Hoya families, but in a different way. They may not have had their grandparents go to Georgetown, but they are having their first grandchild go to Georgetown, and they are special in *that* way. They are Hoyas in that way."

Agnes's point about these families also being special and offering a new kind of "legacy" for first generation families serves as a reminder that appropriate, sensitive, and honest family inclusion— without the strings of fundraising attached—demonstrates respect for the families who supported these students, who are now poised to do great things with their lives. First generation participants were just as likely as their continuing generation peers to express gratitude to their parents and to credit their parents with their personal and academic successes. Thus, they critiqued an implicit message that attending an elite university either created or revealed some fundamental difference between themselves and their non-college-going family members.[5]

Jackie made this point very clearly in her senior interview. Coming from a low-income background, a neighborhood with a high crime rate, and a public high school strained for resources, she was quick to underscore how involved her parents were in her life and successes. She pointed out that they were the ones who grounded her, cheered her on, and believed in her before anyone else did. If she worried about an exam grade or a major assignment, they were the ones who told her to "take a chill pill" while also encouraging her to access resources she needed to succeed. They delighted in hearing about the discussions she had in class, and the relationships she built with her professors. They cheered her on from a thousand miles away, never missing a moment.

Jackie thoroughly believed that her parents should participate in her academic achievements, and she enacted that belief on a daily basis by keeping them informed and involving them as much as possible in her college experience. While she emphasized, "I am without a doubt incredibly grateful for being here" and "it's a great place in terms of its name and what it can do for you," she was adamant that, "[the university] is also fortunate to have chosen the people it has. It wasn't Harvard that made me. It was my parents that made me. Harvard is not the hero. My parents are." Jackie's point serves to remind university officials that many parents of first generation students play a significant role in their academic trajectories, and that their children would like to see the university acknowledge their parents' influence. Narratives of personal uplift and transformation through educational achievement, made possible by the university and its abundant opportunities, even when offered with the best of intentions, often risk eliding those "hero" parents who have been instrumental in their children's success.

---

5. For more in-depth analysis of the negotiated sensemaking of similarities and differences between first generation students and their parents, see Rondini, "Healing the Hidden Injuries of Class?"

Jackie's comments also serve as a reminder that gratitude in the educational context can and should flow in two directions: while students are expected to be grateful for the opportunities afforded them, the institution itself is enriched by the students who elect to attend.

When asked what the university could do to support the parents of their students, continuing generation participants most commonly asked that the university either do nothing or help them to explain to their parents that the choices they make are their own—especially with regard to academic decisions and pre-professional planning. Some students, like Paul, whose father also attended his university and studied in a similar field, asked for help individuating from his father. "Sometimes I would trick myself into behaving like my dad or like I imagined what they expected rather than being myself. I had to decide how I want to behave and who I want to be. I had to stop comparing myself to my dad." Others, like J.B., joked that his parents might prefer "a padded room" for him rather than his own post-college plans. He wondered aloud whether the university could nudge parents to relinquish control over their children's professional choices. If continuing generation participants like Paul and J.B. wanted assistance from the university, it was to separate from their parents as they shaped their futures.

By contrast, first generation students wanted to bring their parents along with them into their futures, despite challenges in translating academic majors and scholarly concepts to parents with little to no familiarity with academia.[6] They advocated for parent newsletters, perhaps with translated sections in Spanish, Chinese, Arabic, and other languages commonly spoken in first generation

6. It is important to note the actual range of parental familiarity with college occluded by this statement. Some first generation participants explained that their parents were familiar with college, had themselves attended college without graduating, or were the children of college-goers. That is, a few first generation participants in this sample were the grandchildren of college graduates even though their parents did not complete college.

households. They also suggested paper and digital copies of parent guidebooks and occasional phone calls home to answer general, nonconfidential questions about important upcoming decisions their children may make (e.g., study abroad, summer internships, postgraduate fellowships). Specific newsletter topics, such as how students spend their time in college, why four or five courses per semester is considered a "full load," the importance of extracurricular involvement for career development, and how different courses and majors relate to various career paths would provide useful conversation starters for family discussion. Many first generation participants explained how their parents, some of whom had never heard of the university before their children were granted admission, were now avid followers and fans of their children's *alma mater*. While they expressed a range of actual parental involvement—some parents traveled regularly to visit their children, while others had not yet seen the college; some parents regularly read the newsy e-mails delivered about campus life, while others expressed no time for such frivolities—in general, they hoped the university would assure their parents that they were safe, that the choices they were making were salubrious and informed ones, and that their time away from home would prove "worth the effort."

For those first generation participants whose parents felt included by the college, that parental inclusion assisted their own social adjustment. Even low-cost symbolic efforts, when well-conceived, were appreciated. The newsletter with a first generation student story, the phone call home to a concerned parent in the family's native language: these inexpensive trust-building efforts paid off in family support and students' increased satisfaction, whereas socially insensitive activities, such as parties hosted at the local country club for newly admitted students or a parents' weekend that focused on fundraising or selling college paraphernalia, often set the stage for alienation of both parents and their children. Indeed, those first generation participants who rated their social experiences low also told of witnessing their parents' alienation during admitted students' parties, move-in day, parents' weekend, or other official university events that appeared not to have them or their children in mind. Parents' negative experiences with the college indicated to their children a lack of true care for them as students. While it is unclear whether the link between students' perceptions of their parents' treatment by the university and their own satisfaction with the college-going experience is causal or correlative, these findings serve as a reminder that universities should carefully consider the explicit and implied messaging associated with parental engagement as a part of their engagement with students. The two are entwined, as students benefit by knowing their parents are respected and appropriately included but suffer when their parents are overlooked or estranged.

Pre-college Connections

University officials and higher education experts tend to take it as a given that first generation students on their campuses have little prior knowledge of campus life.[7] While this generalization ultimately fit for some first generation participants, others spoke of having significant prior college connections that helped them recognize, interpret, and act on experiences early in their college career and allowed them to avoid initial setbacks so commonly described by their peers. While knowledge of campus life and practices such as attending office hours, knowing when and how to ask faculty for help, and accessing campus resources early and often, can help all students, regardless of the university they attend, it may be the case that more first generation students enrolled in highly selective colleges arrive equipped with these skills

7. For instance, in a 2018 interview with *Inside Higher Ed*, Shannon LaCount, a senior official at the educational research firm Campus Labs explained, "It's true that first-generation students may not know the structure of the language or follow the higher education culture because [they] haven't been exposed. . . . [They] may be naïve walking in, but it doesn't mean [they're] not capable." See Smith, "First-Generation College Students More Engaged Than Peers."

than those enrolled in other colleges and universities. As early high achievers, they may have been identified as gifted in their K–12 years and selected for opportunities such as summer enrichment camps at a nearby university, college preparatory programs, and in some instances, scholarships to well-resourced private high schools. By entering a pipeline of high achieving college-bound students, these first generation students self-identified as prospective candidates for competitive colleges while still in high school and were therefore afforded academic support, preparation, and crucial familiarization with the technical, social, and behavioral processes and expectations associated with competitive academic environments.

Those first generation students who participated in pipeline programs such as the federally funded TRIO programs, the nonprofit private school network Prep for Prep, the nonprofit foundation Leadership Enterprise for a Diverse America (LEDA), and the college admissions partnership Quest Bridge all reported greater familiarity and higher social satisfaction with their college experiences, compared to those who had no pre-college connections.[8] While participation in these programs did not automatically correlate with greater feelings of satisfaction toward their college experiences, students from these pre-college programs reported having mentors outside of the university they could turn to for both social and academic advice, as well as pre-college exposure to the college context to ease the transition. Veronica, for instance, explained that her participation in LEDA during high school provided her with a "great support system." After thinking

8. The Posse Program, founded in 1989 by Deborah Bial, is another example of a highly successful national pipeline program for low-income and underrepresented students aiming for elite college admissions. Its foundation operationalizes peer and near-peer support systems through a cohort model, sending approximately ten students to the same university, providing them with extensive training before matriculation, and mandating annual retreats for additional training, reflection, and peer bonding. Neither Harvard nor Georgetown were Posse partner schools at the time of this study.

about who she turns to for support in college, she concluded, "I still talk to people in [LEDA] when I have problems, or need assistance or guidance. I would say I go to them before I go to anybody here." Participants in these external programs were also quicker to ask for help on campus and to develop habits to "access the resources" designed to support student growth, including attendance at office hours, regular departmental tutorials and study sessions, and academic services such as the writing center or tutoring center.

Even more than participation in a college preparatory or pipeline program, first generation participants with siblings who had attended a similar type of college, or the same college, offered the strongest source of social and academic preparation. Such support was strongest among those with older siblings because the younger ones could model their habits on lessons from the older ones' prior experiences. For instance, when describing who he turned to when learning to navigate college, Barney explained, "My sister went here so I called her a lot. My [peer mentor] was really good but I would call my sister over my [peer mentor]." Once the younger sibling began college, both siblings benefited from their ability to commiserate with one another and share tips. As Aaron put it, "I am advising my freshman brother now. I keep telling him to be careful about course selection and to listen especially to his older peers. They have been through it and are probably more believable than others." Approximately fifteen percent of the first generation participants in this sample had older siblings who attended the same or a similarly selective university and who offered specific advice and support about the process of transitioning to college. All of these participants reported high social and academic satisfaction. They were also more likely than other first generation students to express that they experienced no challenges while in college. Again, Barney provides a fitting example. In his sophomore year, he enthusiastically reported, "I love Harvard," and enumerated all of the opportunities he embraced, from joining competitive extracurriculars to traveling abroad the summer after freshman year. He also knew that his sibling connection facilitated his sense of comfort with the campus: "Because of my sister, I had visited here before, and I felt at home from day one."[9]

Similar to having a sibling at the same or a comparable university, those with other relatives or older friends from home attending the same university benefited from advice and social support during the college transition. Near-peers from the same high school served as informal mentors, especially for those traveling long distances. Such connections were not as durable as sibling support, but they provided temporary assistance, particularly at the start of college. Jina, an Asian American pre-med student from a suburban public school in Texas, explained that a near-peer from her high school helped her with some of her worst challenges:

> I have a friend from back home who is also at the school. She is a senior this year, and I think she could relate very well to how difficult it is to transition. She gave me a list of courses that she really enjoyed and found helpful, and we're on the same track, pre-med. We were in the same orchestra in high school. The whole school was very excited when she got in, . . . and when I got in, the first person I contacted was her. . . . She offered me a position in a service organization, and I jumped at the offer. I think it was very, very helpful to have someone from my high school who was also on the struggle boat, and it was very comforting to know that someone else had gone through the struggles I had gone through as a freshman.

These pre-college connections, either through older siblings or by participation in college preparatory or pipeline programs, serve

9. In contrast to having older siblings at the same or similar college, those with younger siblings still at home, those with older siblings who did not attend or finish college, and those who were the first or only student from their high school to attend a highly selective college out of state were more likely to describe challenging and often isolating transitions to college.

as crucial reminders of the variety of ways that first generation students may gain experience, acquire habits, and learn skills associated with successful transitions to elite universities. These transitions, in turn, affect how first generation students perceive their overall college-going experience. Shared academic expectations and similar demographics between a first generation student's high school and college can provide a third powerful precollege connection. In his powerful account of low-income and mostly first generation students at an elite college, sociologist Anthony Jack describes the significant advantages that students attending elite private high schools on scholarship have over their public school peers.[10] Jack's overarching claim is that diverse paths to an elite college shape divergent experiences upon arrival, and that not all "poor" students have the same attitudes, tastes, needs, or desires even when they come from similar family contexts, economic circumstances, and early life histories.[11] He indicates that low-income students with elite private high school experiences, what he calls the "privileged poor," have already benefited from the opportunities and faced the challenges of transitioning to an elite educational setting while young and relatively pliant.[12] By contrast, the "doubly disadvantaged," those who come from underresourced public high schools, encounter such

10. Jack, *Privileged Poor*.

11. This argument could be extended. Even those who come from the same family have different perspectives, attitudes, needs, and desires. Pediatric psychiatrist W. Thomas Boyce has conducted decades of research unraveling the differences among children from similar contexts who respond differently to adversity. See Boyce, *The Orchid and the Dandelion: Why Some Children Struggle and How All Can Thrive*.

12. Khan made a similar claim when describing black scholarship students at St. Paul's School: "Black students from St. Paul's do exceptionally well in the college admissions process. They tend to come from a background of disadvantage and in graduating from St. Paul's have learned to negotiate higher institutions of privilege. Disadvantaged students from boarding schools allow colleges to tell a story they like to tell: they are educating not just the elite but also the truly disadvantaged. Yet unlike most students from disadvantaged backgrounds who are likely to struggle in a rich, elite college environment, students from boarding schools have already shown

privilege, including its tacit sorting and judging of those less privileged, for the first time in college.

The advantage that the "privileged poor" have is recognition. That recognition works in two directions. First, they recognize their surroundings and the behavioral expectations associated with that context. They are not bewildered by the newness of an elite college, with its marble halls and cavernous libraries and dining facilities, and therefore are able to ignore the slights, avoid the shocks, and embrace the opportunities faster than their "doubly disadvantaged" peers. Second, they are recognized as insiders by their wealthier peers for knowing how to engage in "small talk," organize their time, and participate in or at least not flinch at the potlatch-style conspicuous consumption of designer labels and expensive meals out. Their ability to fit in and follow the tacit codes allows them to avoid the appearance of calling into question the naturalness or inevitability of the link between America's economic and the academic elites. Jack's doubly disadvantaged, by contrast, suffer the slights and ignorant assumptions of their wealthier peers while also standing out and struggling to adapt to new academic and social norms associated with success at an elite college.

This study confirms and extends Jack's primary argument that universities should not automatically assume students from similar economic or ethnic backgrounds will have similar needs or encounter similar challenges. The pre-college experiences and unique personal traits and motivations of each student coalesce to foster different attitudes, habits, and interpretations of similar experiences. The "privileged poor" and "doubly disadvantaged" appear to hail from two extremes in America's high school landscape: the elite boarding school with its arcane traditions, Socratic pedagogical style, and hefty endowments versus the impoverished, overcrowded, and teach-to-the-test obsessed public high school.

---

that they know how to make it through this kind of educational culture." Khan, *Privilege*, 189.

In this sample, most students described high school experiences somewhere in between those extremes. Not all who attended private schools considered themselves "privileged," in part due to the considerable variation in resources and resource allocation among private schools across the country. Likewise, first generation students who were happy with their public high school experiences commonly expressed an easy transition to college. On the topic of which factors external to the college context affect how first generation students perceive their college experiences, those who felt challenged and prepared by their high school, regardless of its ranking or name recognition, appeared more apt to transition well.

Stone, who was from a rural corner of Connecticut and whose small public high school was not especially well known or highly regarded, provided an example of what I mean here. Sitting in a sunlit café one spring afternoon with a pile of books stacked neatly beside her chair, she told me, "I think my high school did a really good job. My small town has a lot of doctors and engineers, and they poured money into my STEM classes in high school. I feel like I was really prepared in that." She jumped right in to college research, developed relationships with faculty mentors, and built a community on campus. She rated her college experiences as a 9 or 10 out of 10 and foresaw a bright career with medical school in her near future.

Other students from different areas of the country shared similar stories. Ironman, whose southern public high school did not typically send students out of state, nonetheless felt as though he was well prepared for an elite college experience: "At my high school, they were very good at letting students pursue whatever they want to, and I was able to take a lot of courses." Jason, whose parents were divorced and whose mother made significant sacrifices to secure her children's place at a top-rated public high school in a tony zip code, explained, "My high school prepared me incredibly well for college. Because I grew up in the right area, I had extraordinary resources available." Like Stone, Ironman and Jason rated their social and academic experiences in college very high, a

9 or 10 out of 10. These students' reflections on the value of a high quality, even if not necessarily elite, high school experience add to the growing body of research linking high school experience with college satisfaction. Students' appraisal of fit, belonging, and achievement have roots that far predate college, even when the fruits are borne out after matriculation.

While attendance at an elite private high school has long been understood as a path to a successful transition into an elite college,[13] other pre-college experiences, such as summer academic enrichment camps, pipeline programs, college preparatory programs, siblings with similar college experiences, and, I would argue, attendance at a public high school with decent resources in the student's area of study, also serve as emollients to the college transition and precursors to feelings of satisfaction with the college experience. If admissions deans were seeking predictors of successful transition, or were inclined to consider admissions preferences to recruit and retain high performing first generation students, these experiences may be useful factors to consider. On an individual level, first generation students with these types of pre-college connections may experience greater social satisfaction because they see people like them thriving in college and grow to believe success is possible for them as well. Near-peers in their siblings, high school classmates, and national networks formed through programs like LEDA and Quest Bridge serve to form informal cohorts of students from similar backgrounds supporting one another academically and socially. As these networks expand, students who partake in them will serve as mentors, role models, and eventual donors to broaden the pipeline for future cohorts.

---

13. Historian Jerome Karabel has documented the history of elite colleges admitting students from low-income minority backgrounds and then sending them to elite boarding schools to extend their education before college matriculation. See Karabel, *Chosen* and "How Affirmative Action Took Hold."

Post-college Plans

A third factor associated with first generation students' academic and social satisfaction in college related to whether they knew what they would be doing after graduation at the time of our senior interview. It may seem an obvious point that students express greater satisfaction with their college experiences when they are not anxious about what comes next, but this factor is not always taken into consideration in interview-based studies of student life. The university does not exert control over post-college outcomes, although it strives to support the best possible results for each of its graduates. First generation students, perhaps more than their continuing generation peers, may judge the quality and worthiness of their education by their immediate postgraduate plans. Their judgment of college experiences, from social life in the residence halls to class discussions with peers, are commonly framed by whether they allow themselves to take the following leap of faith: that an elite education leads to a remunerative and rewarding career.

First generation participants, often because they witnessed the struggles of parents and other family members, were more likely to critique their peers' assumptions that hard work confers professional rewards. Moreover, they did not always believe the promise that education has a direct influence on life outcomes. Senior year was a time for whistling in the dark, or as Fay so crisply put it, "Let's hope this experience was worth it. Just because we're here, that doesn't necessarily change anything after college for us. You're always between two different worlds." Students with this perspective often pointed out that their career choices were shaped by family exigencies and personal desires. As Fay explained:

> We feel like we need to get a job to make enough money to help our parents, but we also want to be happy. I feel like it's not addressed that much, how we can't always do everything we want, and sometimes the decisions we make have to do with personal connections back home rather than personal motivation . . .

> There is this tension between "follow your passions" and take a job, any job, because it's more than your parents would make. . . . I hope I can make the most out of my education. I don't want to do something you don't need a college education to do.

The pressure to support one's family was a common theme for first generation students and unheard of among their continuing generation peers, who instead spoke of the relentless pressure to live up to their parents' expectations. First generation participants wanted to lift up their families, but were sometimes frustrated that their parents could not help them define or access the means to do so. Eliza explained:

> I feel the pressure of taking care of my parents and giving them something to fall back on. Graduating in May for me won't be, "I did the college thing." I think, "Where does this go? How do I thank my family?" I have to take this privilege that I have and put it to use.
>
> Also, all the consulting talk makes [me] anxious. They're recruiting now, and I'm still not sure what I want to do. I've been here for four years. What does it all mean? What am I going to do? And my parents don't have the skills to guide me.

While the pressure to support their families was real, those who saw a clear pathway to do so generally rated their college experiences higher than those who did not yet have a clear plan. Senior first generation participants who had post-college plans were more likely to reflect back positively on their entire experience in college and to give high ratings for their academic and social experiences in college. Those with jobs in hand during senior interviews expressed vindication for their hard work and sacrifices throughout college. Jackie, whose job in finance was secured early in the fall of her senior year, practically gushed when she described the pieces of her life coming together and the good fortune she felt:

> I know how privileged I am. As a first generation student coming from an impoverished background with immigrant parents,

I have a six figure salary lined up for right after graduation! Doors are continuing to open for me, which is not true for so many people. I've been fortunate enough.

Likewise, Ironman, who in the early fall of senior year told me that he was "very happy with everything" and felt like he was "leaving college a better person," beamed when asked about his greatest academic accomplishment. Hands down, it was "doing well enough to be in a place where I have a job already. I'm most proud of that."

Of course, there are multiple possible reasons for a strong correlation between having a job lined up and feeling contented with one's overall college experiences. Students who rated their social experiences highly were also likely to be more integrated into the university and therefore better able to take advantage of preprofessional opportunities the university offers. They were also more apt to cultivate a wide network of friends who could assist with their post-college planning. However, the halo effect[14] must also be considered: having a job offer or a plan for post-graduation during senior year may alleviate personal anxiety and incline participants to rate their overall college experiences high.

However, a job in hand does not resolve the pressure first generation students feel to support their families. A first job out of college is not always the dream job, but it could still be a pathway to success and securing a stable future. Ironman explained that he would one day like to work in a nonprofit organization that supports young adults with autism. As someone with family experience with autism, he has witnessed the challenges that young adults with neurodevelopmental disorders face, and he has the drive and vision to do something to improve their lives. For now, he will go to work on Wall Street so that he can build the financial

---

14. This form of cognitive bias, where a positive response to a single aspect of a person, place, or thing engenders a positive overall assessment, was first described by psychologist Edward Thorndike, "A Constant Error in Psychological Ratings" (1920).

resources he needs to realize his goals. When asked whether his parents assisted in his job search, he shook his head: "My parents have no idea what I do, how many interviews I did, how many people I networked with in order to get this job. They don't know what stress means here." Later in the interview, he sighed and looked pensive as he sought to explain his complex emotions about the future:

> Sometimes I feel overwhelmed by what I've gotten myself into with investment banking. I also feel overwhelmed by the pressure to support my family when they're older. They don't have savings. I knew I wanted to do investment banking because of the money, but I had no idea what it was going in. I don't have parents who are CFOs or CEOs. I was totally lucky to land this job.
>
> But one thing, I never stopped to think what *I* was interested in. I don't know how you preface people with that. Some people come in with life experiences and things they knew that I wasn't exposed to growing up. I have a different point of view because my experiences come from [my major] and internships.

Given Ironman's goals of a stable financial future for himself and his family, his academic choices and postgraduate plans make sense, and his university helped him get there. The question remains whether the university also could have helped him explore ways to carve out time and consider, as he put it, what *he* was interested in. Is there a role for the university as a source of lifelong learning and career exploration in the lives of alumni like Ironman?

Regardless of whether having a job in hand is the cause or outcome of feeling satisfied with one's college experiences, the link between post-college plans and deeming one's college experiences satisfactory is undeniable. Those first generation participants who did not know what they would be doing after graduation, approximately twenty-five percent of the sample, may have benefited from earlier and ongoing postgraduate planning. The benefits that accrue from career counseling integrated into the academic departments may not only help academically but also socially. For graduates who make early career decisions to ensure financial stability but pivot later in their careers, it would also make sense that the university involve itself in some way with their ongoing career goals.

External Factors: Those that Help, Those that Hinder

Parents, pre-college connections, and post-college plans affect how first generation students perceive and evaluate their college experiences. How they are described may lead one to consider these factors as discrete and isolable. However, a more accurate depiction would be that there are of a welter of factors, some that help and others that hinder first generation students' satisfaction and sense of fit or belonging.

For instance, Stone, who described her high school experiences as facilitating a smooth transition to college, also discussed her fears over not knowing for certain whether she would achieve her goals postgraduation. She talked about the expense of preparing to apply to medical schools and the fear of rejection despite high grades and extensive laboratory experience. She wished she had an outlet "to talk about the pressure and anxiety surrounding going to an elite school as a first generation student." She felt the tension of living up to disparate expectations at home and school, and, given that our interview took place on the cusp of graduation, her thoughts veered toward the gap between the career she wanted and the lives of women she knew in her hometown:

> Going to college and leaving people behind: that was really hard my freshman year and sophomore year. Working at the horse barn, those girls are in community college. You feel bad that your parents didn't get to go to college. I remember talking to people at GSP about it, and I didn't know how to talk. . . .

When you don't want to lose that connection to where you come from. It took a while to reconcile, "No, I'm still me, I come from that community."

I know friends from here, when they go home they don't want to say that they go to Georgetown because they worry that people will judge them. I don't know women that have careers where I come from. They have jobs or stay at home, but not careers. That made it hard to figure out *what do I want to do*, because you don't have anything to base it off of. There are no role models at home for this kind of life.

And maintaining that integrity and wholeness in my life: it's challenging, but it is important to me. And reminding myself, it's the differences in our lives that make us interesting. We're not all cookie cutter. We don't have the same experiences. We don't come from the same backgrounds, and that's a good thing.

Privilege and disadvantage exist along a continuum, while the perception of one's place along this continuum changes based on context. Perhaps even more accurate, first generation students who have made it into highly selective colleges express a mixture of privilege and obstacles that may not neatly fit into the labels we create for them. Many of these are related to high school experiences, with those who felt strongly about the quality of their high schools—regardless of whether they were public or private, elite or average—more likely to describe a quicker and smoother transition to an elite college setting. Others are related to how they saw the institution interacting with their parents and whether they feel their families are respected and included in the college conversation. Still others are related to pre-college connections and postgraduate plans. To be reminded and to remind others that "we don't come from the same backgrounds, and that's a good thing," is a simple yet powerful and often challenging mantra to live by at an elite college, where competition, evaluation, and judgment are commonly held as virtues. It is nonetheless worth remembering.

Francis reminded me that. We had spent an afternoon together, first at a secluded café table in a quiet outdoor terrace (we chose this spot for its privacy, as I later guessed that he knew he might cry) and later meandering through the trimmed and blooming spring campus in the final weeks before graduation. After sharing his painful early experiences, the sacrifices he and his family made to get him there, all of the slights and misunderstandings he felt at critical junctures, and all of his fears for postgraduation, Francis, tears wetting his cheeks, concluded:

> As hard as it's been, I love Georgetown. . . . I don't regret coming here. I get chills thinking of the opportunity and privilege of attending this school. When I worked off campus, I always anonymously sent $17.89 of my paycheck to the 1789 Scholars Fund. And when I make it big, this will be one of the places I support financially in a big way.

Francis, with his teary, wan smile, expressed the frustration and internal conflict over the tangle of privilege and disadvantage, obstacles and opportunities, that many first generation students navigated through college. Giving back and paying it forward, they underscore that the academic process is often one of give and take, of gift and regift, and of the impossible but absolutely necessary work that universities must daily do to try to live up to their mission and the aspirations they have for every matriculating student.

7

Advice to Campus Leaders from First Generation Students

ONE OF THE MAIN goals of the *First Generation Student Success Project*, the four-year study upon which this book is based, was to seek advice from first and continuing generation students on a host of issues that shaped their academic and social lives while attending a highly selective, historically elite, and often tradition-bound college. The colleges studied here implemented some of the suggestions participants provided during the years of the study or soon after its conclusion, and have incorporated other advice into longer term strategies to improve access, equitable opportunities, and inclusion within their academic and social spaces. In this concluding chapter, I synthesize participants' suggestions to administrators seeking to improve inclusion and belonging. Some of these are no- or low-cost changes to current programs and practices, while others are potentially more cost-intensive and will require careful and deliberative consideration of university priorities.

While these suggestions emerge from the particular context of two universities at a specific moment in time, 2012–16, they are offered here in the spirit of building conversations with any campus seeking to foster greater inclusion among its first generation students. Questions such as "*Does this make sense given the makeup of students on my campus?*" will help campus leaders discern which of the following suggestions might be useful to consider at their own institution. Of course, attempting to adopt a policy or practice borrowed from another institutional context without a clear understanding of how this will integrate into a university's mission, context, and history could backfire or result in an unanticipated or undesirable change in the campus culture. Taking the time to ask students themselves what they want and need from their university, just as this study did with Harvard and Georgetown, is an important early and iterative step that should coincide with honest consideration of university priorities, goals, and the interests of university leadership, faculty, staff, alumni, parents, and the surrounding community.

In the following pages, I organize the advice from the student participants of this study into three broad categories, each of which is subdivided into smaller units: *guidance for improved transitions*, which includes ways to frame college, support for improved geographic and demographic transitions, and the pros and cons of academic preorientation programs; *recommendations to enhance academic experiences*, which includes early intervention, ongoing proacademic cocurricular programming, opportunities to explore earlier and select a major later, participation in high impact practices, fixing the pipeline, and affirming the importance of academic mentorship; and *recommendations to enhance social experiences*, which includes choice and leadership opportunities in extracurriculars, reduced financial barriers to social inclusion, inclusion of parents of first generation students, and nuanced and ongoing discussions regarding social diversity and inclusion on campus.

Guidance from Students for Improved Transitions

First and continuing generation participants from Harvard and Georgetown offered advice for improved college transitions ranging from reducing the number of graded courses in the first semester to instituting faculty-led programs that would include formal meals and excursions to theatrical and musical performances to introduce incoming students to the social norms and habits associated with aesthetic appreciation in elite contexts. Here, I highlight three types of advice from first generation students concerning how to best support the transition to college: framing college with an inclusive and honest discourse about what to expect and how to seek help, supporting geographic and demographic transitions through modeling and signage, and considering academic preorientation programming for students from underresourced high schools.

Framing College

Many first generation participants who arrived feeling less prepared for college also described a double bewilderment of not knowing what to expect from the college transition while also feeling misrecognized or misunderstood based on their pre-college life and educational experiences. Attending a university like Harvard or Georgetown was generally not part of their overall life plan. In fact, many explained that they applied to elite schools on a whim, never expecting to be accepted. When the letter of admission arrived, they were surprised, confused, but also compelled by the promise of a transformational experience not only for themselves but for their families and communities. More than the letter of admission, most first generation students who were also from low-income households described not being able to say no to the generous financial aid offer. It would have been more expensive for their families if they attended their public flagship than it was for them to commit to four years at Harvard or Georgetown. Considered a whim at the point of application, attending an elite college later became a giddying, elating, and sometimes terrifying opportunity they felt they could not turn down.

The opportunity to frame their expectations for college before they matriculate, and the time to speak with different representatives from the university about the purpose of college, could help first generation students feel more at ease with the college transition. Visitation weekend could be a prime opportunity to make such options available through increased recruitment and financial aid that would allow first generation and low-income students to participate in a pre-college visit. Likewise, multiple visitation weekends could be offered rather than a single one. Providing several dates for a pre-college visit would reduce the stress associated with altering work schedules and other commitments to accommodate a single weekend.[15] Explicit workshops run by local alumni chapters and interactive online videos covering what students might expect, as well as what the university expects from them, could help all students to ideate on their preferred approach to the college experience.

Likewise, many universities host themed preorientation programs designed to foster community and a shared sense of purpose before students begin their first year. Outdoor adventure trips, international student programs, and volunteer and community outreach projects have all been successfully deployed to enhance first-year integration and comfort with the transition to college. These preorientation programs are short in length—usually no more than a few days to a week—and not expressly aca-

15. Castleman and Page's research on "summer melt," or the tendency for low-income and first generation students to apply for and select a college while still enrolled in high school but fail to matriculate anywhere once the summer between high school and college ends, offers suggestions for supporting these students' follow-through on meeting important deadlines along the way to college enrollment. In one experiment, near-peer mentors, recruited as paid representatives of a university or nonprofit organization, were tasked with calling and periodically checking in with potential students to underscore the importance of attending particular events or meeting university deadlines for financial aid or course enrollment. Those students who were paired with peer mentors enrolled at higher rates than those who simply received text message reminders or periodic mailings. Likewise, peer mentors reported gains in their own commitment to the university through the process of helping a neophyte navigate territory once foreign to themselves. See Castleman and Page, *Summer Melt: Supporting Low-Income Students through the Transition to College.*

demic in focus. Universities like Harvard and Georgetown have sponsored preorientation programs such as these for close to forty years, while some form of outdoor or service-focused bonding experience has been a feature of orientation programming dating back to the nineteenth century.[16] In recent years, such pre-orientation programs have not been considered an opportune venue to introduce themes related to first generation student adjustment, but they could be a perfect time to introduce first generation students to one another, to their continuing generation peers, and to encourage honest and empathetic interactions among students from different economic, social, cultural, ethnic, and racial backgrounds. Considering the potential benefits of pre-orientation programming, Leila reflected: "It's important for first generation student[s] to not think that they are less qualified or that they don't have something to offer. . . . I think Harvard is a much better place when you are confident, and if there were a pre-orientation program where you could work on building that sense of self, that would be useful." Such programs could incorporate formal and informal exercises to help first generation students—and all students, really—prepare for and frame their expectations of college.

First generation participants in this sample participated in their university's preorientation programs at lower rates than their continuing generation peers, so recruitment and robust financial aid would be required to effectively marshal these activities in the service of first generation inclusion and integration.[17]

16. See Finnegan and Alleman, "The YMCA and the Origins of American Freshman Orientation Programs."

17. During the four years of this study, 2012–16, undergraduate student groups and alumni who identified as first generation advocated for a centralized first generation focused preorientation program at Harvard. At first it seemed as though the administration resisted this centralized model of support, instead seeking ways to advertise and provide financial aid for first generation and low-income students to participate in preorientation programs that served all students. After years of debate and critique from the student newspaper, student groups, and first generation

If attendance at preorientation programs is not feasible for all first generation students, then express programming during orientation should be. Framing exercises during college orientation workshops that allow incoming first generation students to hear stories from and ask questions of successful students from similar backgrounds, as well as hearing advice framed in the context of a personal narrative of trial and error delivered by a diverse representation of students, can aid the process of self-empowerment by helping students feel more comfortable about asking for help.[18]

---

alumni, Harvard College launched a new preorientation program in summer 2018, First-Year Retreat and Experience (FYRE), designed specifically to support first generation, low-income, and students from high schools not traditionally represented in the Ivy League. The program would be open to all students but with the message that students from the certain demographics were particularly encouraged to attend. It would be free of charge and compatible with Fall Clean-Up (also known as "Dorm Crew"), an opportunity to earn money on campus before the start of the semester. However, if students selected FYRE, they would not be able to participate in the other preorientation programs, such as those that sent groups of freshmen on outdoor camping trips, exposed students to urban issues around Boston, or welcomed international students. FYRE promised to introduce incoming students to stellar faculty, offer tips on maximizing their advising resources, provide them with practice engaging in the rituals of office hours and networking with faculty and administrative leadership, and introduce them to Harvard and the surrounding region through excursions and activities on and off campus. A similar program at Georgetown, Preparing to Excel (PEP), was established before the launch of this study and was routinely described by Georgetown first generation study participants who participated in PEP as a highly beneficial introduction to the campus and its resources, to Georgetown's academic expectations, and to the surrounding Washington, DC, area. At Georgetown, however, many PEP participants also recognized that the program tacitly encouraged them to self-select friends from similar demographics, and many first generation participants who chose against participating in PEP spoke of the downsides of programs that siloed one demographic from the rest of campus.

18. Experimental research testing the effectiveness of near-peer narratives of success, offered to freshmen in workshop settings during college orientation, has shown a positive effect on first-year academic outcomes. These low-cost activities may foster belonging and establish role modeling throughout the first year and beyond. See Stephens, Brannon et al., "Feeling at Home in College" and Stephens, Hamedani et al., "Closing the Social-Class Achievement Gap."

Assigned readings and focus groups during orientations are often powerful opportunities to frame college. Of course, merely talking about issues related to students' diverse pre-college backgrounds does not solve structural problems or promise to alter peers' insensitive or ignorant behavior. However, talking, and particularly the iterative power of framing and reframing one's personal experiences in a way that honors one's values and goals for college, can have a powerful effect on one's confidence, sense of belonging, and willingness to seek help when difficulties inevitably arise. Such a format would give students the floor and thus encourage them to discuss issues of diversity among their peers in a structured, informed, and empathetic way.

In addition to the suggestions on college-framing for incoming students, first generation participants suggested opportunities to encourage high school students to consider what life might be like at a highly selective college. Building a first generation alumni base of support throughout the country could help current high school students from first generation backgrounds prepare for matriculation at an elite university. Peer mentor partnerships, high school visits, and public social gatherings that include families and friends may help high-performing first generation students to conceive of universities like Harvard or Georgetown as within their reach. These do not have to be sponsored by a specific university. Rather, a network of first generation alumni who attended highly selective universities could reach out to high schools within their geographic region to offer workshops, social events, and informational meetings that cover standardized test preparation, high school course selection, financial aid form deadlines and guidance, and application support. A focus on the opportunities and challenges of earning a college degree from a highly selective institution, as well as troubleshooting tips and an emphasis on the strengths that individual students and their experiences can bring to bear in the classroom and around campus, can help normalize the process of applying to and taking seriously the possibility of an elite college education for first generation students and their families nationwide.

Support for Improved Geographic and Demographic Transitions

First generation participants commonly underscored the geographic and demographic differences between Harvard or Georgetown and their home communities. The weather, the physical landscapes, architecture styles, and the racial, ethnic, cultural, and economic makeup of the community were all features frequently raised as challenges first generation students had to overcome, and not so much for their continuing generation peers. Georgetown's Healy Hall or Harvard's first-year dining facility, Annenberg Hall, fondly nicknamed "Hogwarts," were described as initially arresting, overwhelming, and representative of an intimidating gulf between those who take wealth and privilege for granted and those for whom college is their first encounter with such physical manifestations of privilege. Manicured quadrangles, specimen trees, or, as S. put it, "all that brick" signaled a lifestyle and aesthetic that sharply contrasted with their public high schools and home neighborhoods. It often surprised many first generation participants that so much money would be funneled into the beautification, furnishing, and maintenance of an educational institution.

Watching their peers move through the campus in the first days and weeks, first generation participants described looking for students like themselves inhabiting these spaces. They also observed students who appeared at ease in the dining halls, classroom, and library spaces, picking up tacit rules and either altering their behavior, critiquing unspoken norms, or both.

Some first generation students had prior experience on an elite college campus, either through high school summer programs or extended preorientation programs. These students described feeling at home with, or at least not arrested by, the physical transition to college. Likewise, the physical transition was smoother for first generation students who attended elite private high schools or well-resourced public high schools, who grew up near the campus, or who had older siblings attending the same college. First generation students with these experiences can offer informal assistance to those who arrive on campus less familiar with an elite residential campus setting. A corps of first generation guides, paid through work study or incentivized in another way, could be added to current program efforts designed to introduce new students to campus. They could be partnered specifically with new first generation students, but they could also be recruited as part of a diverse team of campus tour guides, peer mentors, and support staff who provide assistance to all first-year students. The value in recruiting first generation students to serve as campus guides to all incoming students rather than targeting their services exclusively to other first generation students is the normalization of the first generation narrative for all incoming students and a raised expectation of the legitimacy of diverse experiences and trajectories on an elite campus.

In addition, improving descriptive signage on campus; the creation of interactive, user-friendly campus guides and smartphone apps; the diversification of campus tour guide staff; and changes in the content of campus tours to incorporate diverse perspectives and backgrounds, are all efforts that can be made to improve the legibility, inclusivity, and responsiveness of a campus to all its members and guests. Findings from recent and ongoing historical and archival projects led by faculty and students to unearth their university's complex legacies related to slavery, institutional racism, and exclusion, but also unearthing untold stories of diverse founders, faculty, and students, may be incorporated into a broader narrative delivered at orientation sessions and convocation speeches. Likewise, when appropriate and if accurate, stories of students who were first in their family to attend college may be woven into an historic narrative of student experiences on such campuses. These would not serve as mere palliatives or public relations tools but as prescriptions to critically examine college-going experiences at these institutions—from the inspiring to the shameful—in order to redefine the parameters of belonging on our nation's most selective campuses.

Academic Preorientation Programs

This study has demonstrated a higher percentage of first generation students arrive feeling less prepared for college than their continuing generation peers. The way students talk about preparation, however, indicates that first generation status does not appear to be as much a categorical reason for perceived lack of preparation but rather an issue of intensity. First generation students who feel less prepared for college are more likely to worry about belonging, achievement, and lack of academic fit, but they associate these concerns more with their high school experiences than with the condition of being first generation. While they tout their parents and teachers as "heroes," they identify straitened school systems, lack of advanced coursework opportunities, and poorly motivated peers as potential hurdles in their successful transition to a demanding academic setting.

First generation students are more likely than continuing generation students to have these kinds of high school experiences coming into an elite college. However, recruiting for an academic support program that is labeled a first generation program may confuse or alienate those first generation students who feel well prepared for college, as well as those continuing generation students who lacked a rigorous high school experience.

Targeted academic programming in advance of the first term may afford students who worry about the academic transition an opportunity to practice the skills, habits, and academic frame of mind that can ease the transition to a rigorous classroom experience. At Georgetown at the time of this study, there were both short preorientations designed to provide students with a crash course in academic habits useful for college (time management, speed reading, library research, etc.) and a longer five-week program dedicated to supporting low-income students from underresourced high schools who might need additional tools and social networks to thrive in college. Both of these programs were highly regarded by Georgetown's first generation participants, and approximately half of Harvard participants requested similar programs. Georgetown's five week program, the Community Scholars Program (CSP), has delivered workshops and orientation programming alongside classes for academic credit for more than fifty years, and has an impressive record of producing excellent graduates while also helping the university achieve its social justice goals.[19] Students in the CSP program who also participated in this study spoke highly of their experiences with CSP and with the opportunities to bond with one another and their faculty before the fall freshman term. However, not all first generation students who expressed academic concerns chose to attend CSP. Some worried about the potential for self-segregation, while others could not afford to take five weeks from work before college. Still others preferred to spend their final summer at home with family and friends, knowing they would not be able to return for Thanksgiving, and in some cases, even Winter Break. Financial concerns loomed large, with fears of being stereotyped or shamed as "less prepared" taking a close second.

In addition, first generation students who arrived well prepared for college asked whether funds might be identified to provide them access to summer internships, laboratory experiences, or independent research opportunities that they could not otherwise afford. Their requests serve as a rejoinder to the vision of academic preorientation programming as exclusively restorative or remedial. Georgetown did offer a pre-college summer program for advanced students as well, and the first generation students who participated in it spoke highly of its organization and their improved confidence and research skills upon entering college. Is there a way to meaningfully, sensitively, and productively mingle the cohorts of those preorientation programs designed for the high achievers as well as those who need additional academic support before they

19. See https://cmea.georgetown.edu/community-scholars#

start freshman year? I have no definitive solution, but if underscoring the diversity of a highly selective campus—including students' varied talents and life experiences—is a priority, then I believe structuring activities for students at different preorientation programs to mingle on campus is a goal worth considering.

Harvard does not currently offer an extended academic preorientation program before the fall term. When asked whether they would have considered such a program if it were offered, approximately fifty percent of the first generation participants in this study responded favorably, often remarking that it might be beneficial but that they would not personally choose to enroll. However, the topic was controversial. Some first generation participants who had felt lost in the first year of college were in favor of an academic preorientation. S. responded to the idea, "That would be cool. But being very real. Look, schools that don't send kids to the Ivy League do not prepare kids for the Ivy League. When you come from a school like that, like I did, you were a big fish in a small pond. And now, coming to Harvard, we get to this ocean and they're like '*Swim, motherfucker!*'" Ashleigh, who like S. did not feel well prepared by her public high school, nonetheless was adamantly against an academic preorientation just for first generation students: "I did not want to appear different, I wanted to be seen as part of the pack." She continued, "Nobody wants to be singled out as needing more help. . . . Even the name 'first generation students' sounds remedial in some way, and the message that you need additional support makes me very uncomfortable." Gretchen, who felt well prepared by her private high school, reacted against the idea, "I wouldn't want people knowing I was first gen. Yes, for other people who struggle academically coming in, but that wasn't me. I wouldn't have signed up if something was offered my freshman year." Continuing generation participants were also divided over an academic preorientation. Bailey offered her thoughts, "I think that would be helpful, but it shouldn't be targeted. I don't like it when Harvard targets low-income or black and Latino students only. I think that everyone would benefit." Rita replied, "We talked about this in *The Crimson* once. On the one hand, it's Harvard, aren't the kids supposed to be smart? Do they need remedial help? But on the other hand, I get the rationale. But I worry about the stigma, you are a student who needed help. . . . I'm not sure how it would affect the brand."

An academic preorientation, either extended like Georgetown's Community Scholars Program or short like Preparing to Excel, would require sensitivity and advance framing that such a program was not "remediation" but advance exposure to resources and techniques not available in many of our nation's public high schools. Universities planning to establish these types of pre-orientation programs should be sensitive to potential pitfalls associated with targeting and messages of remediation.

Recommendations from First Generation Students to Enhance Academic Experiences

In chapter 3, I explored how the first and continuing generation students at Harvard and Georgetown spoke about their academic experiences in college. The participants in this sample were generally very highly motivated and accustomed to success, as they had been the valedictorians, salutatorians, and top performers in their high schools. For first and continuing generation participants alike, their high school preparation influenced their college academic pathways. Given that more first generation than continuing generation students attended lower resourced high schools, more first generation than continuing generation participants discussed feeling limited in college by their high school experiences. Through dint of their own motivation and effort, many of these first generation participants described an academic turnaround, usually after sophomore year, that included feelings of greater confidence and pride in their successes by early senior year. But how can highly selective colleges and universities do more to support first generation success earlier in their college experience? What follows are a few recommendations offered by first generation participants to jump-start positive academic experiences in college.

Early Intervention

For many of the first generation participants, the first semester in college was their first exposure to a staggering variety of course options and potential career paths. They were unprepared for the volume of possibilities afforded them in college. If highly selective colleges and universities, from small private colleges to large public flagships, want to ease the entry to college, then an important first step is to spend more time visiting high schools or having high school students visit these institutions. College representatives could spend time not only recruiting promising candidates, but explaining the wide variety of career pathways available upon graduation. Students could familiarize themselves with college campuses, classrooms, and syllabi long before they matriculate. Government-sponsored early intervention programs such as the US Department of Education's GEAR UP and TRIO afford low-income students these types of opportunities. Likewise, nonprofit organizations like LEDA and Quest Bridge, as well as university programs for high school students like the Princeton University Preparatory Program, have provided tremendous opportunities for selected high school scholars from low-income backgrounds. Such programs could be expanded into regions that currently do not receive such support. They could also widen their target population to include all first generation students, regardless of parental income. Likewise, colleges across the United States, Harvard and Georgetown included, already sponsor programs designed to foster relationships with schools in their region, inviting middle and high school students to tour the campus, take part in a lecture or debate, or view a performance. Such relationships could be deepened, for instance, by offering repeated visits for the same students over a course of several years. Or they could be expanded to include all schools in a district rather than a select handful. Advice from first generation students suggests such program expansion would benefit those with little prior exposure to college in their home communities.

Ongoing Proacademic Cocurricular Programming

In addition to targeted preorientation programming, many first generation participants requested more proacademic social programming throughout the first two years of college, especially sophomore year. These may include workshops in how to speak effectively in class, incentives for visiting office hours, opportunities to engage one-on-one with faculty in low-risk settings, time management tips, and multiple opportunities to reduce stress, express vulnerability, and remind students that it is both normal and okay, even instructive, to fail at challenging tasks. Such programs already exist at many colleges and universities, but reiteration of their value, demonstrated by continued investment in quality programming of this sort, is essential. Georgetown's GSP members reported enjoying competing in a scavenger-hunt-style challenge to complete proacademic tasks—say, visiting a professor's office hours, attending an academic services workshop, or bringing a paper to the writing center—for incentives such as coffee gift cards and tickets to sporting events. Even short informational sessions that expose students to stories of struggle and ultimate success, alongside discussions of how socioeconomic status, race, religion, gender status, sexuality, and other identities factor into the college experience, provide powerful opportunities for students to narrate their experiences and take control of their academic destinies.[20]

High Impact Practices

Overwhelming evidence suggests that "high impact practices" such as study abroad, internships, and laboratory and independent research all offer the potential for transformative experiences in

---

20. See Stephens, Brannon et al., "Feeling at Home in College" and Stephens, Hamedani, "Closing the Social-Class Achievement Gap." Also, Dweck's research on fixed versus growth mindsets and demonstrating to students how to assess their current learning strategies and pinpoint new ones when their original ones fail are also relevant to helping first generation students regain trust in their academic capabilities after early setbacks. Dweck, *Mindset: The New Psychology of Success.*

college. However, first generation students tend to participate in such practices at lower rates than continuing generation students. Discovering the specific barriers to participation in such opportunities that first generation students face and devising solutions to attenuate or eliminate these barriers would help level the academic playing field for first generation students. During the final year of this study, Georgetown's GSP was able to secure funding to offer up to eight stipends for first generation students to take on unpaid summer internships, and some departments and academic programs also offered stipends for such work. Such funding could be expanded to increase the number of first generation students who benefit. Study abroad is generally covered by the student's tuition, but parents of first generation students may be wary of sending their children abroad and are apt to question its value and fit with their children's future goals. Outreach to parents explaining the effect of study abroad on a student's academic and career trajectory could be a low-cost and effective solution. Laboratory work is theoretically available to all willing and capable students regardless of parental educational background. Nonetheless, psychological and practical barriers persist, usually having to do with the need for paid work. If specific preorientation or term-time programs were established to introduce first generation and low-income students to laboratory opportunities, then first generation students would likely be more inclined to consider, apply to, and self-advocate for such opportunities as they progress through college.

Opportunities to Explore Earlier, Select a Major Later

A higher proportion of first generation participants than continuing generation participants either selected a major they did not originally intend or switched their major between sophomore and senior year. Some of these students narrated the switch in purely positive terms, but many others expressed disappointment or frustration with their early academic experiences in college. Providing students with ample opportunities to meaningfully explore their options and to select a major later than their sophomore year may reduce their anxiety about choosing the "right" major when they are still undecided. Freshman seminars, which are often taken pass/fail, are examples of lower risk opportunities to explore new academic interests. Team-taught introductions to academic fields are also useful, but they are less readily available. Mandating that at least one course be taken pass/fail freshman year and tweaking the timeline for major selection are other possibilities.

Fix the Pipeline

Fix the pipeline: this is an argument being made among student activists, scholars, writers, research institutes, and political and community leaders across the United States at present.[21] Numerous sophisticated arguments have been made regarding increasing opportunities for low-income and minority undergraduates to gain access to highly regarded preprofessional pathways, as well as increasing the number of university faculty and staff from underrepresented backgrounds that serve as mentors and models for undergraduates. One goal is to increase the number of minority and low-income students who pursue advanced degrees—PhDs, JDs, MDs, MBAs, etc.—and are then hired into these professions. This study concurs with the larger body of literature arguing for increased representation of minority, low-income, and first generation professionals on faculty and staff at all universities, and at highly selective universities in particular, as well as opportunities for these faculty and staff to share their stories with undergraduates both formally and informally. As first generation students often put it, they long for more faculty who "get it," to whom they can relate and by whom they feel validated and supported. These faculty do not have to be first generation themselves, but should understand the challenges that first generation students face and be committed to their ongoing achievement.

---

21. One example of research on this topic is a report from the US Department of Education, "Advancing Diversity and Inclusion in Higher Education."

Academic and career advisers who were themselves first generation or who have a long-standing history supporting such students would also benefit undergraduates through their modeling and support. Finally, ongoing training of current faculty in the kinds of obstacles that first generation students face in their classrooms and beyond would allow well-meaning but often unaware faculty to improve their teaching and the ways they relate to all of their students.

Affirm the Importance of Academic Mentorship

While many first generation participants longed to see faculty who looked like them and shared similar childhood experiences, many others underscored a more generic need for authentic academic mentorship regardless of shared personal history. As one first generation participant put it, "having those mentors reminding you that they know who you are and know you exist" makes a world of difference when students are facing personal and academic struggles. This study did not examine the significant challenges that faculty face when balancing scholarship, service to their university, and teaching, but it did suggest that a university's commitment to rewarding engaged teaching and mentorship would likely yield outsized benefits to first generation students.

Recommendations from First Generation Students to Enhance Social Experiences

Chapters 4 and 5 explored how first and continuing generation students described their social experiences in college, in particular, how well they felt integrated into their university's overall structure. In general, both first and continuing generation students reported high levels of social satisfaction, particularly by their senior year. First generation participants described greater and more frequent fluctuations in their social satisfaction over time, but through involvement in extracurriculars and building friend groups, they fashioned supportive and rewarding communities they believed would sustain them beyond graduation.

First generation participants were more likely to express concerns about social and personal integration, to discuss financial barriers to social life on and off campus, and to express complex misgivings around belonging at elite universities. Continuing generation students were more likely to raise issues related to open social spaces and sexual assault on campus, or were inclined to critique or defend apparently classist or exclusionary social practices such as "comping" (or requiring competition to gain entry into extracurricular organizations) and participation in unrecognized or closed membership social organizations. The following pages outline four recommendations provided by first generation participants to support positive social experiences and outcomes in college: increased choice and leadership opportunities in extracurricular commitments through reduced barriers to entry; reduced financial barriers to social life; authentic involvement of first generation parents; and more frequent and intentional discussions of race, class, privilege, and feelings of belonging on campus.

Choice and Leadership Opportunities in Extracurriculars

Participation in a select few extracurriculars, and eventual leadership in at least one organization, was a clear recipe for social satisfaction among first and continuing generation participants alike. First generation participants did not always anticipate the significant social, academic, and preprofessional rewards to joining clubs and campus organizations. Clear messaging to first generation students and their parents that extracurricular participation can support all aspects of a student's college life would be beneficial. Students who felt that they had ample choice—say, the ability to join an ethnic organization that supported them even if they did not match the demographic, or the ability to launch a club or Greek chapter that served a niche not yet filled—were more likely to report feeling fully part of the campus community. By their senior year, those who found themselves at board or cabinet levels in one or two organizations also felt greater empowerment elsewhere in their social lives. Information to incoming first generation students and their parents about the rewards of choice and leadership in extracurricular engagement would likely provide a clearer roadmap for social integration and important talking points for discussions between students and their parents about how they spend their time outside of class.

Despite the abundant benefits of extracurricular engagement, the competitive nature of many organizations at elite universities threatens to corrode those benefits, especially when newcomers view the competition for entry as arbitrary, discriminatory, or opaque. Across the board, first and continuing generation participants requested reduced pressure associated with entry to extracurricular organizations, or as continuing generation Emily put it, "leveling the extracurricular field." The university could consider sending introductory flyers that explain the competitive or "comp" process and provide a brief informational blurb and application deadlines for many of the most well-known competitive organizations on campus. Sending these flyers to students' homes before the start of fall semester would provide them a chance to learn about the "comping" process and its myriad deadlines without the added social anxiety of moving, meeting new roommates, and navigating an unfamiliar campus. They would have an opportunity to consider the merits and hurdles associated with "comping," thus mitigating bewilderment upon arrival.

Alternatively, universities could clarify the purpose of competitive entry. Those organizations that follow an apprenticeship model, where students learn valuable skills while also trying out new roles alongside older peers who are both instructing and assessing their growth, appear more in-line with highly selective college and universities' missions to cultivate leaders. Administrators could step in to establish standards designed to reduce arbitrary barriers to entry and cultivate a healthier cycle of competition and peer judgement, as well as encouraging growth among noncompetitive extracurricular organizations. One example of such an action might be to give increased funding to extracurricular organizations that establish and then demonstrate achievement toward equity goals among their members and leaders. Such a monetary incentive might encourage club leaders to review their policies and processes for potential implicit biases that systematically exclude or create unnecessary barriers to entry. It might also encourage active recruitment at the club level to align more closely with universities' broader diversity and inclusion goals.

Reduced Financial Barriers to Social Inclusion

The majority of participants in this study, regardless of income background or first generation status, wanted to see a reduced focus on money in social life on their campuses. While they acknowledged that the university could not meddle in the spending habits of its students, on-campus activities could be planned and regulated with accessibility in mind. Students asked for "more free things to do" and ways to "get out of the [insert university name here] bubble," like group hikes or tours of the surrounding city. Periodic large, open-access events on campus ritualize a sense of community and place, but so too do smaller events throughout the year, such as house concerts where student bands can perform for free, and access to on-campus clubs and pubs for students over the age of twenty-one. Administrations should not be afraid to get more involved in the training and advising of extracurricular organizations on how to reduce financial barriers to their activities. As continuing generation participant Z. put it, "If there were college support, advising support for extracurricular groups, that would solve a lot of these problems. The college should be more involved, should provide more structures." Similarly, talking more about financial barriers to social inclusion promises to destigmatize moments when students say "I can't afford that." It also opens up opportunities for students and administrators to consider alternatives to spending. For example, if an event requires planning and execution to put on, then have student volunteers "earn" their entry through the work to create it, or create an extracurricular bank where volunteer hours at one event can earn one's entry into another, and so on. The best ideas are student generated, and students will be more forthcoming when they believe that campus officials are invested in their inclusion.

Inclusion of Parents of First Generation Students

Increased communications with parents of first generation students that are not related to financial aid or fundraising may help first generation students to feel more included on campus. Their parents, too, will feel more included. First generation participants requested brochures or newsletters home, preferably translated into a few key languages, that would include vignettes about first generation student achievements; specific information about important sites around campus (e.g., one issue could cover study spaces in the library, while another would describe the financial aid office or the writing center); where students go to attend to their daily needs such as meals, laundry and wellness; the importance of extracurricular activities and leadership; and how individual courses relate to degree programs and postgraduate pathways. Daniel echoed a general first generation student concern not commonly raised by continuing generation participants: "I found myself pretty often, especially with my dad, having to answer questions like, 'What do people do with their time if they only take five classes?' They don't understand how we spend our time." Consistent messaging that addresses the use and misuse of time in college should be a guiding theme.

Despite a lack of specific knowledge of the college-going process, first generation parents often play a crucial role in their children's integration into college. They offer support, guidance, and cheerleading from afar—they are the boosters, as one observer recently put it, in "the invisible row of bleachers" behind each of these students. As Veronica remarked, "If there were people who were here who made an effort to meet parents, talk to parents, and made it feel like a community that includes them as well, that would be great!" However, inclusion of first generation parents must be conducted in ways that respect their personal biographies, too. Some parents do not read email, and so any materials such as flyers, pamphlets, and guidebooks should be sent by mail. Language can be a barrier, so translation into the most common home languages of first generation students is recommended. Phone calls in the parents' first language also promise long-term benefits. Fundraising to support parent trips to campus for orientation and graduation would be beneficial, and first generation liaisons (either students or recent alumni) could organize workshops and social events for fellow parents to ask questions, trade advice, and make personal connections with one another.

First generation students often worry that through their elite education they will grow increasingly distant and disconnected from their families. Including parents in ongoing communications and activities sends a powerful message that the university values both first generation students and their parents in the same way it values continuing generation students and their parents. It sends the message that when they entrust the futures of their children to the university, first generation parents are also participating in the college journey.

Frequent, Nuanced, and Integrative Discussions of Race, Class, Privilege, and Belonging

First and continuing generation participants alike addressed the urgent need for all students to have frequent, formalized, and meaningful opportunities to talk about and learn from each other's experiences across intersections of race, gender, ideology, class, and privilege. College students, or at least the traditional eighteen- to twenty-four-year-old residential college-going type, are in a unique moment in their lives. Newly separated from their families, brought together on a residential campus with diverse peers, they are often purposefully placed into situations that will test, stretch, and possibly fundamentally alter their pre-college beliefs, values, and assumptions about all sorts of issues, including the discernment of truth and beauty, the definition and parameters of justice, the qualities of virtue, the privileges and corruptions of power, and the pragmatics of compromise. In the classroom, the residence halls, and in safe and brave spaces throughout campus,[22] students are both yearning and afraid to talk and to listen to one another, without immediate judgment and without the ranking and sorting actions they know all too well as winners of a grueling and capricious contest to gain admission into one of America's elite universities.[23]

Faculty and staff also have an important role to play in these conversations, allowing that while they have much to impart, they too are participants in the multistage pageant we call higher education. These discussions should not be an exercise in vacuous self-congratulatory antiprejudice designed to reaffirm elite institutions' "moral worth."[24] Rather, honest and nonjudgmental conversations

22. For an analysis and practical guidance on how to foster brave spaces in multiple collegiate contexts, see Arao and Clemens, "From Safe Spaces to Brave Spaces."

23. Warikoo's comparative analysis of students' ideologies and framing language around the nexus of diversity and educational opportunity at Harvard, Brown, and Oxford offers many subtle and powerful lessons here. At the start of her analysis, she points to the crux of the American meritocracy conundrum: we believe that education offers a mobility ladder, but the most selective of educational institutions— those we tend to presume or at least gloss as populated most densely with our nation's most talented or tenacious young individuals—are also our least diverse. Those who win the admissions lottery at our nation's most selective institutions "understandably feel a huge sense of accomplishment and believe they are surrounded on campus by the best of the best. . . . This belief in meritocracy blinds students to the vast inequalities in society—by both class and race—and in particular to the way higher education is complicit in reproducing that inequality, in part through admissions systems." See Warikoo, *Diversity Bargain*, 7.

24. Warikoo, *Diversity Bargain*, 113. Elizabeth Lee also critiques what she calls "the semiotics of class morality" as the unspoken but widely acknowledged moral

about discrimination and privilege in America—driven by specific examples and concrete data rather than generalizations and hearsay—offer a real opportunity to learn from all participants at the institution about the true diversity of the American experience. Granted, elite colleges like Harvard and Georgetown are no microcosm of the United States, but as proving grounds for many of our nation's next generation of leaders, such institutions should make it their goal to encourage their students to find their authentic voice, to feel empowered to share their perspectives and experiences, to learn from one another, to critique long-held assumptions and given wisdom, and when necessary, to bravely change their minds. There is mounting evidence that this is not happening, or at least not to the extent that university leadership and higher education experts believe it should.

First generation students in this study crisscrossed multiple categories and represented varied responses to the pressure to assimilate to explicit and tacit norms on their elite campuses. They spoke out, hid out, celebrated, lamented, adapted, and augmented in different ways and at different times, depending on the company they kept and were called to keep. Their stories can add significant nuance to the necessary conversations regarding diversity on campus, as they often intersect and even transcend multiple campus categories. Often considered an "invisible" group on campus, their choice to disclose or to pass and under what conditions they choose to do so is another important aspect of this ongoing conversation. As Alex lamented, "Visibility is an important thing on campus. Just knowing that others are going through similar issues makes you feel less alone, less isolated. . . . I think Harvard is doing a good job trying to bring in diversity and inclusion, but just having more of us around, and knowing who is first gen, who's not just the other Latinos, that would make us feel less alone and more a part of campus." While personal circumstances and demo-

---

judgments associated with a prioritization of upper-class social norms on elite college campuses. See Lee, *Class and Campus Life*, 6–9, 117–18.

graphic features shape individual experiences, they do not wholly define them, and they do not by their nature have to alienate students from one another. As one first generation senior, Paola, put it, "The first gen experience isn't the same for everybody. Issues of social class, race, sexuality, gender, those things are so intertwined that you can't necessarily say this is happening to me because I am first gen. . . . That said, half of my close friends come from a very different background, are very privileged. They are all great, loyal friends, and can differentiate between me and my circumstances." Colleges and universities around the country are engaged in critical discussions about race, class, gender, privilege, and discrimination inside the college gates, and first generation students add powerful (and varied) voices to those important conversations. Action is of course also important, but deliberation holds pride of place in America's campus *cum* forum and town square.

Questions, Participants, Methods, and Analysis

THIS BOOK is the result of my participation in a four-year multi-institutional effort to identify specific activities—some that participating universities were already doing, and others they might consider adopting—to foster equitable opportunities, experiences, and outcomes for first generation students at traditionally elite or "legacy" campuses. While extensive research had been conducted on first generation college students in the United States, most of this research was carried out where the majority of first generation students attended college: large public flagships and regional state colleges, community colleges, and technical or vocational training centers. The organizers of the *First Generation Student Success Project*, which I joined as a graduate student in my second year at Harvard, presumed that the challenges first generation students might face at a university renowned for its traditions and associated with a history of power and privilege in the United States would be, in at least some fundamental ways, quite different than those faced by first generation students attending our nation's public and less selective institutions. Having attended nonelite public schools from kindergarten through college, and then two elite private universities for my graduate degrees, I had witnessed and experienced what I took to be very different tacit norms, unspoken rules, and pedagogical assumptions associated with who

members of an institution believe comprise its student population. I suspected that the administrators involved in this project
were on to something, and I wanted to get involved.

The *First Generation Student Success Project* was convened in
2012 by a group of approximately a dozen senior administrators,
including deans of admission and financial aid as well as senior
leaders in student affairs and divisions of diversity and inclusion,
from Brown, Duke, Georgetown, and Harvard. The group was led
by Richard J. Light, an endowed professor, director of the Harvard
Assessment Seminars under multiple university presidents, and a
long-time advocate of in-depth interviews with students to identify meaningful advice for improving undergraduate academic and
social experiences. For a prior project that later served as the basis
for his widely read *Making the Most of College: Students Speak Their
Minds*, Light spent time on dozens of university campuses, conducting interviews and focus groups with undergraduates to identify specific, actionable steps that administrators could implement
to improve student achievement (as defined by the students, university leaders, and the campus mission and vision) and satisfaction with their college experiences. Galvanized by recent reports
that first generation college students, now attending highly selective universities at significantly higher rates than the prior three
decades, were either falling behind, being overlooked, or simply
not participating in the many opportunities their campuses offered, Light and these administrators sought advice for how to
institutionalize equal access and improve engagement. They
wanted to know how first generation students at their universities
felt about and assessed their academic and social experiences on
campus, whether they considered themselves included in the
wider university, and what specific counsel they would offer to
administrators to ameliorate barriers to thriving that might build
a more inclusive and supportive campus. The working group participants agreed to gather interviews with first generation students
at each of their campuses and to share findings in the spirit of
learning from one another how best they might support and in-

clude first generation students both academically and socially. While the administrators agreed that their universities' distinctive contexts and histories would likely lead to varied conclusions in terms of how best to support first generation students, they nonetheless believed that sharing lessons learned from their individual campuses could yield insights and benefits far beyond their gates.

The *First Generation Student Success Project* met annually each May from 2012 to 2016, after a period of data collection and analysis on each campus. At first, the goal was to learn more about specific challenges first generation students faced in the transition to college, both academically and socially, and to compare their insights with a comparison group of their continuing generation peers. Members from each participating university agreed to interview sophomores reflecting on their transition and first year in college. By the spring of 2014, each of the campuses had recruited participants and collected interviews from two cohorts of students, the classes of 2015 and 2016. We then made the decision to return to the same students, now entering their senior year, to reflect on changes in their experience over time. This crucial decision enabled a longitudinal approach to understanding first generation college transitions. By completing interviews in their sophomore and senior year, participants were able to reflect on the arc of college, but they also had the opportunity to adjust or clarify statements made in their sophomore interviews. This enabled a more nuanced assessment of first generation students' change over time and allowed for revision of extemporaneous comments from initial interviews.

While all four campuses agreed to seek similar information from the interview process, the interview teams at Harvard and Georgetown ultimately agreed to follow the same interview protocols and recruitment methods. The interview team at Brown University implemented its own interview protocol and recruitment, graciously sharing their findings and raising important questions and critiques at each of the annual meetings. The interview team from Duke University did not continue on the project once it turned to longitudinal analysis, but their insights were extremely helpful in the first two years of the endeavor. While the lessons learned from first generation participants at Brown and Duke were invaluable to the *First Generation Student Success Project* as well as on their own campuses, ultimately leading to the creation of their own first generation student centers,[1] they are not included in this book due to variations in participant recruitment and data collection.

Participant Recruitment

Interview participants were recruited at Harvard and Georgetown through the following process. The office of admissions generated two random lists of student names, one of first generation and the other of continuing generation sophomores. First generation was defined as a current college student with neither parent having graduated from a four-year baccalaureate program, while continuing generation was defined as a current college student with at least one parent with a baccalaureate degree. These names were adjusted with replacement to approximate the gender and ethnic representation of the population of first and continuing generation students at each institution. Next, a member of the research team sent a brief email invitation to approximately fifty names on each of the lists, explaining the purpose of the project and asking if they would be willing to participate in a one-hour interview about their experiences in college. Those students who responded affirmatively were then assigned an interviewer who emailed the student a second time to schedule and complete an interview somewhere on or near campus. With the goal of interviewing approximately thirty first generation and twenty continuing genera-

1. Brown launched the U-FLi Center (Undocumented, First-Generation College, and Low-Income Student Center) in 2016, in large part based on their research findings from this study, while Duke launched the Washington Duke Scholars Center in 2016, later renamed as the David M. Rubenstein Scholars Center.

tion students on each campus for each of the cohort years (classes of 2015 and 2016), additional invitations were sent from the original list until the target number was reached.

Richard J. Light and Anya B. Bassett, two Harvard faculty members on the project with extensive in-depth interview experience with undergraduates, developed the interview protocol used at Harvard and Georgetown, with minor adjustments to account for differences at the two universities. In addition to Light's leadership and veteran status with undergraduate assessment, Bassett's extensive research, teaching, and advising experience provided keen insights into questions of inequality and opportunity inside elite college campuses. She served as the inaugural faculty adviser for the First Generation Student Union at Harvard and was a strong advocate for first generation student support. At Harvard, five interviewers—myself, Richard Light, Anya Bassett, Thomas Dingman (the dean of freshmen), and Jasmine Waddell (resident dean of first-year students)—completed ninety-three interviews during the first two years of the study. Interviewers represented a mix of university positions, including two administrators, two faculty members, and a graduate student. I served as the primary interviewer, completing more than sixty percent of the total interviews each year. I collected, coded, and analyzed all interviews at Harvard and created preliminary findings reports to distribute for discussion at our annual meetings. At Georgetown, two graduate students, Jennifer Nguyen and Christopher England, completed well over one hundred interviews during the first three years of the study. During the fourth year of the study, I was granted permission to serve as the sole interviewer on the Georgetown team, where I completed approximately thirty interviews. I was given access to code and analyze all interviews from Harvard and Georgetown between 2012 and 2016 to create final reports for each university. This analysis served as the basis of my doctoral dissertation and now this book.

It is worth noting that this study faced an early obstacle in participant recruitment among continuing generation students at

Georgetown. The goal of this project was to discern whether and to what extent first generation students spoke of their transition to and progression through college differently than their continuing generation peers. It was important to use similar framing language about the purpose of the study when recruiting participants for each group. In the first two years of the study at Georgetown, continuing generation students responded to initial recruitment emails at very low rates. Upon review of the initial recruitment email, the Georgetown interview team concluded that the wording of the invitation may have discouraged continuing generation students from seeing this study as relevant to their experiences. In 2014, Georgetown interviewers adjusted their recruitment language to match the Harvard recruitment email—which explained the purpose as seeking to better understand students' experiences in college and to elicit advice about how to improve academic and social life—and were successful at recruiting a higher number of continuing generation participants. However, given that the final analysis was framed as a longitudinal study, most of the additional continuing generation participants at Georgetown were not able to be included. Thus, while more than seventy continuing generation students at Harvard and Georgetown participated in at least one interview and provided essential feedback to campus leaders about how to best support students in their transition to college, only thirty-five were incorporated into the final sample.

As table A.1 indicates, participants returned for a second interview at high rates. They often thanked their interviewer for the opportunity to share their story and provide advice to administrators on academic and social matters. Nominal compensation for initial interviews was restricted to snacks, coffee, or a light meal during the interview, while follow-up interviewees were offered small gift cards as a token of appreciation for their gift of time, insight, and concrete advice.

The final sample analyzed in this book includes ninety-one first generation and thirty-five continuing generation repeat

TABLE A.1. First and Continuing Generation Student Invitation and Participation Rates

	Cohort 1				Cohort 2			
	Sophomore Invitation	Sophomore Participation	Senior Invitation	Senior Participation	Sophomore Invitation	Sophomore Participation	Senior Invitation	Senior Participation
G FG	50	28 (56%)	32	30 (94%)	55	33 (60%)	28	25 (89%)
G CG	40	2 (5%)	4	2 (50%)	100	4 (4%)	52	28 (53%)
H FG	50	28 (56%)	28[a]	22 (79%)	65	27 (42%)	24[b]	22 (92%)
H CG	40	18 (45%)	20	17 (85%)	55	20 (36%)	18	16 (89%)

CG, continuing generation; FG, first generation; G, Georgetown; H, Harvard

[a] One first generation participant from the original 2012–13 cohort (seniors of 2014–15) took a one-year leave of absence and so was incorporated into the following cohort year (seniors of 2015–16).

[b] The original 2012–13 first generation cohort included students who took extended leaves or left the university between their sophomore and senior year. The lower number of invited seniors reflects this cohort's attrition.

TABLE A.2. Repeat Participants, by Cohort (2015, 2016)

	Cohort 1	Cohort 2	Total
Georgetown Repeat FG	17	30	47
Georgetown Repeat CG	0	2	2
Harvard Repeat FG	22	22	44
Harvard Repeat CG	16	17	33
Total	55	71	126

CG, continuing generation; FG, first generation

participants. Table A.2 indicates the number of repeat participants from Georgetown and Harvard by cohort year (2015, 2016).

Participant Demographics

When comparing first and continuing generation students at Harvard and Georgetown, one immediate question is whether the population demographics between first and continuing generation students are similar by such measures as gender, ethnicity, and high school type. A second important question is whether the students who agree to an interview, and thus who shape the sample, represent the first generation or continuing generation population at the university. While every effort was made to recruit a representative sample of participants, the final sample is ultimately comprised of those who agree to participate.

As shown in table A.3, female, Latinx, and African American students were somewhat overrepresented among first generation participants compared to the overall undergraduate population at Georgetown and Harvard. First generation participants attended public high schools at a higher rate than their continuing generation peers. Among continuing generation participants, white students were slightly overrepresented and Latinx students were slightly underrepresented compared to the overall undergraduate population at Harvard and Georgetown. The different demographic makeup of the samples could indicate that first generation students at Harvard and Georgetown comprised a different pro-

TABLE A.3. First and Continuing Generation Participant Demographics

		First Generation	Continuing Generation
Gender	Female	62 (68%)	17 (49%)
	Male	29 (32%)	18 (51%)
Race/Ethnicity	White	23 (25%)	24 (68%)
	Black/African American	12 (13%)	3 (9%)
	Asian/Asian American	22 (24%)	7 (20%)
	Latinx	31 (34%)	1 (3%)
	Multiracial	3 (4%)	0
High School	Public	67 (74%)	23 (66%)
	Private	24 (26%)	12 (34%)

portion of ethnicities and high school types than the overall population at these schools. Specifically, the modal first generation student at these universities may be a female, Latinx, public high school graduate, as this sample indicates.[2] This study did not ask students to disclose their socioeconomic status in the interviews, nor did I have access to students' financial information. As such, any economic comparisons could only be made if and when participants voluntarily raised issues of socioeconomic differences in the interview context.

Data Collection

The primary source of data for this study was the one-hour semi-structured interview, conducted once during students' sophomore year and again during their senior year. These contained a mixture of open-ended and content specific questions designed to blend student narratives of their experiences on campus with recommendations for improvement or adjustments to campus policies.

2. Spiegler and Bednarek found this pattern to be true in general among US first generation college students in their international review of research on first generation college students. See Spiegler and Bednarek, "First Generation Students: What We Ask, What We Know and What It Means," 322–33.

The questions focused on students' assessments of their own academic and social achievements and challenges, with a focus on how the institution could best support students navigating different spheres of college-going—the classroom, the residence hall, extracurricular environment. I and the other interviewers deployed an interpretivist-constructivist lens, allowing students to craft their own narrative while also providing them the opportunity to act as auto-experts when delivering advice to the university.[3] This interview strategy is akin to what anthropologist James Beebe calls "directed conversation,"[4] and intentionally placed the participant in the position of collaborator in order to identify relevant policy solutions.

Each university's Institutional Review Board (IRB) protocols regarding audio recording of interviews were followed according to our permissions. At Georgetown, interviewers were allowed to audio record the interviews with participants' consent. They also took notes on laptop computers during the interview. At Harvard, interviewers took notes and transcribed student responses on laptop computers during the interviews but were not permitted to use audio recorders. In write-ups of student responses, interviewers indicated which responses were direct quotes and which were paraphrases. While audio recordings are ideal for securing accuracy of quotes, the three primary interviewers on the Harvard interview team were all extensively trained in qualitative and interview techniques to ensure the accuracy of note-taking and interview write-ups. I, for instance, was able to draw on my advanced graduate training in anthropology and qualitative methods when note-taking in the interviews.

At the outset of each interview, participants were asked to select a pseudonym by which their interviews would be saved and according to which they would be identified in all reporting, including this book. Participants were given the opportunity to change

---

3. See Schwandt, "Constructivist, Interpretivist Approaches to Human Inquiry," and Charmaz, *Constructing Grounded Theory*.

4. See Beebe, *Rapid Assessment Process*.

their pseudonym if they wished, and, in a small number of cases, their pseudonym was shortened to initials if it was later deemed that the originally chosen pseudonym was too easily identifiable or was trademarked in some way.

Next, all interviewees were asked the same battery of questions during each interview phase, with the exception that first generation participants were asked how the university could better support its first generation students while continuing generation participants were asked how the university could better support all students. Continuing generation students who inquired about the purpose of this study were told that the goal was to find ways to improve the experiences of first generation students in particular, and all students in general. As such, some continuing generation participants may have tailored their responses with that goal in mind, while others responded in more general terms with ideas to improve the undergraduate experience. First generation participants who did not consider their first generation status as relevant to their college-going experiences were encouraged to explain why they thought so during the open-ended portions of the interview. Thus, as interviewers, we intended to allow students to craft their own narrative and not embrace any specific framework that they might consider false, partial, or constraining. This openness in conceding that the labels under which we researchers operated might not be valid to the participants themselves allowed for greater flexibility in interpretation and distinguished this study from prior ones that assumed first generation students would naturally embrace that moniker or frame of research.

Analysis and Review

Data analysis began with the interview write-ups themselves. The interviewers at Harvard and Georgetown delivered to me write-ups with direct quotes or, when noted, paraphrases of student responses to interview questions. I considered these write-ups as raw data for the purpose of analysis, but was also aware that transcribed interviews are already in some way digested and interpreted in the process of transcription. I made note when a participant response was recorded as a direct quote versus a paraphrase, and only included direct quotes in the qualitative portion of the analysis.

Once all interviews were delivered, I read each write-up in full twice in order to get a feel for its pacing and general tone. Interviewers sometimes made notes about the interview itself, and I incorporated these notes into my assessment of the write-up. Once I ascertained a general feel for the interviews as a group, I then created a spreadsheet to organize, code, and compare all first and continuing generation responses. Focusing on each question in turn, I then reorganized these responses into emergent themes, reviewed the themes and recategorized them into general theme groups. I then conducted a hand count and compared the percentage of students whose responses fell into each of the theme groups in order to differentiate primary and secondary themes. For any questions that involved quantifiable responses, such as satisfaction scales, major selection, or responses to yes/no questions, I created comparative tables to visualize the scope, range, and shape of response types.

Once a basic digestion and component breakdown was conducted for both first and continuing generation participant responses, I then set out to compare first and continuing generation responses. I noted points of overlap and divergence, and where I found divergence, I tested whether differences were meaningful or slight. For anything that could be tested by a simple two-by-two contingency table—such as questions regarding whether a student felt "more/as" or "less" prepared for college than their peers—I conducted a simple statistical test (the Fisher's Exact Test for statistical significance) to determine whether differences in categorical response were significant. Given that this is a small sample study yielding primarily qualitative data, I deployed contingency tables specifically to provide another layer of context to the qualitative findings. This simple statistical tool proved useful when discerning which responses were more common across the groups and which were primarily associated with one group or the other.

At this stage, the analysis was primarily descriptive and interpretive. Its perspective was largely *emic*, or shaped by the participants' point of view. Without judging the validity of truth claims offered by participants, it sought to unearth themes in how students themselves interpreted their experiences in college and to compare their responses by first and continuing generation status. The basic guiding question to shape the analysis included: what are the similarities and differences between how first and continuing generation students talk about their experiences of college-going at an elite university, and what sorts of advice do they offer their university to improve the college-going experience? The analysis focused on the ways in which students spoke, presuming that their speech in the interview context would correlate to a large extent with what they desired the university to know about their experiences and how they wished their experiences to shape future practice and policy at the institutional level.[5]

In order to check my initial interpretations for researcher bias, I sought input from the interview team and from interested students, administrators, and alumni at each of the universities. I cross-checked the emergent themes and my interpretation of the interviews with the entire interview team by delivering preliminary analyses at the end of each study year, inviting responses and

5. One should not assume that the way students talk about their college experience directly reflects their actions and experiences. Ethnographers such as Khan and Jerolmack point out that students often say and do very different things, especially regarding concerns of meritocracy and privilege. This book does not intend to reveal what students *do* but rather what they want administrators to *know* about them and how they want to be treated by representatives of their university—faculty, administrators, fellow students. For an extended critique of relying on interviews to analyze student behavior, see Khan and Jerolmack, "Saying Meritocracy and Doing Privilege" and "Talk Is Cheap: Ethnography and the Attitudinal Fallacy." For a defense of interview methods in cultural analysis, see Vaisey's rejoinder in the same journal, "The 'Attitudinal Fallacy' Is a Fallacy."

incorporating changes in the following round of research and analysis. During the years when Georgetown interviewers conducted their own analysis, I also discussed preliminary findings with their team to check for validity and transportability. I attended student roundtable discussions and alumni events focused on first generation student issues. I followed the student newspaper and other university periodicals, and attended campus events related to social class diversity, inequality on campus, and first generation students. These events provided an opportunity to further contextualize interview findings and enable ongoing data triangulation.

Data Reporting

The write-up phase of this project was iterative and cumulative, beginning with the end-of-year reports delivered to *First Generation Student Success Project* members and discussed at each of its annual meetings. Each exercise in synthesizing the findings of this study afforded me the chance to share and receive feedback on the research, as well as to offer direct programmatic advice to the involved institutions. At this point, the analysis evolved from descriptive to prescriptive, as I provided programmatic and policy guidance aimed at administrators and program staff interested in developing and/or improving relevant student support services. Several of these suggestions were incorporated into subsequent programming at Harvard and Georgetown, providing participants with the experience of having their voices heard and witnessing change of policy during their course in college.

In delivering the findings, I selected quotes from students that were either typical of more common responses in the sample, or were distinctive in some way. I then explained as a framing device how this student's response was either typical or distinctive. I chose to maximize students' voices by showcasing students' own narratives of their experiences in college while also providing relevant information about each participant whose quotes were used.

It was my intention to keep quotes intact whenever possible, allowing each student's insights to be read and analyzed in full. While it is more typical for social scientists to provide their readers with shorter, more digested quotes that support their argument, I eschewed this strategy when possible to maximize autonomous conclusions from the reader. This strategy provides the reader with direct access to the participants' tone, style, and message. It also allows the reader to analyze the data I use in the analysis in order to draw their own, potentially divergent, conclusions. I invite the reader to actively participate in the analysis and to judge whether the students' voices were properly rendered.

Rapport and a Note about My Status as It Relates to This Research

This study could not have been conducted without the trust and willingness of its participants, who committed to sharing sometimes painful details about their college experiences not once but twice over their four years in college. The research team was acutely aware of both the importance of this research to improving undergraduate experiences for future cohorts and the risks entailed in participants' disclosure of uncomfortable elements of their personal lives, including housing insecurity, personal or family members' undocumented status, family financial and health-related issues, or dealing with racism, sexism, and classism in their everyday encounters. Considerable efforts were made during the interviews to build rapport between interviewers and participants. Examples include polite e-mail notes reminding students of upcoming interviews and thanking them for their ongoing commitment to the project; offers of scheduling at the students' convenience and not the other way around; and gifts of coffee, light meals, and for seniors, a small monetary gift ($10 gift card) as a token of thanks for their time, commitment to the project, and considered responses to requests for advice. During the interviews, each interviewer made an effort to listen deeply, to encourage honest responses without fear of judgment, and to take careful notes and ask follow-up questions in the event of confusion.

However, given that some participants interviewed with senior administrators and others interviewed with graduate students, it is possible that participant responses differed according to interviewer type. For instance, some social scientists suggest that interview participants are more inclined to speak frankly about their challenges when they perceive the interviewer to be close in age, to have had similar experiences, or to share a connection based on race, ethnicity, or social class. The range of interviewers meant that the participants might not feel a connection with their interviewers based on age or social status, and so the interviewers made an effort to build rapport through other means, such as attentive listening and an emphasis on collaboration in the interview. In order to discern whether the interviews were skewed by any perceived power differentials between the participant and interviewer, I compared the interview write-ups by interviewer type and found no significant differences between interviews conducted by administrators and those conducted by graduate students, and likewise no significant differences between interviews conducted by interviewers who had been first generation college students and those who had not (approximately half of the interviewers were first generation college graduates). The resulting similarity in the range of interview responses may be the result of extensive rapport building in the interview context, or it may be because the stated purpose of this project—to identify ways to best support first generation and all college students at highly selective universities—is an issue that our participants care deeply about and are willing to discuss regardless of the position the interviewer embodies at the university.

Given the increasing concern regarding whether researchers have the authority to speak for their research subjects, particularly when those research subjects are minoritized or marginalized in some way and the researcher is an outsider to the group, I wish to note that as a college student I was neither first generation nor what someone would call an "elite" student. I am an outsider to both statuses.[6] I came to this research because I am deeply invested in increasing access to and success in quality postsecondary education for all students and for marginalized and minoritized students in particular. I believe that high-quality education is a necessary ingredient for thriving democracies, and that all members of a society have a right to the education they seek and have the capacity to obtain, regardless of their race, religion, gender, social class, immigration status, age, sexuality, or any other category that has historically been used to bar qualified students from entry. I am also convinced that ground-up longitudinal research seeking student input on improving the college-going experience provides necessary nuance to other forms of research on student outcomes (e.g., survey data or quantitative analysis of standardized test scores). I believe that I was able to convey how much I care about this research to the participants involved, and I was careful to disclose that as a college student I was neither "elite" nor "first generation."

6. However, it would be false to claim that I had no prior personal knowledge of these two statuses and how they might interact. My parents were both first generation college students who ultimately earned advanced degrees, and they often spoke of the challenges associated with being the first in their family to go to college. And as a graduate student at two highly selective private universities, Duke and Harvard, I taught and worked with undergraduates experiencing the enormous shift in personal identity that often accompanies the recognition that one is becoming a member of the "educated elite." So while not quite an insider, I was never purely an outsider to these categories either. For the case of being an insider-outsider in qualitative research, see Dwyer and Buckle, "The Space Between: Being an Insider-Outsider in Qualitative Research."

BIBLIOGRAPHY

American Academy of Arts and Sciences. "The State of the Humanities 2018: Graduates in the Workforce and Beyond." Accessed May 1, 2019. http://www.amacad.org/sites /default/files/academy/multimedia/pdfs/publications/researchpapersmonographs /HI_Workforce-2018.pdf

Arao, Brian, and Kristi Clemens. "From Safe Spaces to Brave Spaces: A New Way to Frame Dialogue around Diversity and Social Justice." In *The Art of Effective Facilitation: Reflections from Social Justice Educators,* edited by Lisa Landreman, 135–50. Sterling, VA: Stylus Publishing, 2013.

Aries, Elizabeth. *Race and Class Matters at an Elite College.* Philadelphia, PA: Temple University Press, 2008.

Aries, Elizabeth, and Richard Berman. *Speaking of Race and Class: The Student Experience at an Elite College.* Philadelphia, PA: Temple University Press, 2012.

Armstrong, Elizabeth, and Laura Hamilton. *Paying for the Party: How College Maintains Inequality.* Cambridge, MA: Harvard University Press, 2013.

Bain, Ken. *What the Best College Students Do.* Cambridge, MA: Harvard University Press, 2012.

Ballantine, Jeanne, Floyd Hammack, and Jenny Stuber. *The Sociology of Education: A Systematic Analysis.* 8th ed. New York: Routledge, 2014.

Banaji, Mahzarin, and Anthony Greenwald. *Blindspot: Hidden Biases of Good People.* New York: Delacorte Press, 2013.

Beebe, James. *Rapid Assessment Process: An Introduction.* Walnut Creek, CA: Altamira, 2001.

Black, Sandra, Jane Lincove, Jennifer Cullinane, and Rachel Veron. "Can You Leave High School Behind?" *Economics of Education Review* 46 (June 2015): 52–63.

Bourdieu, Pierre. *Distinction: A Social Critique of the Judgment of Taste.* Cambridge, MA: Harvard University Press, 1984.

———. *Practical Reason.* Stanford, CA: Stanford University Press, 1998.

———. *The State Nobility: Elite Schools in the Field of Power.* Stanford, CA: Stanford University Press, 1996.

Bowen, William, Matthew Chingos, and Michael McPherson. *Crossing the Finish Line: Completing College at America's Public Universities.* Princeton, NJ: Princeton University Press, 2009.

Bowen, William, Martin Kurzweil, and Eugene Tobin. *Equity and Excellence in American Higher Education.* Charlottesville: University of Virginia Press, 2005.

Boyce, W. Thomas. *The Orchid and the Dandelion: Why Some Children Struggle and How All Can Thrive.* New York: Knopf, 2019.

Bronfenbrenner, Urie. *The Ecology of Human Development.* Cambridge, MA: Harvard University Press, 1979.

Caplan, Bryan. *The Case against College: Why Everything You Have Been Taught about College Is Wrong.* Princeton, NJ: Princeton University Press, 2018.

Capó Crucet, Jennine. *Make Your Home among Strangers.* New York: St. Martin's Press, 2015.

Carnevale, Anthony, Ban Cheah, and Andrew Hanson. *The Economic Value of College Majors.* Washington, DC: Center on Education and the Workforce, 2015. https://cew.georgetown.edu/cew-reports/valueofcollegemajors/

Cary, Jennifer. "Tradition and Transition: Achieving Diversity at Harvard and Radcliffe." PhD diss., Harvard University, 1995.

Castleman, Ben, and Lindsay Page. *Summer Melt: Supporting Low-Income Students through the Transition to College.* Cambridge, MA: Harvard Education Press, 2014.

Chambliss, Daniel, and Christopher Takacs. *How College Works.* Cambridge, MA: Harvard University Press, 2014.

Charmaz, Kathy. *Constructing Grounded Theory: A Practical Guide through Qualitative Analysis.* Thousand Oaks, CA: Sage, 2006.

Chetty, Raj, John Friedman, Emmanuel Saez, Nicholas Turner, and Danny Yagan. "Mobility Report Cards: The Role of Colleges in Intergenerational Mobility." *National Bureau of Economic Research Working Paper No. 23618,* July 2017. https://www.nber.org/papers/w23618

Choy, Susan. *Students Whose Parents Did Not Go to College: Post-secondary Access, Persistence, and Attainment.* Washington, DC: National Center for Education Statistics, 2001.

Collier, Peter, and David Morgan. "'Is That Paper Really Due Today?': Differences in First-Generation and Traditional College Students' Understandings of Faculty Expectations." *Higher Education* 55, no. 4 (2008): 425–46.

Crenshaw, Kimberlé. "Demarginalizing the Intersection of Race and Sex: A Black Feminist Critique of Antidiscrimination Doctrine, Feminist Theory and Antiracist Politics." *University of Chicago Legal Forum* 1989, no. 1 (1989): 139–67.

Cuba, Lee, Nancy Jennings, Suzanne Lovett, and Joseph Swingle. *Practice for Life: Making Decisions in College.* Cambridge, MA: Harvard University Press, 2016.

DeAngelo, Linda, Ray Franke, Sylvia Hurtado, John Pryor, and Serge Tran. *Completing College: Assessing Graduation Rates at Four-Year Institutions.* Los Angeles: Higher Education Research Institute UCLA, 2011.

Delbanco, Andrew. *College: What It Was, Is, and Should Be.* Princeton: Princeton University Press, 2012.

de Novais, Janine, and Natasha Warikoo. "Colour-Blindness and Diversity: Race Frames and Their Consequences for White Undergraduates at Elite U.S. Universities." *Ethnic and Racial Studies* 38, no. 6 (2014): 860–76.

DiLuca, Juliana. "Last Paper Study Card Day." *Sustainability at Harvard University,* February 27, 2015. https://green.harvard.edu/news/last-paper-study-card-day

Duckworth, Angela. *Grit: The Power of Passion and Perseverance.* New York: Simon and Schuster, 2016.

Duffy, Elizabeth, and Idana Goldberg. *Crafting a Class: College Admissions and Financial Aid, 1955–1994.* Princeton, NJ: Princeton University Press, 1998.

Dweck, Carol. *Mindset: The New Psychology of Success.* New York: Ballantine Books, 2006.

Dwyer, Sonya, and Jennifer Buckle. "The Space Between: Being an Insider-Outsider in Qualitative Research." *International Journal of Qualitative Methods* 8, no. 1 (2009): 54–63.

Eismann, Louisa. "First-Generation Students and Job Success." *National Association of Colleges and Employers,* November 2016.

Engle, Jennifer, and Vincent Tinto. *Moving beyond Access: College Success for Low-Income, First-Generation Students.* Washington, DC: The Pell Institute, 2008.

Ettekal, Andrea, and Joseph Mahoney. "Ecological Systems Theory." *The SAGE Encyclopedia of Out-of-School Learning,* edited by Kylie Peppler, 239–41. Thousand Oaks, CA: Sage, 2017.

Finnegan, Dorothy, and Nathan Alleman. "The YMCA and the Origins of American Freshman Orientation Programs." *Historical Studies in Education* 25, no. 1 (2013): 95–114.

Griffin, Kimberly, and Samuel Museus, eds. *Using Mixed-Methods Approaches to Study Intersectionality in Higher Education.* San Francisco: Jossey-Bass, 2011.

Guinier, Lani. *The Tyranny of the Meritocracy: Democratizing Higher Education in America.* Boston: Beacon, 2015.

Hamilton, Laura. *Parenting to a Degree: How Family Matters for College Women's Success.* Chicago: University of Chicago, 2016.

Harper, Shaun. "Am I My Brother's Teacher? Black Undergraduates, Peer Pedagogies, and Racial Socialization in Predominantly White Postsecondary Contexts." *Review of Research in Education* 37, no. 1 (2013): 183–211.

———. "Black Male College Achievers and Resistant Responses to Racist Stereotypes at Predominantly White Colleges and Universities." *Harvard Educational Review* 85, no. 4 (2015): 646–74.

Harper, Shaun, and Christopher Newman. "Surprise, Sensemaking, and Success in the First College Year: Black Undergraduate Men's Academic Adjustment Experiences." *Teachers College Record* 118 (2016): 1–30.

Horowitz, Helen. *Campus Life: Undergraduate Cultures from the End of the Eighteenth Century to the Present.* Chicago: University of Chicago Press, 1987.

Hoxby, Caroline, and Christopher Avery. "The Missing 'One-Offs': The Hidden Supply of High-Achieving, Low-Income Students." *Brookings Papers on Economic Activity* 2013, no. 1 (Spring 2013): 1–65.

Hoxby, Caroline, and Sarah Turner. "Expanding College Opportunities for High-Achieving, Low-Income Students." *SIEPR Discussion Paper*, No. 12-014 (2013): 1–57.

Hu, Shouping, Lindsey Katherine, and George Kuh. "Student Typologies in Higher Education." *New Directions for Institutional Research* (2011): 5–15. https://doi.org/10.1002/ir.413

Hurtado, Sylvia, M. Kevin Eagan, Minh Tran, Christopher Newman, Mitchell Chang, and Paolo Velasco. "'We Do Science Here': Underrepresented Students' Interactions with Faculty in Different College Contexts." *Journal of Social Issues* 67, no. 3 (2011): 553–79.

Inzlicht, Michael, and Toni Schmader, eds. *Stereotype Threat: Theory, Process, and Application.* Oxford: Oxford University Press, 2011.

Jack, Anthony Abraham. "Crisscrossing Boundaries: Variation in Experiences with Class Marginality among Lower-Income, Black Undergraduates at an Elite College." In *College Students' Experiences of Power and Marginality*, edited by Elizabeth Lee and Chaise LaDousa, 83–101. New York: Routledge, 2015.

———. "Culture Shock Revisited: The Social and Cultural Contingencies to Class Marginality." *Sociological Forum* 29, no. 2 (2014): 453–75.

———. "(No) Harm in Asking: Class, Acquired Cultural Capital, and Academic Engagement at an Elite University." *Sociology of Education* 89, no. 1 (2015): 1–19.

———. *The Privileged Poor: How Elite Colleges Are Failing Disadvantaged Students.* Cambridge, MA: Harvard University Press, 2019.

Jenkins, Anthony, Yasuo Miyazaki, and Steven Janosik. "Predictors that Distinguish First-Generation College Students from Non-First Generation College Students." *Journal of Multicultural, Gender, and Minority Studies* 3, no. 1 (2009): 9p.

Jimenez, Francisco. *Reaching Out.* New York: Houghton Mifflin Harcourt, 2008.

———. *Taking Hold: From Migrant Childhood to Columbia University.* New York: Houghton Mifflin Harcourt, 2017.

Kahlenberg, Richard. "How Low-Income Students Are Fitting in at Elite Colleges." *Atlantic*, February 24, 2016.

———. *Rewarding Strivers: Helping Low-Income Students Succeed in College.* New York: The Century Foundation, 2010.

Karabel, Jerome. *The Chosen: The Hidden History of Admission and Exclusion at Harvard, Yale, and Princeton.* New York: Houghton Mifflin, 2005.

————. "How Affirmative Action Took Hold at Harvard, Yale, and Princeton." *Journal of Blacks in Higher Education* 48 (Summer, 2005): 58–77.

Keller, Morton, and Phyllis Keller. *Making Harvard Modern: The Rise of America's University*. New York: Oxford University Press, 2007.

Kett, Joseph. *Merit: The History of a Founding Ideal from the American Revolution to the Twenty-First Century*. Ithaca, NY: Cornell University Press, 2013.

Khan, Shamus. *Privilege: The Making of an Adolescent Elite at St. Paul's School*. Princeton, NJ: Princeton University Press, 2011.

Khan, Shamus, and Colin Jerolmack. "Saying Meritocracy and Doing Privilege." *Sociological Quarterly* 54, no. 1 (2013): 9–19.

————. "Talk Is Cheap: Ethnography and the Attitudinal Fallacy." *Sociological Methods & Research* 43, no. 2 (2014): 178–209.

Kirp, David. *Improbable Scholars: The Rebirth of a Great American School System and a Strategy for America's Schools*. Oxford: Oxford University Press, 2013.

Kuh, George. *High-Impact Educational Practices: What They Are, Who Has Access to Them, and Why They Matter*. Washington, DC: Association of American Colleges and Universities, 2008.

LaDousa, Chaise. *House Signs and Collegiate Fun: Sex, Race, and Faith in a College Town*. Bloomington: Indiana University Press, 2011.

Lareau, Annette. *Home Advantage: Social Class and Parental Intervention in Elementary Education*. Lanham, MD: Rowman and Littlefield, 2000.

————. *Unequal Childhoods: Class, Race, and Family Life*. Berkeley: University of California Press, 2003.

Lareau, Annette, and Amanda Cox. "Class and the Transition to Adulthood: Differences in Parents' Interactions with Institutions." In *Social Class and Changing Families in an Unequal America*, edited by Marcia Carlson and Paula England, 134–64. Stanford: Stanford University Press, 2011.

Lee, Elizabeth. *Class and Campus Life: Managing and Experiencing Inequality at an Elite College*. Ithaca, NY: Cornell University Press, 2016.

Lemann, Nicholas. *The Big Test: The Secret History of the American Meritocracy*. Cambridge, MA: Harvard University Press, 2000.

Light, Richard. *Making the Most of College: Students Speak Their Minds*. Cambridge, MA: Harvard University Press, 2001.

Lubrano, Alfred. *Limbo: Blue-Collar Roots, White-Collar Dreams*. Hoboken, NJ: Wiley and Sons, 2004.

McCabe, Janice. *Connecting in College: How Friendship Networks Matter for Academic and Social Success*. Chicago: University of Chicago Press, 2016.

Menand, Louis. "The Graduates." *New Yorker*, May 27, 2007. https://www.newyorker.com/magazine/2007/05/21/the-graduates

————. "Why We Have College." *New Yorker*, June 6, 2011. https://www.newyorker.com/magazine/2011/06/06/live-and-learn-louis-menand

Moffatt, Michael. *Coming of Age in New Jersey: College and American Culture*. New Brunswick, NJ: Rutgers University Press, 1989.

Mullen, Ann. *Degrees of Inequality: Culture, Class, and Gender in American Higher Education*. Baltimore, MD: Johns Hopkins University Press, 2010.

Museus, Samuel, Robert Palmer, Ryan Davis, and Dina Maramba. "Racial and Ethnic Minority Students' Success in STEM Education." *ASHE Higher Education Report* 36, no. 6 (2011): 1–140.

Orfield, Gary, Erica Frankenberg, Jongyeon Ee, and Jennifer Ayscue. "Harming Our Common Future: America's Segregated Schools Sixty-Five Years after Brown," March 10, 2019. https://www.civilrightsproject.ucla.edu/research/k-12 -education/integration-and-diversity/harming-our-common-future-americas -segregated-schools-65-years-after-brown

Pascarella, Ernest, Christopher Pierson, Gregory Wolniak, and Patrick Terenzini. "First-Generation College Students: Additional Evidence on College Experiences and Outcomes." *Journal of Higher Education* 75, no. 3 (May–June, 2004): 249–84.

Pianta, Robert, and Arya Ansari. "Does Attendance in Private Schools Predict Student Outcomes at Age 15? Evidence from a Longitudinal Study." *Educational Researcher* 47, no. 7 (October 2018): 419–34. doi:10.3102/0013189X18785632

Pike, Gary, and George Kuh. "First- and Second-Generation College Students: A Comparison of Their Engagement and Intellectual Development." *Journal of Higher Education* 76, no. 3 (May–June, 2005): 276–300.

Polanyi, Michael. *Personal Knowledge: Toward a Post-Critical Philosophy*. Chicago: University of Chicago, 1958.

Putnam, Robert. *Our Kids: The American Dream in Crisis*. New York: Simon and Schuster, 2015.

Radford, Anne. *Top Student, Top School? How Social Class Shapes Where Valedictorians Go to College*. Chicago: University of Chicago Press, 2013.

Redford, Jeremy, and Kathleen Hoyer. "First-Generation and Continuing-Generation College Students: A Comparison of High School and Postsecondary Experiences." *National Center for Education Statistics*, September 2017. https:// nces.ed.gov/pubs2018/2018009.pdf

Reeves, Richard. *Dream Hoarders: How the American Upper Middle Class Is Leaving Everyone Else in the Dust, Why That Is a Problem, and What to Do About It*. Washington, DC: Brookings, 2017.

Rivera, Lauren. *Pedigree: How Elite Students Get Elite Jobs*. Princeton, NJ: Princeton University Press, 2015.

Rodriguez, Richard. *Hunger of Memory: The Education of Richard Rodriguez*. New York: Bantam, 1982.

Roksa, Josipa, and Daniel Potter. "Parenting and Academic Achievement: Intergenerational Transmission of Educational Advantage." *Sociology of Education* 84, no. 4 (2011): 299–321.

Rondini, Ashley. "Healing the Hidden Injuries of Class? Redemption Narratives, Aspirational Proxies, and Parents of Low-Income, First-Generation College Students." *Sociological Forum* 31, no. 1 (March 2016): 96–116.

———. "Negotiating Identity: Elite Institutions, Low-Income First Generation College Students, and Their Parents." PhD diss., Brandeis University, 2010.

Rosenberg, John. "'Authentic' Versus 'Constrained' Choices in the Classroom." *Harvard Magazine*. September 28, 2017. https://static1.squarespace.com/static /589ddbf646c3c44e76bbd0ee/t/5b2177ed562fa7589de8c60f/1528920045370 /Harvard+Magazine-+_Authentic_+versus+_Constrained_+Choices+in +the+Classroom.pdf

Ryan, James. *Five Miles Away, A World Apart: One City, Two Schools, and the Story of Educational Opportunity in Modern America.* Oxford: Oxford University Press, 2011.

Schwandt, Thomas. "Constructivist, Interpretivist Approaches to Human Inquiry." In *The Landscape of Qualitative Research Theories and Issues*, edited by Norman Denzin and Yvonna Lincoln. London: Sage, 1998.

Smith, Ashley. "First-Generation College Students More Engaged Than Peers." *Inside Higher Ed*, June 26, 2018. https://www.insidehighered.com/news/2018/06/26 /re-evaluating-perceptions-about-first-generation-college-students-and-their -academic

Soares, Joseph. *The Power of Privilege: Yale and America's Elite Colleges.* Stanford, CA: Stanford University Press, 2007.

Spiegler, Thomas, and Antje Bednarek. "First-Generation Students: What We Ask, What We Know and What It Means: An International Review of the State of Research." *International Studies in Sociology of Education* 23, no. 4 (2013): 318–37.

Steele, Claude. *Whistling Vivaldi: How Stereotypes Affect Us and What We Can Do.* New York: W. W. Norton, 2010.

Steinberg, Jacques. *The Gatekeepers: Inside the Admissions Process of a Premier College.* New York: Penguin, 2002.

Stephens, Nicole. "A Cultural Mismatch: The Experience of First-Generation Students at Elite Universities." PhD diss., Stanford University, 2013.

Stephens, Nicole, Tiffany Brannon, Hazel Ruth Markus, and Jessica Nelson. "Feeling at Home in College: Fortifying School-Relevant Selves to Reduce Social Class Disparities in Higher Education." *Social Issues and Policy Review* 9, no. 1 (2015): 1–24.

Stephens, Nicole, MarYam Hamedani, and Mesmin Destin. "Closing the Social-Class Achievement Gap: A Difference-Education Intervention Improves First-Generation Students' Academic Performance and All Students' College Transition." *Psychological Science* 25, no. 4 (2014): 943–53.

Stevens, Mitchell. *Creating a Class: College Admissions and the Education of Elites.* Cambridge, MA: Harvard University Press, 2007.

Stuber, Jenny. *Inside the College Gates: How Class and Culture Matter in Higher Education*. Lanham, MD: Lexington Books, 2011.

———. "Talk of Class: The Discursive Repertoires of White Working- and Upper-Middle-Class College Students." *Journal of Contemporary Ethnography* 35, no. 3 (2006): 285–318.

Stuber, Jenny, Joshua Klugman, and Caitlin Daniel. "Gender, Social Class and Exclusion: Collegiate Peer Cultures and Social Reproduction." *Sociological Perspectives* 54 (2011):431–51.

Terenzini, Patrick, Leonard Springer, Patricia Yaeger, Ernest Pascarella, and Amaury Nora. "First-Generation College Students: Characteristics, Experiences, and Cognitive Development." *Research in Higher Education* 37, no. 1 (1996): 1–22.

Thorndike, Edward. "A Constant Error in Psychological Ratings." *Journal of Applied Psychology* 4, no. 1 (1920): 25–29. http://dx.doi.org/10.1037/h0071663

Tinto, Vincent. *Leaving College: Rethinking the Causes and Cures of Student Attrition*. 2nd ed. Chicago: University of Chicago Press, 1993.

———. "Stages of Student Departure: Reflections on the Longitudinal Character of Student Leaving." *Journal of Higher Education* 59, no. 4 (1988): 438–55.

Trejo, Sam. "An Econometric Analysis of the Major Choice of First-Generation College Students." *Developing Economist* 3, no. 1 (2016): 1–21.

Turner, Victor. "Betwixt and Between: The Liminal Period in 'Rites de Passage.'" *The Proceedings of the American Ethnological Society: Symposium on New Approaches to the Study of Religion* (1964): 4–20.

US Department of Education. "Advancing Diversity and Inclusion in Higher Education: Key Data Highlights Focusing on Race and Ethnicity and Promising Practices." November 2016. https://www2.ed.gov/rschstat/research/pubs/advancing-diversity-inclusion.pdf

Vaisey, Stephen. "The 'Attitudinal Fallacy' Is a Fallacy: Why We Need Many Methods to Study Culture." *Sociological Methods & Research* 43, no. 2 (2014): 227–31.

Vance, J. D. *Hillbilly Elegy: A Memoir of a Family and Culture in Crisis*. New York: HarperCollins, 2016.

Veblen, Thorstein. *The Theory of the Leisure Class*. Oxford: Oxford University Press, 2009. First published 1899.

Vuong, Mui, Sharon Brown-Welty, and Susan Tracz. "The Effects of Self-Efficacy on Academic Success of First-Generation College Sophomore Students." *Journal of College Student Development* 51, no. 1 (2010): 50–64.

Warburton, Edward, Rosio Bugarin, and Anne-Marie Nuñez, "Bridging the Gap: Academic Preparation and Post-secondary Success of First-Generation Students." In *National Center for Educational Statistics*, 1–67. Washington, DC: United States Department of Education, 2001.

Warikoo, Natasha. *The Diversity Bargain: And Other Dilemmas of Race, Admissions, and Meritocracy at Elite Universities*. Chicago: Chicago University Press, 2016.

Weis, Lois, Kristin Cipollone, and Heather Jenkins. *Class Warfare: Class, Race, and College Admissions in Top-Tier Secondary Schools*. Chicago: University of Chicago, 2014.

Westover, Tara. *Educated: A Memoir*. New York: Random House, 2018.

Wildhagen, Tina. "'Not Your Typical Student': The Social Construction of the 'First Generation' College Student." *Qualitative Sociology* 38, no. 3 (2015): 285–303.

Williams, Dennis. "Joe and Jane Hoya Must Go." *Hoya*, October 24, 2008, https://www.thehoya.com/joe-and-jane-hoya-must-go/

INDEX

academic advisor(s): electronic signature system to reduce meeting in person with, 57n6; institutional context and interactions with, 56–57n5; unfortunate experience with, 54–56

academics/academic experiences: challenges faced by all students, 82; challenges faced by first generation students, 82–86; as a continuum over time for continuing generation students, 87; evolving over time for first generation students, 86–94; extracurricular, 66–67, 68n19; of first and continuing generation students, similarities and differences in, 58–59; "high impact practices," 68, 190–91; major, choice of (*see* major, choice of); recommendations from first generation students on enhancing, 188–93; satisfaction with, 60–62; self-doubt and fear of failure, 80–82; sophomore struggles and "slump," 85–86

academic success in college: academic turnaround and ongoing academic achievement, distinction between, 75–76; academic turnaround by first generation students, 77–79, 85; experienced by first and continuing generation students, 68–75; high school quality and, 35n24; ongoing academic achievement by continuing generation students, 79–80

advice from first generation college students, 176–77; academic mentorship, 193; academic preorientation programs, 185–88; discussion of race, class, privilege, and belonging, 198–201; early outreach to potential students, 189; enhance academic experiences, 188–93; enhance social experiences, 193–201; extracurriculars, choice and leadership opportunities in, 194–96; financial barriers to social inclusion, reduction of, 196–97; fix the pipeline, 192–93; framing college expectations for incoming students, 178–83; high impact practices, eliminating barriers to participation in, 190–91; ongoing proacademic cocurricular programming, 190; parents, inclusion of, 197–98; selecting majors later to provide opportunities to explore, 191–92; support for geographic and demographic transitions, 183–85; transitions, improving, 177–88

Ansari, Arya, 24n8

Apple, Michael, ixn1

Bain, Ken, xiii

Bassett, Anya B., 207

Bednarek, Antje, 43n30, 211n2

Beebe, James, 212

Bial, Deborah, 162n8

Black Lives Matter movement, 141n6

Bourdieu, Pierre, 5n8, 129n2
Bowen, William, xii
Boyce, W. Thomas, 165n11
Bronfenbrenner, Urie, 38n25
Brown, Michael, 141n6
Brown University, 205–6

Caplan, Bryan, 66n17
Castleman, Ben, 179n15
Chambliss, Daniel, 56
Chetty, Raj, 97n1
Choy, Susan, 3n4
continuing generation college students:
    academic experiences of (see
    academics/academic experiences);
    parents of, role played by, 149–52;
    parents of, separation from,
    159; preparation for college (see
    preparation for college, self-
    assessment of)
continuing generation college students,
    comments by: academic success,
    narratives of, 74–75, 79–80; campus
    belonging, feelings of, 143–47;
    extracurricular organizations, exclu-
    sivity and values of, 110–15; financial
    concerns raised by, 138–39; self-
    assessments of preparation for
    college, 38–42, 74; self-doubts and
    fear of failure, 80–81; transition to
    college, challenges of, 23–27
Crenshaw, Kimberlé, 32–34
cultural capital, academic preparation
    and, 49–50
cultural mismatch, 42n29

Deacon, Charles, 62, 119
Dingman, Thomas, 207
disclosure conundrum for first
    generation students, 15–21, 127–28
"doubly disadvantaged," 165–66
Duckworth, Angela, 79
Duke University, 205–6
Dweck, Carol, 79, 190n20

ecological systems theory, 38n25
economics: academic preparation
    and, 48–49; choice of major
    and, 58, 65–66; middle class,
    absence of, 139–40; post-college
    plans and, 169–73; social life of
    first generation students and
    concerns about, 134–40; value of
    different majors, 67n18. See also
    wealth
elite colleges and universities: college
    conferring the degree matters more
    than the major, belief that, 63;
    experiences of first generation
    college students at, 6–9, 12 (see also
    first generation college student(s));
    recruitment of first generation
    students, 9–12; risks of enrolling in,
    9. See also Georgetown University;
    Harvard University
England, Christopher, 207
equality of opportunity, 2n3, 112
external influences on first generation
    college student experiences: parents,
    roles of (see parents of first
    generation college students);
    post-college plans, 169–73;
    pre-college connections, 161–68;
    satisfaction with college experience
    and, 173–75
extracurricular experiences/involve-
    ment, 66–67, 68n19; challenges
    to access and participation in,
    108–15; enhancing knowledge of
    and access to for first generation
    students, 194–96; first generation
    specific organizations, 116–22; first
    generation specific organizations,
    dilemma of involvement in, 122–26;
    fraternities and sororities, 113;
    secret societies, 111–13; social
    satisfaction and, 103–8; types of
    for first and continuing generation
    students, 103–5

first generation college students: academic experiences of (*see* academics/academic experiences); advice from (*see* advice from first generation college students); complexity of the preparation and experience of, 51; continuing generation college students and, comparisons between, 21–22; definitions/identity of, 3–5; at elite institutions, experiences of, 6–9; external factors in the college-going experience of (*see* external influences on first generation college student experiences); graduation rates of, 6–7n11–12; identity disclosure conundrum/negotiation for, 15–21, 127–28; at less selective institutions, goals of, 5–6; misrecognition of, 128–29n2; numbers of, 3–4n5; parents of (*see* parents of first generation college students); preparation for college (*see* preparation for college, self-assessment of); privilege and disadvantage for, tangle of, 173–75; recruitment by elite institutions, 9–12, 76n24; social lives of (*see* social life); study of, 7–8 (see also *First Generation Student Success Project*); transition to college (*see* transition to college); ubiquity of the term, 2–3

first generation college students, comments by: academic accomplishment, narratives of, 72–74, 77–78; academic challenges faced by, 83–85; academic preorientation programs, concerns about, 187–88; classroom participation, anxiety associated with, 70–71; confidence won from experience for seniors, 21; conflation of academic merit with parental careers, experience of, 17–18; ethnic organizations, joining, 107; evolution of approach to academics,

87–94; extracurricular organizations, exclusivity and values of, 108–11; friendships through extracurricular involvement, 105; GSP support at Georgetown, 120–21, 124–25; interacting with people from different backgrounds, challenges of, 106; major, change in and academic experiences, 52–58; parents, college's treatment of, 155; parents, inclusion of, 157–58, 197–98; parents, relations with, 156; payoff for the hardships, anticipation of, 175; post-college prospects and concerns, 169–72; pre-college connections, experiences with, 162–64; preorientation program, need for, 180; privilege and disadvantage, tangle of, 173–74; self-assessments of preparation for college, 36–38, 44–48; social class, experience of, 18–19; social life, experience of, 95, 101–2; social life and demographic transitions, experience of, 129–34; social life and financial concerns, experience of, 135–39; stigma associated with first generation student groups, fear of, 122–25; studying abroad, value of, 69–70; transition challenges faced by, 13–16; visibility and diversity of first generation college students, 200–201

First Generation Student Success Project, xiii, 176, 203–6; data analysis and review, 213–16; data collection, 211–13; data reporting, 216–17; participant demographics, 210–11; rapport between interviewers and students, variability in, 217–19; samples and interview procedures, 7–8, 206–10

Foy, Missy, 119

friendships: from extracurricular involvement, 105–6; of first and continuing generation students, differences between, 99–103

GEAR UP, 189
gender, first generation student identity and, 132
Georgetown Scholarship Program (GSP), 11, 62, 86, 116–21, 191
Georgetown University: Community Scholars Program, 11, 101–2n4, 186; first generation support, approach to, 116–21; graduation rates of first generation students, 60n10; *Joe and Jane Hoya* stereotype, 69; longitudinal study of first and continuing generation students (see *First Generation Student Success Project*); preorientation at (Preparing to Excel (PEP)), 181n17; racial oppression and exploitation, examination of historical involvement with, 141n6; recruitment and support for first generation students at, 11; senior thesis rate for first and continuing generation students, 61n11; sophomores, support for, 86; "The Corp," 111, 113; "The Hidden Curriculum," 86
graduation rates: of first generation college students, 6–7n11–12; of Georgetown and Harvard undergraduates, 59–60

"Harvard bubble," 26
Harvard Financial Aid Initiative (HFAI), 10
"Harvard State," 25–26n10
Harvard University: "final clubs," 113, 115n5; first generation students, recruitment and inclusion of, 10–11; First Generation Student Union (FGSU), 117–18, 121–22; first generation support, approach to, 117–18, 121–22; graduation rates of first generation students at, 60n10; longitudinal study of first and continuing generation students (see *First Generation Student Success Project*); low-income students,

financial aid for, 10; preorientation at (First-Year Retreat and Experience (FYRE)), 181–82n17; racial oppression and exploitation, examination of historical involvement with, 141n6; senior thesis rate for first and continuing generation students, 61n11; social culture at, 25–26; startup fund for incoming students from lower-income families, 140n5
hidden curriculum: definitions/meanings of, ix–xi; speaking up in class as part of, 71n21; "The Hidden Curriculum" course at Georgetown, 86
high impact practices, 68, 190–91

insiders, x, 166
Institutional Review Board (IRB) processes, xviii
Institutions, legacy. *See* Georgetown University; Harvard University
intersectionality theory, 32–34

Jack, Anthony, 165–66
Jackson, Philip, ixn1
Jerolmack, Colin, 215n5

Karabel, Jerome, 2n3, 168n13
Khan, Shamus, 71, 75n23, 147, 165n12, 215n5
Kurzweil, Martin, xii

LaCount, Shannon, 161n7
Leadership Enterprise for a Diverse America (LEDA), 162–63, 168, 189
Lee, Elizabeth, 27, 199–200n24
legacy students, 23, 150
Light, Richard J., xiii, 204, 207
liminality, 127n1
Lubrano, Alfred, 5

major, choice of: changing by first generation students, accounts of, 52–58; economic value of different majors, 67n18; by first and continuing generation students, comparison of, 61–67; later selection of to provide opportunities to explore, 191–92; lucrative careers and, 58, 65–66; popularity of specific majors, 63–64; professor rather than discipline, majoring in, 56

mental health, academic pressure and, 81–82

mentors/mentorship, 193

merit: academic major as a signal of, 66; academic turnaround and, 79; as a class weapon, 154; cultural mismatch and, 21; educational achievement conflated with, xv, 128; equality of opportunity as, 2n3; extracurricular involvement as a signal of, 110; parental careers conflated with, 18, 21

meritocracy, 2, 75, 199, 215

methodology. *See First Generation Student Success Project*

narrative: academic, xiv, 47, 59, 68; deficit, 43, 51; first generation, 2, 10, 184; methodology and, 213, 216; personal, 28, 51, 72, 75, 158, 181

Nguyen, Jennifer, 207

Occupy Wall Street Movement, 141n6

"Opening Days", 10

opportunity: academic/educational, 2, 18, 199n23; equality of, 2n3, 112

Page, Lindsay, 179n15

parents: advantages conferred on offspring, concern regarding, 150n1; hiring of private admissions coaches, concern regarding, 151n2; separation from, continuing generation students' desire for, 159

parents of first generation college students: campus visits of, socioeconomic class insensitivity experienced at, 152–55; careers and

socioeconomic class of, 17–18; elite educational institutions, unfamiliarity with, 19–20; inclusion of, 156–61, 197–98; parents of continuing generation students and, distinctions in roles played by, 149–52, 155–56

Pascarella, Ernest, 68n19

Pianta, Robert, 24n8

pipeline, need to fix, 192–93

Polanyi, Michael, 90

Posse Program, 162n8

preorientation programs, 179–80

preparation for college, self-assessment of: by a continuing generation student, 23–27; ethnicity and, 39n26; geography and, 40n27; intersectionality theory and, 32–35; less prepared, comparison of first and continuing generation students feeling, 41–43; less prepared, continuing generation students feeling, 38–41, 74; less prepared, first generation students feeling, 35–38; stereotype threat and, 32, 39n26; well prepared, first generation students feeling, 43–51, 167

Prep for Prep, 162

Princeton University Preparatory Program, 189

"privileged poor," 165–66

race, first generation student identity and, 130–33

Rivera, Lauren, 75–76n23

Rondini, Ashley, 76n24

self-assessment of preparation for college. *See* preparation for college, self-assessment of

social life: campus belonging, first and current-generation students and, 141–48; demographic transitions and, 128–34; extracurricular activities (*see* extracurricular experiences/involvement); financial concerns and, 134–40; friendships of first and

social life (*continued*)
    continuing generation students, differences between, 99–103; social satisfaction and greatest successes/ challenges of first and continuing generation students, 95–98
social life, recommendations for enhancing, 193–94; discussion of race, class, privilege, and belonging, opportunities for, 198–201; extracurriculars, promoting and easing access to, 194–96; financial barriers, reduction of, 196–97; parents, inclusion of, 197–98
social reproduction, first generation students as a test of, 7
sophomore struggles, 85–86
Spiegler, Thomas, 43n30, 211n2
status: based on accomplishments and potential, assumption of, 16–17; individual merit vs. socioeconomic class, 16–19; middle class, absence of, 139–40; the transition to college and, 15–21
Steele, Claude, 32
Stephens, Nicole, 42n29
stereotype threat, 32, 39n26
Stuber, Jenny, 76n24
Summers, Lawrence, 10

Takacs, Christopher, 56
Tebaldi, David, 10
Tinto, Vincent, 128n1

Tobin, Eugene, xii
transition to college: challenges faced by continuing generation students, 22–27; challenges faced by first generation students, 13–15; the disclosure conundrum, 15–21, 127–28; by first and continuing generation students, differences in, 22, 27–28; preparation for college (*see* preparation for college, self-assessment of)
transition to college, advice from first generation college students on, 177–88; academic preorientation programs, 185–88; framing college expectations for incoming students, 178–83; support for geographic and demographic transitions, 183–85
TRIO programs, 162, 189
Turner, Victor, 127n1

van Gennep, Arnold, 127n1
Veblen, Thorstein, 135n3, 154n4

Waddell, Jasmine, 207
Warikoo, Natasha, 199n23
wealth: collegiate outcomes and parental, 24n8; on display at campus events for parents, 153–55; of students' families at Georgetown and Harvard, 98n1. *See also* economics
Wildhagen, Tina, 3–4, 8n13

A NOTE ON THE TYPE

This book has been composed in Arno, an Old-style serif typeface in the classic Venetian tradition, designed by Robert Slimbach at Adobe.